To Sally

To Ale Karen—

We CAN Change The World

keep up the struggle
for a better world.

Dave Stratman
June 7, 1991

KAREN MANSON
32 West Knapp
Rice Lake, 54868

We CAN
Change The World

The Real Meaning Of Everyday Life

———————————

David G. Stratman

New Democracy Books
Boston

Bertolt Brecht's lines "From a German War Primer," trans. by H. R. Hays, are taken from Bertolt Brecht, *Poems 1913-1956*, revised paperback edition, edited by John Willett and Ralph Manheim, and are reprinted by permission of Methuen London.

New Democracy Books
Boston

ISBN 0-9628566-1-4
ISBN 0-9628566-0-6 (pbk.)
Library of Congress Catalog Number: 90-92305

Printed in the United States of America

1 2 3 4 5 6 7 8 9

Contents

Acknowledgments

This book evolved over many years, and I am indebted to a great many people for their ideas, insights, criticisms, and support. I would especially like to thank Eric Prahl, Steve Raudenbush, and Carol Doherty, who contributed many of the ideas for the book and who read numerous drafts.

Thanks also to Joshua Bradt, Dennis Cerrotti, Brian Conly, Jim Cronin, Cynthia Curtner, Barbara Garson, Carol Glazer, Alice Hageman, Dick Hague, Ann Hurley, Pam Korte, Dave Noble, Darrel Stewart, Jake Stewart, Nancy Stewart, and Taylor Thompson, who read the manuscript and were generous in their suggestions and criticisms. Robin Stratman read the manuscript, and, over the years, she and Justin Stratman have been my sounding-boards and inspiration, more than they know.

I owe the greatest debt to my wife, Sally. Her unflagging support and encouragement, her guidance and suggestions, her tireless hours of reading and re-reading manuscripts, and her confidence in me and in the project, made the book possible.

INTRODUCTION:
HOPE AND REVOLUTION

If there is anything that defines the world as we approach the end of the twentieth century, it is the loss of hope.

The fundamental reason for this loss of hope is that there seems to be no alternative to the capitalist system. Communism provided the fullest articulation of apparently revolutionary ideas in the twentieth century, and it has turned out a disaster. The idea of revolution has been defeated by the reality of it.

Without an alternative to the system, fundamental change seems out of the question. We seem doomed to live in the grip of a system which defines human life in terms of its own imperatives of profit and loss, competition and inequality. It seems that the deepest human values and most important human relationships must forever be subordinated to the needs of the economy and the dictates of the elite.

Hope in the future and belief in the possibility of fundamental change—belief in the possibility of revolution—are inextricably linked. The defeat of the idea of revolution has led to an end to the belief that human beings have the capacity to create a human world.

My purpose in this book is to show that we *can* triumph over the system to create a truly democratic society.

A Note on "Revolutionary Democracy"

Throughout this book I use the term "revolutionary democracy" to describe the society I believe we should aim to create. "Democracy," "socialism," and "communism" have all been corrupted to mean something other than what their original adherents had wished. "Communism" quickly became a caricature of its original vision. "Socialism" focuses too narrowly on economic arrangements to be an adequate term, and in practice has meant little more than planned capitalism. "Democratic socialism" and "social democracy" are terms for welfare capitalism; social democratic parties are simply sophisticated instruments of capitalist rule. "Democracy," to the extent that it means "rule by the people," is the essential element in meaningful social change, but does not by itself convey that, to be democratic, a movement must be revolutionary. Thus "revolutionary democracy."

The Meaning of Revolution

"Revolution" has historically meant different things to different people. In the American Revolution, to bankers, merchants, and slaveowners, revolution meant freedom from British control, to consolidate their power as an elite. To the small farmers and laborers who were its backbone, the revolution meant establishing equality and radical democracy in the New World. Once independence had been won and the rank-and-file were no longer needed, the Founding Fathers moved quickly to limit democracy in the new republic.

To workers and peasants in Russia in 1917, revolution meant equality, radical democracy, and collective freedom, while to the Communist Party it meant something quite different: the ability of the party elite to guide the economic development of Russia. Immediately after the October Revolution, the party took steps to destroy the power of workers' and peasants' committees in field and factory, and to consolidate party control.

The meaning of revolution does not depend only on the economic interests of who is defining it. The capture of political power by the American elite reflected their view of humanity. They saw themselves as the cultured few who were fit to rule. Their rule would eventually benefit the whole society—within a framework which they would direct. Similarly the Communist seizure of power in the Russian Revolution was not mere cynicism on the Communists' part; rather, it reflected their view of who was fit to rule. The party would rule on workers' behalf, supposedly to their eventual benefit.

What we mean by "revolution" then depends largely on our view of people. Democratic revolution and truly democratic society can only be based on a view of ordinary people as fit to rule society.

I believe that the basis for a truly democratic society can be found in the values and relationships of ordinary working people. I maintain that the people who do the productive labor of society—who mine its coal, build its cars, care for its sick, teach its children—have goals and values which fundamentally conflict with the goals and values of the class of people who control the society and reap the rewards of this labor. Ordinary people struggle to achieve their goals in every area of their lives—with their co-workers, their husbands and wives and children, their friends and neighbors. These goals taken together constitute a different vision of what human life should be, a different idea of what it means to be a human being, from the vision of the ruling elite.

Revolution, in my view, does not mean simply a new economic structure, and it does not mean control by a new elite. It means transforming all the relationships in society to accord with the values, goals, and idea of human life of ordinary working people.

There seem to me to be two values which are fundamental to most people's lives and which are critical to creating a new society. Most people believe in equality and in commitment to each other. Revolutionary democracy means changing all the relationships and institutions in society to reflect the values of solidarity and equality.

Revolutions occur when people gain sufficient confidence in their own view of human life and in themselves as the makers of history to shape all of society with their vision.

The Importance of a Revolutionary Conception of Change

The idea of revolution has no legitimacy in contemporary society. Yet a revolutionary conception of society is essential if we hope to understand the world around us or to change it.

The reason for this lies in the nature of the system in which we live. Capitalism is not merely an economic system. It is a system of human relations, which projects and enforces its own view of the world as its primary source of control. The essence of the capitalist view of the world is a view of people: the idea that capitalist society expresses human nature.

According to this view, society is competitive and unequal, driven by greed and self-seeking, because that is the way people are. The goal of society is economic development; the goal of the individual is to produce and consume. Society is a jungle in which only the fit survive, and the most fit rise to the top. Whatever is good comes from the top of the social order. The feudal aristocracy claimed that the order of society was the will of God and therefore eternal. The capitalist class claims that the order of society is human nature, and therefore cannot be changed.

Capitalism holds that self-interest is the fundamental human motivation. Capitalism defines the possibilities of human society in terms of this view, and it shapes the fundamental relationships in society, such as economic relations, to conform to this view. Capitalism means a society constructed on selfishness as the basis of human development.

The culture of capitalism has great power to convince us that the world cannot be different, because "this is the way people are." In this competitive world, we are taught to be always on the defensive. We are forced to compete for grades at school and for jobs when we graduate. The stories we read in the newspaper, the ideas we are taught in school, our experiences on the job can all serve to convince us that people really are just out for themselves.

To understand that the world can be different, we have first to realize that people are different from what capitalism says they are. We have to realize that selfishness is not the fundamental impulse of most people's lives.

The heart of a political vision is thus not a view of economic or political structures but a view of people. The revolutionary vision which I develop in this book is a view of people which shows that most people are moved primarily by goals other than self-interest and thus are capable of creating a new society together.

In addition to an alternative view of people, a revolutionary vision must provide a coherent explanation of social change and a method for analyzing events and issues. Above all, it must furnish a basis for action: it must allow us to understand history in such a way as to change it. In this book I use my alternative view of people to develop a different reading of the present crisis in world affairs and the history which has led to it, and a different view of the way out of it.

There are two tests for the truth of a theory of social change. One is how satisfactorily a theory seems to explain our experience. The second is how successfully it enables us to act. These are the two tests which I believe previous theories of social change have failed. They are also the standards against which the ideas proposed in this book should be measured.

Why Revolution Is Necessary and Possible

Any number of serious problems which we face seem to call for fundamental change. Unemployment and homelessness in the U.S., the continuing slaughter in Central America and South Africa and the Middle East, the destruction of the environment: each of these is linked more or less directly with the operation of the capitalist system. It can be argued that each will require systemic change to solve.

But these problems are divorced from the texture of most of our daily lives, and our sense of the possibilities of human society does not really hinge upon their solution. If all these problems were somehow solved tomorrow, we would still need to create a new society, and we would have precisely as much ability to do so as we have today.

The necessity for revolutionary change does not lie in these important problems. It lies rather in the nature of capitalism as a system of human relations, and in the nature of the attack which capitalism makes daily upon the things most essential to our humanity: our understanding of ourselves and our fellow human beings and our relationships with other people.

All the institutions of capitalist society are geared toward breaking the ties among us from which we derive self-understanding and support, and through which we learn about the world around us and gain the confidence to act with others to change it. The culture of competition and inequality which characterize capitalism influences every aspect of our lives. The education system attacks the self-confidence of our children, to get them to accept their place in an unequal society. Work is designed to undermine the collective relationships and self-confidence of workers, to wrest control of the work process out of their hands. The media systematically misinform us of the real problems in the world and the real solutions. The consumer culture constantly encourages us to judge our personal worth—a sense of worth already undermined by every other aspect of the culture—by the car we drive or the dress we wear or the cigarette we smoke. In every aspect of our lives, our human values are under attack by capitalist culture.

The need for revolution comes from the dehumanizing nature of capitalism in the daily life of all who live within this system.

If the necessity of revolution does not derive from specific problems like unemployment or the destruction of the environment, neither does the possibility of change. The possibility of revolution comes from the values and ideas about human life which most people share, and the nature of the struggle against capitalism in which they are already engaged.

The idea which I advance in this book which most flies in the face of conventional ways of thinking about human beings is this: that the struggle to humanize the world is the most essential of human activities, and one in which most people are engaged in their everyday lives. Most people, in the little part of the world they think they can control, are engaged in a struggle against the dehumanizing influence of capitalism on their lives. When parents try to instill in their children a sense of real values instead of the designer-jean values of television; when husband and wife try to support each other in the face of the assaults of the outside world; when friends help each other rather than compete; when teachers try to raise the expectations of students whom the school is trying to beat down; when workers try to restore some meaning to work that management is trying to render meaningless: when people do any of the many things that they do every day, they are trying, consciously or not, to resist the dehumanizing culture of capitalism. To the extent that they have supportive human relationships in any aspect of their lives, people have created them by struggling to transform capitalist relations into their opposite.

People's motivation in this everyday struggle is not self-interest or hope of gain. It is to do what they think is right, and to act in a way that accords with their idea of what human life should be.

The necessity and possibility for revolutionary change lie in the vast gulf between the world as it is and the world as most people would have it to be. The logical end of the struggles in which most people are already engaged is the creation of a new society which expresses their values and their idea of what it means to be human.

What Do Capitalism and Communism Have In Common?

For all their apparent differences, the societies of the United States and the Soviet Union and China, as well as France and Poland and Germany, are alike in one fundamental respect: they are class societies, controlled by privileged elites, who make more or less show of democracy as they manage disenfranchised populations.

The members of this world elite have more in common with each other than with the ordinary people of their own societies. These elites—corporate leaders and politicians and party "experts"—control the economy and direct development. Capitalists and Communists can differ endlessly on whether "the market" or "central planning" is more effective, yet still agree on the essential point: the need to exclude the mass of people from real political power.

How could it happen that societies that claim to be so different could be at bottom so similar? The answer to this lies in certain fundamental similarities between Marxist and capitalist ideas.

Marx's goal was to end exploitation and alienation in human society. He intended his theories as a "science of revolution," which would discover the fundamental laws of history, and in so doing enable people to understand the dynamics of modern capitalist society and to change it.

Capitalism, according to Marx, was a stage in the history of economic development. Like earlier stages, it was destined to be superseded by a new system, because there would come a point at which the private ownership of the means of production would act as a brake on further economic development. At this point, the capitalist system would be destroyed by the class which it had brought into existence—the industrial working class, the "proletariat." The proletariat would then create socialist society, based upon common ownership of the means of production, in which exploitation would cease to exist.

Marx's model of history did not see working people as conscious agents of change who act on the basis of their own anti-capitalist values. Instead, observing the savage power of industrial capitalism, Marx defined working people primarily as dehumanized and passive victims of economic forces who, when they are moved to action, are moved by these same forces. While he believed the capitalist and the working class to have opposing interests, Marx saw them motivated by essentially the same goal—to get a greater share of the wealth.

Marx's theory of social change did not challenge the capitalist view that self-interest is the primary human motivation. Marx believed with the capitalists that history is driven by economic development, which in turn is driven by greed. Marx maintained, however, that greed leads not to permanence but to revolution. He thought that the actions of the capitalists would lead to revolution and socialism.

Capitalism and Marxism both see ordinary people as the passive victims or beneficiaries of the actions of elites, within a history driven by economic development and self-interest. It is this fundamental similarity in their view of people that leads to the practical similarities between capitalist and Marxist societies.

The Economic Model of History

If it is true that most people are engaged in a struggle to humanize the world, then why have we not seen this struggle before or realized its significance? And if it is true that Marxism has always led to revolutions which contradict the vision of their makers, why has Marxism not simply been rejected by revolutionaries?

The answer to both these questions lies in the nature of the models or paradigms of human behavior and social change through which we understand our experience. Thomas Kuhn describes these paradigms in his book, *The Structure of Scientific Revolutions*. A paradigm is an explanatory model through which scientists interpret their data and make sense of the world which they observe.

Kuhn gives Ptolemy's model of the solar system as an example of a paradigm. Before Copernicus, it seemed obvious to people that the earth was stationary and that the planets and sun revolve around it. The calculations of planetary motion made by Ptolemy and other ancient astronomers were all based on this model.

Once scientists agree upon a model for understanding their observations, Kuhn explains, they must exclude from their field of vision phenomena which do not fit the paradigm. A paradigm in this way is "like a box"; the phenomena which do not fit the box are often not seen at all. Ancient astronomers tended to "see" only those phenomena which fit their conception of the relation between the earth and the heavens.

As science progresses, however, scientists increasingly encounter phenomena which do not fit the model. This "failure of existing rules" leads to a state of insecurity and crisis in the affected scientific field, and leads to a search for new rules—a new model to account for what the old model cannot explain. Ptolemy's paradigm of a stationary earth failed to account for certain observable phenomena, and predictions made on the basis of Ptolemy's model led to unexplainable errors in the calculation of planetary motion. Ancient astronomers began to search for a way to make sense of their observations.

Even though scientists may be confronted by severe and prolonged anomalies—observations for which the accepted model cannot account—says Kuhn, and "may begin to lose faith and even to consider alternatives, they do not renounce the paradigm that has led them into crisis" until a new paradigm is at hand. The paradigm of a stationary earth was clung to for centuries in spite of its obvious failures as a model:

Once it has achieved the status of a paradigm, a scientific theory is declared invalid only if an alternative candidate is available to take its place....The decision to reject one paradigm is always simultaneously the decision to accept another, and the judgment leading to that decision involves the comparison of both paradigms with nature and with each other.[1]

The adoption of a new paradigm is what Kuhn calls a "scientific revolution." A scientific revolution is a "transformation of vision," rather than simply a new interpretation of existing data. It constitutes a new world view. When Copernicus proposed that the earth moved around the sun, his new model accounted for the observed deviations from Ptolemy's model. More than that, however, this new paradigm caused a revolution in men's thinking about the earth and the heavens, and revolutionized the problems and methods of astronomy. Such "scientific revolutions," says Kuhn, come "like a gestalt switch" or "a lightning flash."[2]

Though Kuhn's focus is on scientific revolutions, he suggests that "Something like a paradigm is prerequisite to perception itself."[3] Paradigms provide the structure through which all people, not merely scientists, order and understand their experience.

I have described Kuhn's analysis at some length because it throws light on the present crisis in our capacity to understand the world and to change it.

Capitalist and Marxist theories of history and social development, in spite of their apparent differences, have remained within the same paradigm of history driven by economic development and the same view of people.

Marxism has been the only coherent and systematic model of social change posed as a revolutionary challenge to capitalism. The Marxist model, however, is in fundamental conflict with the revolutionary vision it is intended to fulfill; it cannot lead to the society which it envisions. Marxism is in crisis. Since no alternative revolutionary theory has come along adequate to replace it, the crisis affects a far wider range of people than those who think of themselves as Marxists or who have the scantest knowledge of his ideas. It affects all those who yearn for a better world.

Kuhn shows that people do not abandon an explanation for how the world works, however much their experience may seem to contradict it, unless another paradigm is available. However badly Marxism has failed, no satisfactory alternative paradigm of revolutionary change has come along to take its place. Marxism has thus continued to hover like a dark cloud over the revolutionary imagination of the twentieth century.

The fundamental condition for a new and popular revolutionary movement is a new understanding of the role of ordinary people in society, and a new paradigm of social transformation based upon it. The essential element of a new paradigm is that the struggle to change the world is the most human and most pervasive of activities. Like scientists who have been trained to exclude from the "box" of our vision any experience which does not fit the established paradigm, we simply have not been able to see this struggle going on around us everyday.

The key elements of a new paradigm are that most people have goals and values opposed to those of capitalism and Communism; that, far from being passive, most people are already engaged in a struggle to create a new society; that it is the irrepressible struggle of people to humanize the world, rather than the forces of economic or technological development, that drives history; and that ordinary people, rather than intellectuals or a revolutionary party, are the source of the idea of a new society, and of the values that should shape it.

I should explain what I mean by a "new" paradigm or model of change. The ideas and values which I will discuss have underlain every revolutionary struggle of the past, and are already part of most people's sense of how the world really ought to be. In this sense, there is nothing new about what I will say. At the same time, by fashioning these common feelings into a coherent model for understanding the world, I hope to reveal their revolutionary significance.

For most of the twentieth century, the world has been trapped between capitalism and Communism. With the collapse of Communism, we are presented with an historic opportunity to create human society on a new basis. The first step to being able to change the world is to see it with new eyes.

PART ONE

Part One examines the link between class struggle and people's everyday lives. It shows that, far from being mere passive victims of the system, most people are already engaged in a struggle to create a new world. It shows that the central dynamic of society is conflict over its goals.

1

LEARNING SOMETHING NEW

A number of years ago, from 1974 to 1976, I went through a series of experiences that convinced me that real change in the world is possible. I was learning at the hands of an assortment of parents in Dorchester and other working class neighborhoods of Boston. Many of them were not aware that they were teaching me anything; some of them were very consciously trying to change me.

My wife and I and our two small children moved to Dorchester in 1974, a year after I was "non-rehired"—a polite academic term for "given the boot"—from my teaching job at a small New England college. Beginning in 1967, while still a graduate student, I had become involved in the anti-war movement, and then in civil rights and labor issues. Around 1970 or so, as a young faculty member, I had become convinced that Marxism held an accurate explanation for the terrible things happening in U.S. society and around the world. I became convinced of the need for revolutionary change. While it was clear to me that communism as practiced in the Soviet Union and China contradicted everything I thought a society should be, still I thought that the *ideas* behind communism were basically true, and could lead to a democratic and humanly fulfilling society if they were practiced under the right conditions.

After the movement built up around the war collapsed in the early '70s, like many other people, I began to despair of seeing any real change. I also became firmly against communism of any sort, concluding that there must be something wrong with any tree that always bears bad fruit. But this only made the possibility of change seem even more remote. The system seemed all-powerful. More than that, people themselves seemed to be a big part of the problem.

1974 was the first year of busing in Boston. In the late '60s, a militant movement of black parents had demanded better education for their children. Schools in black neighborhoods, they protested, were rundown, overcrowded, and understaffed. In 1972, the Federal Court

had found that the Boston School Committee had intentionally maintained a segregated school system. September, 1974 marked the first
phase of busing to desegregate the schools, in the face of much opposition from white parents. National and international airwaves were
filled with the angry faces and shouts of whites, some just registering
their opposition to busing, some actually attacking black children
coming into white neighborhoods.

Our daughter was, at the time, just beginning kindergarten at the
Patrick O'Hearn School around the block from our house. The Patrick O'Hearn had been a center of the anti-busing movement in the
Dorchester section of Boston. Now it was to have its first black students.

The principal sent notices home for a preliminary joint Home and
School Association meeting for the three small primary schools under
his direction. I went to the meeting full of concern. I didn't know any
of the other parents yet, and the news was full of reports of violent
racial incidents in South Boston, a short distance away.

There were forty parents there, all of them white. The principal
began by thanking us for coming, saying, with a clear racial implica-
tion, "I guess we can see which parents *really* care for their kids."
Immediately eight parents—not me; I was just watching—jumped to
their feet and attacked the principal for the remark. "You should never have had the meeting in this neighborhood. Of course the black
parents are afraid to come here." The meeting was being held in a
totally white section. They said, "You should have had the meeting at
the White Church"—a church between the white and black neighborhoods. The other parents seemed to agree, and the principal said he'd
hold the next meeting on neutral ground.

A few minutes later, the principal made a remark clearly disparag-
ing the black students. Some of the schools had been greatly overcrowded by desegregation. The Patrick O'Hearn, for example, had
been built for 280 students; under the busing plan, it had 360, with
the gym turned into four "open-space classrooms" of twenty students
apiece, with a Title I remedial class conducted on the stage behind a
portable blackboard. The principal talked about the crowding and
said, "These new students are ruining the school." This time, even
more parents were on their feet, yelling at the principal that, "It isn't
these kids' fault that they're being bused here. It's the bigshots' that
made the plan."

My education had begun. I wasn't particularly surprised when the
principal made racist remarks. But I was very surprised when the par-

ents attacked him for it. This was a working class Irish neighborhood, not different from South Boston, and many of the parents at the meeting were active anti-busers. Something was happening here that was very different from what the newspapers and my academic and leftist background had led me to expect.

A day or two later, I ran into a woman on the street who had been at the meeting. Connie DiAngelo* had lived in the neighborhood all her life and had been very active in the anti-busing movement. She was carrying a copy of a newspaper story of black children being stoned in South Boston, and she was in tears. We decided to contact some of the parents from the preliminary meeting, and to take the initiative in forming an integrated Home and School Association at the Patrick O'Hearn.

Connie and I co-chaired the first meeting of the Patrick O'Hearn Home and School Association as a desegregated school and organization. We wanted the black parents to feel welcome at the school, and we wanted the Home and School to discuss serious education issues.

It so happened that I had just read an interview with a teacher talking about the effects of "teacher expectations" on the self-image and performance of students. I shared the article with Connie, who was very moved by it. I opened the meeting by talking about the effects of teacher expectations and how important it was, particularly with the new black children in the school, that the school start with the assumption that all our kids are smart and treat them that way. Connie eloquently described bad experiences her kids were having at the time with boring and unchallenging classes, which she attributed to low expectations.

Several parents nodded agreement as we spoke. When we had finished, another parent got up and, in an emotion-filled voice, told of always being made to feel stupid in school. She had been persuaded by a guidance counselor that she "was not college material," and felt cheated of an education. Other parents told similar stories.

Then another woman got up with a related problem. She said that every Friday her daughter, who normally liked school, got sick to her stomach and didn't want to go. After several weeks of this, the mother found out what was going on. Every Friday the principal would go to each class and present "Boy and Girl of the Week" awards. Her

---

*Connie's name, like the names of the other parents mentioned in this chapter and the strikers in the next, has been changed.

daughter was made so anxious by the competition that she did not want to go to school.

Other parents got up and said the same thing. Then someone said, "Why do they have to have this competition in school anyway? I thought our kids were here to learn."

And so it happened that the first official act of the newly-integrated Patrick O'Hearn Home and School Association was to pass a unanimous resolution (35-0) calling on the principal to do away with the Boy and Girl of the Week awards, and requiring the newly-installed officers of the association to meet with him to press our demand. When we met with the principal the next day, he was apoplectic, and declared that "Without competition we would never have beat the Russians to the moon." The parents, however, were determined, and he reluctantly agreed to drop the awards.

A couple weeks later, we organized an informal coffee-klatch in one of the parents' living room. We still did not have real relationships with the black parents; the coffee included ten people, all of them white. The question on the floor was, "What are the problems at the school that we should deal with?" One woman said, "I hear the black kids are shittin' in the sink." Another said, "I heard that too, but it's not true. My husband's the plumber there. He says the toilets were backed up because the kids use hand towels to wipe because there's no toilet paper."

Then somebody said, "How come there aren't any black parents here? How can we do anything if we're not together?" "Well, maybe they don't feel welcome, and they didn't even know about this meeting." After some discussion, it was agreed by all: we couldn't accomplish anything unless black and white parents were together. After a few suggestions were rejected, such as addressing every announcement to parents, "Dear Black and White Parents," it was decided to write a letter to all parents listing a few of the obvious problems at the school—such as broken glass in the playground and lack of toilet paper in the bathrooms—and calling a meeting to discuss them.

A couple days later, the parents from the meeting, most of them with pre-school kids in tow, were outside the school, handing each child a flyer about the meeting and telling them to "Be sure to give this to your mother as soon as you get home."

But then something happened. All of the black students at the school were bused in, so a couple of us handed them flyers as they filed into their buses. Seeing what was happening, the vice-principal ordered Joyce Hamilton, a black parent at the school and the bus monitor, to get on the bus and take the flyers away from all the black children.

The white parents were outraged. They saw the vice-principal's action as a clear attempt to keep the black parents divided from the white. We held an emergency meeting, and decided that there was only one thing to do: we would have to go to the homes of the few black parents for whom we had addresses, and talk with them directly. This was a big step. While the black families lived only a few blocks from the school, the line at the time between white and black neighborhoods was clearly marked. None of the white parents had been across Washington Street, and none of them had been in the home of a black person. Given the racial climate in Boston at the time, they weren't sure how they would be received.

But in the three or four homes that we went to, the black parents were only too glad to talk with us. They too were angry that the black children had not been allowed to bring home the flyer, and they wanted very much to have a united parent organization. Joyce Hamilton and her husband Johnny, who was one of the school's bus drivers, made a plan with us to get flyers to all the black children the next day. At the home of one West Indian family, we were offered milk laced with scotch, and talked about schools and life for quite some time.

We started holding regular coffees in people's living rooms, to talk in a more in-depth way than we could in official Home and School meetings at the school. The first of these, when some black parents came for the first time, was a revelation. Many white parents had complained to the school of the slow and boring pace of the schoolwork; they had repeatedly been told that "We have to go slow because the black children can't keep up." At this first coffee with black and white parents, we put the question again on the floor, "What are the problems we should work on at the school." Johnny and Joyce Hamilton both piped up that their kids "are bored because they aren't being challenged; the work was harder at the [all-black] school they had been at before." We were all amazed. It seemed everybody had the same problems.

One of the results of these meetings was a decision that the O'Hearn needed a full-time reading teacher. In addition to not challenging the children, the school also was not providing extra help when needed. The desegregation plan had been a vehicle for budget cuts. Thirty-six schools—almost all of them in black neighborhoods—were shut down in the first two years of busing, and several hundred teachers were laid off. At the very time that students needed more attention, they were getting much less. Besides being overcrowded by the busing plan, the O'Hearn had also lost its reading teacher.

We began a Home and School Newsletter, and published the reading scores at the Patrick O'Hearn from the last available year—the year *before* busing, when the school was all white. The scores showed that, while the students read at the national median when they came into the school, by the time they left it at the fifth grade, they were reading on average 1.5 years below grade level. These scores were important, because they showed that 1) the school was a disaster before busing; and 2) the problem in the students' performance was not in the "culturally deprived" working class families of Dorchester. The constant refrain of school officials when we complained of poor academic achievement was that the problem was in the students themselves or in their "background": they watched too much television, their parents didn't care, they came from "broken homes," etc. The reading scores showed that the problems got worse the longer the children were in school. The problem, in other words, was not in the kids or their families: it was at school.

School officials reacted angrily to our publishing the reading scores. The vice-principal stormed into a meeting at the school called to discuss them, and declared that "Parents are not allowed to criticize the school." We were informed next day that, as "punishment" for our effrontery, the parent-teacher Open House we had been preparing had been cancelled. We responded with a leaflet to parents, discussing the issues and criticizing the principal for his decision. Then the School Department downtown mailed a letter to every O'Hearn parent. It described the "serious situation" at the school being caused by some troublemakers, and invited parents to a meeting at the Grover Cleveland Middle School.

Things were heading toward a show-down. It was very clear to us that school officials, from the principal to the superintendent downtown, were determined to shut down our parents' group. As the night of the show-down approached, we held a series of house meetings to plan our strategy. We decided to give the officials two or three minutes to state their case. Then we would take over the meeting, and turn it into a discussion of reading scores and conditions at the school.

The School Department pulled out all the stops for the meeting. In addition to the principal and vice principal of the O'Hearn, the entire teaching staff of our school (we had very short-sightedly not devel-

oped our relationships with them; the principal brought them as his
allies) was assembled, plus the president of the Boston Teachers Union, the director of the Boston Home and School Association, and the
associate superintendent of schools for our area.

Things did not go exactly according to plan. The principal of the
O'Hearn opened the meeting. Within seconds, Breda O'Brien was on
her feet, shouting, "Sit down and shut up, you dorty bleedin' liar."
The other white parents chimed in. The principal turned bright red
and began to mumble. The associate superintendent, Rollins Griffith,
told him to sit down. He would take over.

Griffith was very smooth-tongued and slick. He was also black.
The parents had made an unspoken division of labor. Not wishing to
offend each other, the black parents kept silent while the white parents attacked the white principal; when the black associate superintendent took the floor, Monique Matson, a black mother of two at the
school, rose from her seat and cried, "Sit down and shut your stupid
mouth." The other black parents joined the chorus, much to the de-
light of all. I got up, to demand that we be able to speak. Then Mary
Kelly, in a voice that momentarily silenced the auditorium, demanded
that I be able to address the meeting. This was followed by much
cheering and applause.

Taken aback, Griffith held up his hands for silence. After a couple
minutes, he was able to say that, if we gave him a few minutes to
speak his piece, then we could take the floor to speak ours. After we
gave him his say, I took the floor. I reported our findings about reading scores and some of the problems we saw at the school, and began
recognizing parents in the audience to talk of their children's experiences. Some parents who had been previously uninvolved started to
express their feelings, and several teachers began to nod in agreement
and to make their own statements supporting us.

Then it was the turn of Roseanna McCord, director of the citywide
Home and School Association—which is funded by the Boston School
Committee—to take the floor. She had come dressed to the nines, in
suit and flowered hat. She said that "Home and School" meant that
parents should work *with* school authorities, and reiterated that parents were not allowed to criticize the school. This brought such a
storm of hoots and catcalls that she quickly thanked the superintendent and sat down.

Jack Doherty, the president of the Boston Teachers Union, then
took the floor. He had come there as an ally of the superintendent. It
was very clear, however, which way the wind was blowing; he got

up and said how good it was that parents were involved and that he hoped we could work together.

Finally, after more discussion of the need for a reading teacher at the school, Rollins Griffith apologized for any "misunderstanding," said that of course we could have our Open House as planned, that he would do what he could about a reading teacher, and how much he welcomed "parent input." (Shortly after the meeting, the principal took early retirement.)

The parents cheered and hugged each other as the meeting broke up. It was the first real victory anybody could remember at the school. A group of us drank coffee brandy and milk far into the morning hours, telling and retelling the events of the night. Connie DiAngelo's social worker came to her house the next day and said, "Connie, did you hear what happened? Three hundred parents took over a meeting at the Grover Cleveland..." Actually, there had only been thirty-three parents, only twelve of them from our regular group; we had been outnumbered by teachers, administrators, and other officials. But the tale caused so much excitement in the neighborhood that it grew rapidly in the retelling.

Better Education Together

The Patrick O'Hearn, of course, was only one small school in a city in turmoil. In the fall of '74, twenty parents—ten black and ten white—from 18 different schools, formed an organization to deal with the desegregation crisis. We called ourselves "Better Education Together" (BET).

In the Boston school desegregation case, politicians and "community leaders" on opposite sides of the busing issue agreed on only one thing: the issue in the Boston schools was *race*. As black and white parents, we said that the issue was not race but *education*; the issue was what was happening to all our children in school everyday.

We felt as parents that we were trapped between two bad alternatives. On the one side was the Boston School Committee, which had used a segregated school system to deliver inferior education to Boston children for many years. On the other side was the Federal Court, which was using desegregation as a means of closing schools, laying off teachers, and breaking ties between people and their schools; by shifting students around from year to year and school to school, and by lay-offs and the frequent transfer of teachers within the system, the Federal Court was destroying the relationships among parents and students and teachers that gave them some power.

BET went to Court. We petitioned to become a party to the desegregation case, and submitted analyses of the impact of the desegregation plans on our children. By the fifth grade, white students in Boston were on average 1.7 years below grade level; black students averaged over two years behind. We argued that all our children had been injured by the segregated system, and that an adequate remedy would have to include educational improvements designed to bring all students up to grade level. The Court accepted in principle our argument that the plan for Phase II of desegregation would have to improve the schools, and it threw out the NAACP plan and the School Committee plan, both of which focused entirely on race; but the Court did not allow us to become a party to the suit.

On May 10, 1975, the Court adopted a plan for the next phase of desegregation which was both disruptive and destructive to education. With the focus no longer on the Court, the parents in BET were left trying to find a strategy for reaching other parents around the city. We decided to enter the upcoming race for Boston School Committee; I was graciously nominated for the job by the group.

I was a total novice to electoral politics, and none of the other parents had any experience either. We had very little money, and my family had lived in Boston for only two years and in our precinct for less than a year. I registered to vote on the same day I signed up as a candidate. I only had part-time work, was not Irish, and had left the Catholic Church. I had no connections with any of the politicians or neighborhood associations which abound in Boston. I also was not a brilliant speaker; the day after my maiden campaign speech, to a Home and School meeting at another school, the president of the local association who had hosted the meeting said, "You're a nice guy, Dave, but, Jesus, are you boring." In short, I had none of the usual qualifications for running for office.

Our group of twenty parents had one thing going for us, however: we had a message that we felt 90% of the people in Boston agreed with, and were dying to hear. The politicians, the *Boston Globe*, and all the behind-the-scenes powers who run Boston, had divided the city on the question, "Are you for or against forced busing?" By making busing and race the issues, they had kept people from discussing what they had in common. No one was speaking to what was on the minds of ordinary decent people.

We began a campaign that indicted both the School Committee and the Federal Court. We said that black parents and white parents had the same hopes and fears for our children, that we felt trapped between the Court and the School Committee, and that nobody was going to look out for our children but us. We said that as parents what was most important about us was what united us: our children's intelligence and ability and character, our hopes for their futures and our determination that they succeed in spite of the daily attacks on them from a school system which served none of them well. We needed a united movement of black and white parents to fight for our children.

We put out campaign literature that featured the pictures of four black and four white parents, each explaining why he or she was in the campaign. We went to every neighborhood in the city—to white South Boston and white Dorchester, to black Dorchester and Roxbury, to East Boston and Hyde Park and Brighton. In every neighborhood we got the same response: "I'm so glad to see this. I didn't think anybody felt this way but me." We began the campaign in the first week of June with twenty campaign workers, and ended it in November with over three hundred volunteers.

We didn't win, of course; the odds were much too great for that. We came in ninth in a field of nineteen, contesting five places on the Committee. We were out-spent and out-organized and out-experienced. But our campaign had a huge effect. We succeeded in forcing every candidate in the race to respond to what we were saying: that the issue in the schools is not race but education. In a summer when racial fighting was repeatedly breaking out in Boston, when black people were being attacked at Carson Beach and cars driven by whites were being stoned in some black neighborhoods, we began a movement that brought together people from every neighborhood and race. We showed that a totally different approach to the issues and to each other was possible, and that it relied on the common sense and decency of ordinary people.

The next summer, after the second year of busing had concluded, the School Committee held a series of three meetings to discuss raising the class size limits; hundreds of black and white parents flocked to School Committee headquarters to be heard. At two of the meetings, the anger of the parents was so intense that the School Committee, experienced demagogues though they were, had to flee the room. Parents continued these two meetings on their own, blacks from Roxbury and whites from South Boston cheering each other as they rose to denounce the Committee and to demand better education for their children.

What I Learned

The meaning of these two years of experience was not immediately clear to me. Certain things were apparent, to be sure. It was soon clear that there was more decency, honor, good sense, and just plain goodness in the working class people of Boston of whatever color than there were in all the forces ranged against them: the politicians white and black, the School Committee, the Federal Court, the Church, the Harvard and Boston University "experts," the *Boston Globe*, the liberals and the leftists.

I had never realized before just how much about the system people understand, and at the same time, how contradictory an individual's thoughts might be. In a society in which people are systematically misinformed, and in which no organized working class movement exists, it seemed possible for the same person to have bizarre misconceptions about, say, another race, or about the problems of the education system, and at the same time to have the most piercing insights into education and a deep fund of goodwill toward working people of another race. Individual consciousness seemed to me to be fragmented, in something like the way the society is fragmented. But when people were together, and could talk collectively about a problem, the most startling and compelling ideas began to emerge.

I also had learned more about how the elite act to control people. Liberal reform designed and managed from the top—"social engineering"—was as effective as conservatism as a means of social control. Desegregation could be used as well as segregation as an instrument to attack people.

The desegregation plan, with its deep cuts in educational services, coupled with its fracturing of the relationships between people and their schools, was actually a sophisticated plan for increased domination of the working people of Boston by the corporate and government elite. And yet, because it was done in the name of reform and racial justice, it was very disarming. White parents who opposed the plan were branded as racists; in addition, they were left with no leaders acknowledged by the media except politicians who really were racists. There was widespread unpublicized opposition to the busing plan among black parents, who, like white parents, felt that they were losing whatever small influence they had over their children's education; white parents at the O'Hearn were amazed to hear black parents' bitter denunciations of the busing plan in our meetings. But black parents in general were immobilized by the plan, because to oppose it meant "to side with the racists."

Desegregation in Boston was a brilliant reversal of roles for the federal government. Just one year after the U.S. government had ended its open role in the slaughter in Vietnam, here was the same government taking the lead supposedly on the side of racial justice. National media coverage of busing in Boston, which consistently represented the white working people of the city as racists, was deeply demoralizing to many people around the country; it seemed to confirm the most negative beliefs about working people. I suspect that it confused many people about the role of the government, and convinced many people, including many who had just become active in social change movements during the war years, that fundamental change is not possible because people are just no good. It helped lay to rest the movement which had come out of the '60s.

The focus on desegregation pitted people against each other, and inevitably made desegregation a numbers game destructive of the education of the very children who had been most victimized by segregation.

A movement for change in the schools based among white and black working class parents—and teachers and students—such as we had begun with Better Education Together, would have done away with segregation, but it would have made education, not race, the priority. A movement from below would have focused on the many things that people have in common: shared goals and values and shared experiences of exploitation that run very deep. The first chance that black and white parents had to talk about education together at the Patrick O'Hearn, they attempted to take competition out of the system. Here were people who had an idea of education that profoundly contradicted what existed. These parents together could have designed an education system changed to its very core, not just superficially, and could have eliminated not only segregation but racial conflict and many other attributes of an anti-working class education system.

My feelings about the left had also changed. The various left-wing organizations around Boston had been outspoken in their support of busing and strident in their attacks on anyone who opposed it as racist. Leftists seemed blind to the reality before their eyes—that people were being cynically manipulated against each other by the government in the name of reform. They also seemed profoundly elitist. They *assumed* that the opposition of white working class parents to busing was racist, and they ignored or were ignorant of black parents' opposition. The contempt of the left for ordinary people led it ironically into alliance with the corporate and government elite. The left played no small role in enabling the elite to present itself as the positive force in society, and ordinary people as the negative.

I began to see more clearly that the system worked by trapping people between bad choices, neither of which met their aspirations: "Are you for or against forced busing?" "Are you for Bush or Dukakis?" "Democrats or Republicans" "Capitalism or Communism?" Heads I win, tails you lose. If they controlled the agenda, they won. We could only win by changing the game.

I felt moved by my experience, but it wasn't clear that anything could come of it. We had won a couple of small victories, but we had lost on all the big issues. My political training from the anti-war years had taught me to measure political success not by incidental wins and losses but by the growth of the conscious movement. We had made a beginning at building a conscious movement, in a way; but this measure of political success only makes real sense if you have a realistic long-term goal of fundamental change. It had become more obvious to me than ever that the society was controlled by a small and brutal elite which held the money, the power, and the cards. But it seemed to me that they would always win, and we would always lose. I believed that revolutionary change was necessary, but not possible.

It was only after a year or so of reflection on these experiences, and extensive discussion with a number of friends, that the full significance of what these parents were doing emerged.

I had been amazed from the start that, subject to a constant barrage of racist misinformation, the white parents whom I met for the most part felt a strong affinity and sympathy for the black parents. What was surprising was not that some anti-black feelings had been generated, but how superficial these feelings were in most people, and how ready they were to work together. I had been fully prepared to see the black parents in a favorable light; seeing the white parents in this way was new.

I was forced to wonder where they got the resources to reject so much of the indoctrination to which they were constantly subjected by the system. These were not political people. As far as I am aware, they had no previous political experience, and they certainly had little education. How could they have better ideas and better sense about these things than all the institutions which affected them—Church and school and political party?

At the same time, the black parents contradicted all the stereotypes. Whether their families had two parents or one—as had many of the white—and in spite of the poverty that they had in common with the white parents, they had a strength and devotion to their children that belied all the slanders of the media and the education system. These were thoughtful, committed, serious people, but when they demanded to know why their children were doing badly at school, they were told, "It's because they are from bad families." At a follow-up meeting about getting a reading teacher, one black parent demanded of the (black) associate superintendent, "Why can those parents in Newton (a wealthy suburb of Boston) get things like that for their kids and we can't?" He replied, "Because they care more about their kids than you do." The parents were better than anyone expected them to be, in defiance of a system that told them they didn't care.

It also became clear that there was something about the personal lives and the relationships among people in the working class neighborhoods that was different from and better than the general culture of the society. Not that the parents had blameless or trouble-free personal lives or relationships—far from it. But there was a certain continuity between the values they believed in and tried to practice in their lives, and the values they thought should characterize the schools and the society. They were against competition and they were against big-shots and manipulators. They believed strongly in equality, and they believed strongly in solidarity. The story of the night that the parents took over the school meeting was told and retold in the neighborhoods on both sides of Washington Street. People had stood up together, and they felt real joy in the fact. These were the values that were important to them, even if their ability to affect the world with them seemed very limited.

And then it occurred to me: these people had values and relationships which contradicted the competitive values and dog-eat-dog relationships of capitalism. Their values could only have come from themselves, from shared efforts to make the world different than it was, in the ways they thought possible. What this meant was that these people, and others like them, were already engaged in a struggle to make a different world. A vision of a new world was implicit in their values and relationships. They were already, without knowing it perhaps, working for revolutionary change.

There was no reason to think that the working people of Boston are any different from working class people the world over. The most important effect on me of those two years was that it changed my view of people, and suggested the basis of a view of history and political change which contradicts both capitalism and Communism.

If these thoughts were true, then the whole game could be changed. There could be a new kind of revolution, which was not only necessary: it was also possible.

2

THE MEANING
OF CLASS STRUGGLE

Marx said that all history is the history of class struggle. The question, however, is what that struggle is about. According to the economic paradigm of history, workers engaged in class struggle—strikes, protest movements, and other forms—have the same goal as their bosses: they are in a self-interested fight for a greater share of the wealth.

My experience with working people in Boston, however, suggested that people's motivations in struggle are different from this, and have more to do with their sense of values.

In the spring of 1986, I talked at length with workers involved in two historic strikes, to find out what they were really fighting for.

One was the strike of meatpackers at the Hormel plant in Austin, Minnesota. In several visits to the union hall in March and April, 1986 I interviewed about twenty-five strikers and their spouses and retired workers active in strike support. They had been on strike since August of the year before. The international union, which had repeatedly attacked the strike, put the local union P-9 into receivership in May of '86 and signed an agreement—representing the strikebreakers—with the company in September. The strikers formed an independent union, the North American Meatpackers Union, and continued their struggle. None of the strikers was rehired.

The other strike was the year-long British miners' strike of 1984-85. In May of 1986, just over a year after the miners had been forced back to work without a contract, I spent two weeks in Yorkshire and South Wales, interviewing thirty miners and their wives and supporters who had played active roles in the dispute.

The British Miners:
"We Were Fighting for the Future Generation"

The year-long strike of the British National Union of Mineworkers (NUM) of 1984-85 was the longest in its history, met by the most thoroughly coordinated attack by the government on any strike in Great Britain since 1926. The miners and their supporters constituted, in the words of the *Financial Times*, "the biggest and most continuous civilian mobilization to confront the government since the Second World War."[4]

The apparent issue in the miners' dispute was the government's determination to close at least 20 (the union predicted 40—rightly, it turns out) of what it considered to be "uneconomic" pits (mines), and the miners' determination to keep them open. Behind the supposedly economic calculation of the government lay its intention to smash the power of the miners as the most highly organized and militant section of the working class in Great Britain. As George Etheridge, a now redundant (laid-off) miner from Grimethorpe, put it:

"It were political really. It had been planned over a ten year period. There was no way that they were going to let us win this strike. If they didn't beat us, they would never beat any other union. That was the main objective. It weren't the coal and the price of it comin' out."

In 1972 the NUM had soundly defeated the government of Edward Heath. Over 15,000 miners and other trade unionists turned back 1,000 police in a mass picket at the Saltley Gate coke depot. The miners effectively stopped the movement of coal in Britain, causing power outtages and displaying in starkest terms the vast potential power of a militant working class. "At the time many of those in positions of influence looked into the abyss and saw only a few days away the possibility of the country being plunged into a state of chaos," one government official said.[5] In 1974, another strike of the NUM forced the collapse of the Heath government. The government soon resolved to break the power of the miners, and undertook massive preparations, detailed in the Ridley Commission report of 1978.

In March, 1984 the government used its pit closure program to force a strike. While the government had prepared for a showdown with the miners for years, the NUM had prepared very little. Still, miners' wives and others organized support groups throughout the coalfields. Towns and villages and workplaces throughout Britain "adopted" pit villages. The miners established pickets and fought pitched battles with police. Police arrested nearly 10,000 miners and their supporters. Over a year after the end of the strike, 50 miners remained in prison on strike-related charges.

In Barnsley, in the heart of the Yorkshire coalfield, a group of six women read that a government official had predicted the strike would not last because "the women will not stand behind their men." "'Oo was the government to tell us we wouldn't stand behind our 'usbands, we wanted to know," one of them said. They put an ad in the local paper asking miners' wives and other interested women to come talk about the strike. They were surprised when nearly 60 women showed up. From this beginning they managed to organize committees in each of the surrounding pit villages, to give assistance to families in applying for social security benefits. These committees went on to collect clothing for children, raise money for food, and organize other activities. Their most important effort was to establish communal kitchens serving regular meals to miners and their families. These communal kitchens became, along with the picket lines, the center of life of the pit villages and the strike. As Hywel Francis, leader of a support group in South Wales, stated, "The support groups created a new welfare state, in defiance of the government."

On March 5, 1985, after a year of struggle and hardship, the striking miners marched back to their pits, led by brass bands and the banners of their local NUM branch. In many branches, the miners' wives marched in the place of honor at the front. The miners had been forced back without an agreement—a bitter defeat, by most standards. And yet, "They went back with style," as one supporter put it. They knew they had fought with unmatched courage and resourcefulness. "It felt terrible when we had to go back," said Jerry Parker, a striker from Nottinghamshire, "but we didn't have our tails between our legs." Arthur Mawson felt that the miners were beaten badly, but "We came through smiling. Everybody's still smiling back at pit." There have been frequent industrial actions at the Frickley pit where Arthur Mawson works since the conclusion of the strike.

This is not to underestimate the extent of the miners' defeat. Certainly in the terms in which the struggle was defined from the outset—pit closures—the miners lost badly. One year after the strike, about 40,000 miners had lost their jobs, with about 35 pits closed. But judged against a larger standard, the miners did not lose; or rather, as Jerry Parker put it, "We lost the battle but not the war."

"If I Get Arrested, Send Me Knittin' Up"

Strikers and their wives were emphatic about the purpose of the strike. "We were fighting for the future generation. That's why it were so important," was a comment made to me repeatedly. "It weren't about money. It were about jobs, and about the children."

In spite of their defeat, people who had been deeply involved emerged from the strike with an astonishing sense of triumph. When I asked a group of miners' wives the question, "Did you win or lose?" they all replied "We won." I asked them how they could possibly say they had won, after the hardships, after the layoffs, after being forced back without a contract. Kathleen Smythe said very simply: "We won because it taught us the meaning of life."

In this strike to save their communities, people found that they themselves created a community and family life closer than they had ever felt before. Kath Townsend, wife of an NUM member and an active member of Barnsley Women Against Pit Closures (WAPC), commented:

> "We went on strike to save our communities. The government were going to shut down our pits and destroy our communities. But it was on strike that we became a real community, more than we ever were. And we found that nothing the government could throw at us could take that away."

For most of the people I talked with, "the community feeling" and "the solidarity of the miners" were the biggest things about the strike.

The strike had important effects on their families. "The strike fetched me and my husband closer, it did. I say that if you got divorced during the strike, then your marriage weren't stable in the first place," Gert Browne, a member of WAPC maintained. During the strike, people broke from traditional roles. Ethel Hogwood, wife of a retired miner, said, "Me family didn't want me to go out on picket line, but I says to them, 'If I get arrested, send me knittin' up.'" Several miners and their wives commented to me that, though their children suffered deprivations during the strike, the effect of the strike on the children was worth it because "It widened their horizons." "Oh, the children were brilliant," said Annie Lean. "They wouldn't ask for treat when their Dad was out of work," and they contributed in the ways they could. "And it got them talking about politics. You couldn't sit down to table without talking about politics."

Some of the most profound effects of the strike were on miners' wives, who had previously been pretty much tied to the kitchen sink. (This is a fact that has been attributed to the supposed "male chauvinism" of the miners. It should rather be seen as how families are forced to adjust to the terrifically exhausting and treacherous work of mining.) Just the fact of organizing had a big effect: "That were a big thing for women, to be able to talk together." When I asked a group of miners' wives what the effects of the strike were on them, they said, "Well, we're here...in a pub during the day talking to a strange man [me]. We wouldn't have done any of these things before the strike." They all agreed that before the strike they would never have had the "courage" to talk with an educated person. As Gert Browne put it, "I'm not afraid to come out now. I've joined the Labour Party, I take part in politics, I speak up at meetin's. Oh, there's no stoppin' us at all now."

Three days earlier, four of the women had traveled to London to take part in a mass picket of newspaper strikers—a picket which was attacked by mounted police. The women see themselves as "the standing army of the working class," ready to be called into action by whoever else needs them. Their support groups continue to meet to discuss working class issues, which to their minds now include everything from unemployment to nuclear disarmament. For many miners, as Arthur Mawson said, "The most important thing about the strike were the women. They made it bearable to stop out."

The Hormel Meatpackers' Strike:
"You Can't Compromise on Right"

The specific issues in the Hormel meatpackers' strike included safety, wages, and the company's effort to impose a two-tier wage system in the plant. The Austin, Minnesota plant was Hormel's flagship, with new facilities constructed on the basis of a $20 million loan extracted from the workers and opened in 1982. In 1978, workers at the plant had been making $10.69 per hour. They took deep wage cuts as the price of keeping Hormel in Austin, so that in 1985 they were making only $8.25 per hour. After opening the new plant, Hormel had subjected workers to ferocious speed-up, with the result that serious accidents occurred in the plant at a rate of 202 injuries per

100 workers in 1984. Hormel wanted to bring wages up only to $10.00, with new hires coming in at the $8.25 rate. The company was unwilling to budge on safety and production goals.

The struggle of Local P-9 was distinguished both by the attack against it by the international union, the United Food and Commercial Workers (UFCW), and by the extent to which the local reached out to other unions and the public for support. Teams of strikers went out all over the country, speaking in union halls and factories, leafletting neighborhoods and shopping centers.

Their struggle struck a responsive chord among rank-and-filers everywhere, and among some union leaders. Supporters raised hundreds of thousands of dollars at plant gates, and thousands of rank-and-file workers converged on Austin to demonstrate their support in rallies and on the picket line—autoworkers from Detroit and Toledo and Kansas; striking flight attendants from Kansas and New York; painters, construction workers, and striking cannery workers from the West Coast; coal miners from West Virginia and Pennsylvania and southern Illinois; striking pressmen from Chicago; railwaymen and electrical workers from Massachusetts; steelworkers from Ohio and Illinois and northern Minnesota; garment workers, communications workers, and hospital workers from New York; shipbuilders from Maine; meatpackers from all over the Midwest and from Texas; caravans of farmers, some of whom had just returned from Nicaragua, who were building a movement against foreclosures; teachers from all over Minnesota; and others. Black and white workers, Hispanic and Filipino, men and women: all came to Austin to take part in the struggle.

The strikers fought for more than a year, through tremendous hardships. Over 200 were arrested, and hundreds more were tear-gassed or otherwise attacked by police. Many lost their homes and cars. Others lost their health and life insurance and had their utilities cut off. All lost their jobs.

Like the British miners, the striking meatpackers understood that far more was at stake than their specific demands. In a speech to supporters in Boston in February, 1986, Pete Winkels, business agent of Local P-9, made this clear:

"Our people are never going to get back what we've already lost financially. We know that. But we're fighting for our families and for the next generation. And we're not going to give up."

Since it was precisely the strikers and their families who suffered the economic and emotional costs of the strike, the explanation that "we're fighting for our families and for the next generation" has to be interpreted in a class context. "For the next generation" was a phrase the strikers used again and again to describe why they were fighting, as if these words encapsulated their feelings about creating a future very different from where things seem headed, not just for their immediate families, but for other people like themselves. Karl Wroczek explained his own activity in the strike by saying, "All the working class people, the rank-and-file type people, have got to realize that they're going down the drain and pull together."

The strikers' sense of family relationships and class solidarity were deeply intertwined. Edward Stafford's family has 300 total years in Hormel. "I'm more bitter than I've ever been in my lifetime," at the company and at the members of the union who scabbed on the strike, he said. "But my family ties are stronger now than they've ever been. They know I don't have a job, and they're here to support me. There's a few families that have broken up because of the strike, but that's just the excuse, not the reason." He stayed on strike "because I made a commitment to be on strike, and I'll be on strike as long as it takes."

The strikers frequently expressed their determination in terms of their sense of morality, of doing what was right from a working class standpoint. Vicki Guyette, wife of Local P-9 president Jim Guyette, said, "I hope I never have to go through another one. But if the situation was the same, I'd be all for it. It's the right thing to do, and you can't compromise on right." Homer Frampton, a retired telephone lineman from Iowa, explained that he was on the meatpackers' picket line every day because "It's the struggle of right against corporate evil."

The participants in the strike felt themselves deeply changed by it. Bill Bartels said, "Before the strike we were just workers." They knew that what they were doing was important, and, as Carol Jarvis said, "It's exciting to make history."

Part of the change was a new sense of the power of people when they act collectively. Scott Weil explained it in this way:

"People have to understand that they are powerful. If just the three or four of us sitting here decided to do something, we could make it happen....I went to school for three years for supermarket management. My professor told me to try to get ahead. They teach you to brownnose. They get the people in the concept that people working together don't work. That's what I was taught. The system is management-orientated. But you can't make it by yourself."

Ron Gomery, another striker, thought that the most important lesson from the strike is that "People working together can accomplish more than you can imagine."

This feeling about the power of people acting together also seemed to affect people's feelings about themselves personally. In the struggle, people strengthened the collective ties which the company and their schooling had sought to break, to weaken them as isolated individuals. Scott Weil described this:

"I was brainwashed in high school, 'If you're not an "A" student, you're nobody. But I learned that you don't have to be the smartest man to get 1500 people moving in the same direction...I have a soul, I have a conscience. They [the company] want to belittle you, to take away the rights of being a human being. It's not just today, it's tomorrow that counts, and how you feel about yourself....The people on strike, we feel good, we feel like a family, and that's what we've got to get around to people."

Scott Weil and Steve Marquette, both younger workers, were part of the roving picket of a couple hundred strikers who went to Hormel plants in Ottumwa and Dubuque. According to Steve, "The Ottumwa people called a meeting and only got nine people there. We said, 'That's OK, that's a start. You just have to talk to more people.' Next time, they had a couple hundred....[The strike] was a big personal change for me. At first, I didn't know what was going to happen when I did this stuff [leafletting, talking with people]. But now I see that people's minds are changing....In that plant, we were just numbers. You climb to the top of the ladder and you find there's shit at the top."

"Getting the Closeness of the Thing"

For many strikers, the most important thing about the strike was the feeling of closeness it created with their fellows. They sounded very much like the British miners as they described it. Ron Gomery had only been minimally involved in the union before the strike. Now he thought the most important accomplishment of the strike was that it created a real community out of the strikers: "We said we were brothers and sisters before. Now we really are."

For Ralph Corman, who wore a "Firee Retiree" button, the best thing about the strike was "Getting the closeness of the thing" from the people in the union. He also felt a new sense of understanding the world: "What I like best about the strike is finding out so many things [going on in the world] I don't like." During the strike, Ralph and his wife Anne and other retirees spent a good deal of time at the Minnesota statehouse in St. Paul, trying to organize support for their cause and also involving themselves in other issues, like the plight of farmers and the homeless. But Anne and Ralph were both troubled by their new knowledge. Anne said, "I worry about the homeless, and about all the people out there who are worse off than we are. I worry about it for the next generation—not my children, but my grandchildren."

It was remarkable when I talked with them that the pain the strikers talked about never seemed to be their own. The older people were in it to the end, to support the younger people. The younger people were sticking with it to protect the older workers. Karl Wroczek was 53 years old and on rehabilitation status, but he was fired during the strike for alleged "strike misconduct" on the picket line. Like most of the older workers, he carries multiple injuries from the plant—cartilage out in his right knee, three crushed discs in his lower back and two in his neck, ulnar nerve damage in his right hand and tendinitis in both shoulders. He said he worried, "not so much for myself, because my house is paid for, but for the young people. They're losing things, houses and cars, and they'll have the bill collector after them for the rest of their lives."

The first sit-down strike of the 1930s had taken place at the Austin Hormel plant in 1933, but Local P-9 had not had a strike since then. Yet like the British miners, the P-9ers understood that, whatever the outcome of their strike, it was the beginning of a long war. Anne Corman commented: "It's the younger ones who are the hard core. The strike's been worth it for the education. These young ones are going to keep on fighting no matter what happens to the strike."

The Meaning of Class Struggle

These strikes by British miners and American meatpackers tested all the resources that the strikers and their families and other supporters could bring to them. In the end, it was only on the basis of their commitment to the larger struggle, rather than a victory for themselves measurable in material terms, that the miners and meatpackers found the courage and resources to push on against overwhelming odds.

There is nothing unique about the concerns and the values which these strikes expressed. They are widely shared by workers and other people in every land. Some media commentators described the solidarity and commitment of the British miners as unique to close-knit mining communities and the shared dangers of the miners' occupation. In this sentimental portrait, the miners' strike represented the last vestiges of a traditional way of life, rather than values and commitments endemic to working class struggle. I asked a meatpacker from a Hormel plant in Ottumwa, Iowa, one of 503 workers fired from their jobs for honoring a roving picket line of strikers from the Austin plant, why he would sacrifice so much for a fight that was not even his own. He replied: "My father fought for my generation, and I'm going to fight for the next one." The miners would have understood his comment perfectly.

The usual explanation of strikes and class struggle—that workers on strike are simply fighting for "a bigger piece of the pie"—does not hold water. While wages or working conditions or particular injustices are usually the *occasions* for strikes or workers' movements, their real goals lead people to make great personal sacrifices in class struggle—sacrifices which make nonsense of any calculus of economic gain—and still count these struggles as victories.

These strikes reveal that class struggle is a struggle over different conceptions of what it means to be human. The goal of contending classes in this struggle is to shape the world with their own conception of values and relationships. In collective struggle, workers create a microcosm of the world as they believe it should be, and draw strength from the realization that they are the source of it. In certain respects, strikes are revolution on a small scale.

Why then were these strikes defeated?

The Miners' Struggle: Dying Past or Revolutionary Future?

For all its use of brute force, the weapons which the British government used against the miners to greatest effect were not physical
but ideological: the government was able to persuade the public that
it was defending the public interest.

The government's tactics chiefly came down to two. One was to
present itself as the voice of progress. The pits which the miners
were defending were "uneconomic." The miners, claimed the government, were holding onto a past which was not viable. It may be unfortunate that miners have to be sacrificed for the larger good, but
that is the only responsible approach the government can take. The
second tactic followed closely from the first. Having successfully
presented the miners as desperately defending a special interest at cost
to the nation, it was not difficult then to depict any violence on the
picket line as the result of the miners' selfish refusal to accept the
inevitable.

The NUM made little organized attempt to answer either of these
charges. Virtually all the resources of the union were thrown into the
picket lines, which had the capacity to consume all the resources the
miners could bring to bear and more. There was no attempt at a mass
education campaign, no attempt to reach the public with an analysis
of the real issues and the significance of the strike for the whole working class. When it did speak of the larger issues, it spoke of the
strike as a defense of the welfare state against Thatcherism—a defensive approach which was entirely incapable of defeating the government's offensive. With the exception of a couple of leaflets produced
locally in South Wales over four months into the strike, there was no
literature produced by the NUM directed to members of other unions
or the general public until the year-long strike was 9 months old.
These few pieces, when they came, were wholly inadequate.

The ideological attack of the government could have been turned
around, but only by exposing the standards of capitalist progress to
another standard.

The future toward which British capital is leading people is grim
indeed, and not just for miners. The most obvious element of that
future is massive unemployment. The industrial North of England, as
well as Scotland and South Wales, experienced devastating "deindustrialization" from 1980 to 1986. Sheffield, for example, the historic
center of specialty steel manufacturing in England, had lost approxi-
mately 80% of its steel-making capacity in the years leading up to the

miners' strike. A member of the Education Committee of Sheffield told me that, 10 years earlier, the committee had been alarmed to find that some three to four hundred 16-19 year-olds were out of work. In 1986, he said, that figure was in excess of ten thousand. Unemployment in all of Great Britain at the time was nearing an historic four million persons.

The real issue for the working class of Britain is not whether five or forty pits will be closed, or whether some steel manufacturing might trickle back, or whether the dole going to 4 million unemployed workers will be sufficient for them to eke out an existence. The issue is that capitalism is incompatible with the lives of the great majority of British people. The attack on the miners was part of a larger offensive by British capital to smash the power of the organized working class, to force it to submit to the idea of civilization imposed by the capitalist class.

An approach which exposed the whole system of social relations in Great Britain, and which proposed the transformation of British society, was the only strategy which could have put logic and the future on the side of the miners. It was the only basis on which the miners might convincingly have argued that they represented not a regressive special interest but the best hopes of the majority of the British people.

The choice for the miners was to accept the government's characterization of being dragged unwillingly into a capitalist future, or to point to a revolutionary future which they, and the rest of the working people of Britain, could create together. That future was already being created by them in a modest way on the picket line and in their communal kitchens, in their enormous effort of mutual support, in their egalitarian relationships, and in their commitment to each other and the next generation. In the values and relationships which were the strength of the strike, the miners and their wives and supporters were creating an image of the world as they believed it should be. They were creating the potential basis for the transformation of the whole society.

The NUM is not to be faulted for not having a strategy calling for revolutionary change. What union does, after all? The NUM carried out with courage and unprecedented determination a traditional trade union strategy of industrial action limited to the picket line.

But that, in a way, is the point. It would only have been in going beyond trade unionism to adopt revolutionary goals, that the importance of reaching out to other unions and the public, or of explaining the relationships among the issues which confront the working class, or of posing the alternative futures which lie open to Britain, or of articulating the vision of a new society implicit in the actions of its members and supporters, would have been clear. Given the determination of the ruling class to break the union, the NUM could only have won by changing the game.

The president of the NUM, Arthur Scargill, was roundly attacked as a revolutionary by "moderate" trade union leaders and conservative press alike. In his address to the annual NUM conference on July 1, 1985 he described the strike as a victory which transformed the lives of those who took part in it, and said:

"The NUM has challenged the very heart of the capitalist system. We have refused to accept that any industry inside capitalist society, whether public or private, has the right to destroy the livelihood of men and women at the stroke of an accountant's pen."[6]

This is a very powerful statement, remarkable for its commitment to challenge capital's right to destroy people's lives for the sake of profit. Yet that is precisely the right which will continue to exist as long as the capitalist system exists. The statement reflects the inevitably defensive posture of the union, in the absence of a viable concept of revolutionary change.

Why Was P-9 Defeated?

There were many factors involved in P-9's defeat. The workers were striking in the face of a general corporate counteroffensive against labor, designed to take back everything workers had won in the 1960s and '70s. The strikers were systematically betrayed by the international UFCW; liberal and "socialist" AFL-CIO leaders closed ranks with the most obviously reactionary leaders to isolate and defeat the strikers.

But the defeat of Local P-9 cannot be explained by external factors alone. In spite of corporate attacks and AFL-CIO betrayal, the huge support won by the strikers from other rank-and-file unionists could have been turned into victory. What went wrong?

The weaknesses of the Hormel strike, like those of the British miners' strike, were a function of the extent to which the real goals of the struggle were not spelled out and acted upon. The P-9ers clearly had both immediate and long-term goals: they wanted to win the strike, and they also wanted to change society in very profound ways. Their determination to accomplish this second goal led them to keep up their strike, with its escalating personal costs, long after any real hope of winning on the immediate issues had disappeared.

In fact the condition for winning either their short or long-term goals was the same: the strikers had to state openly that they were trying to organize a working class movement for fundamental change, and carry out a strategy reflecting this purpose.

The Hormel strikers were a great source of inspiration to workers around the country; the meaning of their struggle was deeply felt, but never made the basis for concerted action. The P-9ers were leading the fight against concessions which companies were demanding from workers everywhere, and the "No More Concessions" slogan was a big part of their campaign. But the local did not attempt to offer an analysis of the corporate attack, or to relate it to a wider analysis of society. The leadership did not try to show that in the values and relationships of the strikers and millions of other people like them lay the seeds of a new world, rather than just a defensive treadmill against concessions.

The idea that 900 people in Austin, Minnesota, could fight the corporate counteroffensive on behalf of the entire U.S. working class was absurd—but that was the idea which the local leaders, their consulting firm, and the leaders of the support coalition promoted. The strike leadership encouraged a relationship between P-9 and other workers based on charitable donations rather than class struggle; P-9 would do the fighting, while other workers sent money and support. The support for the strikers' families which the "Adopt-A-Family" progam raised from other union locals was much needed, but it became a substitute for building a movement.

The way to win the strike was to spread it. The strikers did not need just moral and financial support, but for other workers to take action of their own. P-9ers did briefly attempt to spread the strike with a roving picket line, which was honored at the Ottumwa, Iowa, Hormel plant and several other Hormel installations, but it dropped this tactic at the request of the UFCW International, as the price of reopening negotiations with the company.

After repeated pleas to the International for help in preparing the strike went unheard, P-9 hired a consulting firm, Corporate Campaign, Inc. (CCI). With Corporate Campaign's assistance, P-9ers made an unprecedented effort to inform other workers of their fight;

they distributed hundreds of thousands of leaflets, made hundreds of speeches at factories and plant gates and union halls around the country. Yet none of the literature produced by the local or its consultants truly showed the connections between the strike and the issues confronting other workers, other than to represent the P-9 struggle as a "fight against concessions."

Instead, Corporate Campaign misled people about the meaning of the fight. The literature which CCI produced identified the enemy as "corporate greed," rather than the corporate system. CCI's analysis isolated the Hormel struggle rather than extending it to other workers with similar problems, by presenting Hormel as a special case. It claimed that George Hormel—the founder and previous owner—would never have treated "his" workers in the shoddy way that the current management was doing.

Corporate Campaign directed the strikers away from class struggle and toward pleas for sympathy from politicians and churches. At one point, one of the consultants padlocked the plant gate and mailed the key to the Governor—suggesting that the real power over the outcome of the strike lay in the hands of the Governor, not in the movement which the strikers could organize.

The strikers had succeeded in January in shutting the plant with a militant picket line. The Governor had called in the National Guard in response. After the Guard departed, strikers again wanted to shut the plant. They felt a great deal of frustration when the local president publicly dismissed the idea of militant action.

It may have been impossible for the strikers to shut the plant again, given the heavy police presence. But the alternative strategy presented by the consultant and the local leadership—to boycott Hormel—was no answer. The idea that Hormel could be brought to its knees by a consumer boycott—a boycott which the AFL-CIO was actively organizing against—was silly and disarming. The boycott was used to defuse the struggle which the meatpackers had begun.

The betrayal of Local P-9 by the International UFCW and the AFL-CIO leadership, and the larger significance of this betrayal, cried out for exposure. The P-9 leadership exposed the role of the International in this specific strike, but the role played by the AFL-CIO leadership in the labor movement as a whole was not examined. Support for P-9 was coordinated nationally by an organization calling itself the "National Rank and File Against Concessions"(NRFAC). As far as it was able, NRFAC suppressed criticism within the support movement of the AFL-CIO leadership for their attacks on the strike, and for their overall role in the labor movement. When the UFCW put Local P-9 into receivership, NRFAC dropped its support like a hot potato.

What P-9 and its supporters needed to do to win their strike was not complicated; it simply required a different vision of what the struggle was all about. They needed to do three things:

1. Widely circulate a clear analysis of their strike in the context of class struggle in the U.S. and the world. This would have meant showing the relationship between Hormel's actions and the corporate offensive against other workers, analyzing the role played by the AFL-CIO leadership on behalf of capital, and showing that in the values of equality and solidarity basic to P-9 and to working class struggles everywhere lay a vision of a new society.

2. Extend their strike as widely as possible—to other Hormel plants, and to all other workers with a stake in the outcome of the class war.

3. Make the P-9 strike the focal point for organizing a movement challenging the goals, values, social vision, and power of capitalism.

P-9ers could have acted as organizers and leaders of a spreading working class movement raising fundamental questions about the nature and direction of U.S. society.

They could only have taken this step, however, if they had had a way of thinking about their struggle that made its meaning more clear to them, and a way of thinking about society that told them that fundamental change was possible. These strikes were defeated by the absence of a concept of change capable of expressing their real significance.

3

REVOLUTION
AND EVERYDAY LIFE

Stories like the British miners' and American meatpackers' are inspiring, but they are also unusual. It is not obvious that they have much relevance to most people's lives.

Is there any connection between the unselfish motivations of people involved in dramatic strikes like these and people's everyday lives?

Capitalism and Social Control

We cannot see the extent of people's everyday struggle to change society unless we first understand the enormous pressures brought to bear against them. People are under attack in every area of their lives in capitalist society, by institutions designed to persuade or force them to accept capitalist relations based on competition and inequality as legitimate, and the capitalist social order as unchangeable.

Let's look first at some of the methods which the system uses to dominate people, and then at the ways in which people resist.

Capitalism is first and foremost a system of social control. The vast resources of the capitalist class are directed primarily toward this purpose; profit and economic development are subordinate to this end. Capitalism attempts to secure its control by attacking in everyday life those things which are most fundamental to our humanity: our understanding of ourselves and other people and our relationships with them.

The chief *weapon* of capitalists in their struggle to dominate society is isolation: they strive in every area of life to break the bonds among people from which people draw their understanding of reality and their ability to change it. This socially-imposed isolation is intended to induce doubts in each individual about his or her own worth, and about the viability of relationships which do not follow the capitalist model of competition and exploitation.

Their chief *strategy* is to encourage in each individual, made to feel personally insecure in his isolation, the capitalist view of other people—that other people are mindless and selfish competitors, imbued with capitalist values and engaged in a lonely battle for "success." "Everybody agrees with the way things are going but me. Maybe I should go along too."

Their chief *goal* is to fulfill the capitalist vision of human society, in which the vast majority live lives of brutish passivity, and a capitalist elite produce the material and cultural wealth. Capitalists strive to create a world in which fulfillment comes not from human relationships but from things—from possession and consumption of the fruits of the capitalist economy. They strive to shape all of society with their view of human beings.

Capitalists have enlisted every element of society in their effort to strengthen their control. For example, work has been organized as far as possible to fragment jobs into specialized, routine tasks and to fragment collective relationships among workers. More and more jobs which once required all-around skills have been broken down into smaller parts, in which all the worker does is pull a lever or turn a screw or punch a number; more and more jobs formerly done by groups of workers under their collective control have been reduced to assembly-line or other work in which workers have no control over the pace or manner of work.

Work reduced to mind-numbing routine is robbed of its human qualities. Rather than being a source of fulfillment, in which a person uses and develops his abilities in productive activity, such jobs become a source of mental anguish and feelings of failure. Anyone who has ever worked at a mindless job—and so many of them are—knows the feeling they create. Working at a job that doesn't use your mind makes you feel like you don't have a mind. Working at a job where all you do all day is turn a screw or pull a lever or punch a number makes you feel no better than a screw or a lever or a number.

The design of these jobs is not an accident, and not an inevitable function of industrialism; it is part of a carefully planned strategy, known as "Taylorism" or "scientific management," designed to concentrate knowledge and control over the work process in the hands of management. In his 1911 book, *Principles of Scientific Management*, Frederick Taylor, the originator of scientific management, lists three principles. According to the first, managers should gather up all the traditional knowledge of the workmen, and reduce it to simple rules and laws. By the second principle, "All possible brain-work should be removed from the shop and centered in the planning or laying-out department." By the third, work should be broken into a series of specific tasks, the manner and time alloted for each task to be described by management in written instructions to the worker.[7]

The premise of scientific management is that there is a day-to-day battle between bosses and workers for control of the work process. Taylorism attempts to win this war by breaking the collective work process into an individual process in which every action of each worker is under the direct control of the boss. It attempts to rob the worker of his skills and of his knowledge of the overall work process, to render him interchangeable and expendable. Scientific management attempts to reduce the mass of workers to cogs of a machine controlled by management.

In his landmark book, *Labor and Monopoly Capital*, Harry Braverman comments that, "It is impossible to overestimate the importance of the scientific management movement in the shaping of the modern corporation and indeed all the institutions of capitalist society which carry on labor processes."[8]

Like work itself, technology in capitalist society is designed to strengthen management control, by making the skills of the individual worker more expendable, and by allowing the pace of work to be regulated by centralized decisions. Machinery, as Marx explained, is nothing but "congealed labor." Machinery encodes within its working parts the skills of workers, and replaces these skills in the production process—as the skills of typesetters, for example, have been encoded within computerized typesetting equipment. Management can control the pace of work simply by controlling the speed of the assembly line or the machines which the workers must tend. In his *Forces of Production*, a study of the history of technology and work, David F. Noble concludes that the primary motive force behind the introduction of machinery into the workplace has not been economic efficiency but management control. When confronted in designing machinery with a choice between greater economic efficiency or greater management control, management characteristically opts for greater control. "The drive to automate," says Noble, "has been from its inception the drive to reduce dependence upon skilled labor, to deskill necessary labor, and to reduce rather than to raise wages."[9] Technology is used at the same time to enhance the illusion that it is capital which is the productive element in society.

Even before they enter the workforce, people have been subjected to years of training to encourage them to acquiesce in the attacks on their humanity at work and elsewhere. The education system, for example, has been shaped by the ruling elite—as far as they have been able—to condition students to fit passively into a world over which they will have no control. Rather than developing in students a critical sense of their own ability to understand the world and work together to change it, the education system tends to fragment students' relations with each other, undermine their self-confidence, and distort their understanding of themselves and the world. Competition for grades and approval in school is intended to condition them to compete for jobs and the approval of authority figures when they leave school. The hierarchy of grades and "objective" test scores is intended to teach them to accept their place in an unequal society as properly their own. Concentration on meaningless tasks, which characterizes so much of school work, is meant to prepare them to accept the boredom of meaningless jobs when they graduate.

The culture of consumerism in modern capitalist society complements the dehumanized work process. The advertising culture reduces life to a surface of images to be purchased and consumed. People are encouraged to define themselves by the images that they acquire by consuming products—to become a "Marlboro Man" or a "Gucchi" woman, or to become Michael Jordan by wearing the right brand of sneakers.

As industrial capitalism robs people of their skills and erodes the human relationships on which people's sense of themselves depend, it creates a crisis of identity and self-worth in each individual. Advertising seeks to intensify this crisis of the self, presenting images of flawless "beautiful people," who seem to exist in a carefree world without boring jobs and daily troubles. As people measure themselves and their lives against these images, new, artificial wants are created. To be like the people in the ad, you only have to buy the product. Advertising thus reduces a social crisis—the crisis of a dehumanizing culture—to a crisis of personal inadequacy. At the same time, it reduces the idea of change from social change to personal change, accomplished by buying a different car or mouthwash or cigarette. As the ad says, "Reeboks Let U.B.U." Advertising thus encourages people to "solve" the crisis of personal worth created by capitalism by consuming the products of the capitalist economy. In this way, it becomes a powerful force for social control.[10]

The effect of advertising as a means of enforcing capitalist power is not accidental. In *Captains of Consciousness*, Stewart Ewen explains that, in the face of rising class struggle and revolutionary activity in the wake of World War I, capitalists came to understand that "the social control of workers must stretch beyond the realm of the factory and into the very communities and structures within which they lived." Advertising was conceived as "a new mechanism...of social order in the realm of daily life."[11]

The media—television, newspapers, the radio—further reinforce people's feelings of isolation and inadequacy. The media generate a kind of false community, dominated by corporate values and corporate images of the world. To join your fellow humans in this community, all you have to do is surrender your real feelings and values to agree with whatever it is that the media say that other people think. In the absence of an alternative image of the world with social legitimacy, to refuse to accept the corporate view is to cut oneself off from social reality. Thus however convinced a person may be that the media are full of lies; however disgusted he may be at the image of human life which is presented by them; however contemptuous of the politicians and corporate leaders who parade across the screen: however a person feels about the image of reality presented by the media, he can still be made to feel that "nobody feels this way but me." A person's desire for connection with other people can lead him to acquiesce in the way he's been told to think.

The tendency of the capitalist organization of work, technology, education, and the marketplace to isolate people and encourage them to fulfill themselves through their relationship to things rather than other people is strengthened by the fundamental idea of capitalist culture—competition. In the capitalist view, the individual is alone in the world, struggling to prove his worth in a contest with other individuals. In this war of each against each, the individual defines himself not through his mutual dependencies with other people but in spite of them. Capitalism encourages the individual to see other people as the enemy; in Sartre's phrase in *No Exit*, "Hell is other people." As people are pitted against each other in the competition for grades, jobs, approval, and status, they experience social problems like dehumanized jobs, unemployment, and inequality as personal failures, so that their capacity to act together against the real enemy is undermined.

At the same time, capitalism encourages people to see other people, even their most intimate relationships—with husband or wife or friends—in terms of the disposable consumer culture. Forming relationships is like shopping in a supermarket—or going to a "singles bar." If one relationship doesn't work, throw it away and choose another. Commitment is for saps. In this world you had better look out for Number One. Freedom is conceived in these terms as an essentially negative condition. "Freedom" means freedom from restraint, freedom from obligation or commitment.

Alienation from other people is thus an inherent part of this society. The individual is alienated from society, which acts to restrain him, and from other individuals, with whom he must compete. He is alienated also from himself, since his concept of himself as a person rests upon his relationships with other people, who are the enemy against whom he must define himself. Capitalist relations undermine people's sense of themselves and create profound insecurities in them. In its drive to distort and attack human relationships, capitalism creates a profoundly anti-human culture.

Capitalism is an acid which eats away at all human connections. It seeps into every corner of people's lives, to affect relationships with husband or wife, friends and co-workers, and people's own sense of personal adequacy. The capitalist view of people leads to personal isolation and emotional desperation. The corrosive effects of this culture are in evidence everywhere. Never has there been a society with so much apparent wealth and so much private misery. The divorce and suicide rates, the incidence of alcoholism and drug abuse, the savage criminality of corporate and political leaders at the top of the social order and of drug gangs at the bottom, are all testimony to how brutally anti-human is a culture which must deny human connectedness as its most essential characteristic.

The Battle of Everyday Life

In spite of all the pressures people face every day, we know that not all relationships are competitive or exploitative or disposable. People do create meaningful connections with other people. They do have commitment to each other. While people's self-confidence and values and ideas about the world are under constant attack, still in most instances people find the resources to resist the pressure and keep a sense of themselves and their own values and ideas. Every day we can observe, in our own lives and around us, people being generous and supportive rather than competitive and self-seeking—acting in ways which contradict the values and relationships of capitalism.

People's efforts to establish positive human connections take many different forms. A number of years ago, my wife and I moved to an old farmhouse in rural Maine. My wife was pregnant, and I had yet to draw my first paycheck from my teaching job. The woman who ran the little gas station-market down the road insisted on lending us $10 until I got paid. For the first few weeks, every evening different neighbors would drop by with a hot supper or vegetables from their garden—to welcome us and help us out. This treatment was not just for newcomers. If someone in the community had to go to the hospital, people would go door to door and take up a collection to help with their bills. When someone died, there would be a Grange supper to raise money for funeral expenses. There seemed to be a constant round of collections for the support of one family or another.

In most places, of course, people's efforts to support each other are not so obvious or community-wide as in rural Maine. Still, those efforts are there; they are there in exceptional situations, like the help people give to a family that has had a tragedy like a fire, and they are there in the simple things that people do for each other, not for hope of gain but out of kindness. These acts might involve sacrifice; for example, at the day-care center where our daughter works, several teachers—who make only $8 an hour and have their own families to support—buy food and clothes for some of the children from poorer families. Or they might involve no sacrifice at all, as in my wife's office when secretaries give sympathy and encouragement to a woman who has just been chewed out by her boss. They might be as personal as listening to a friend's troubles and offering advice and comfort, or as public as organizing neighbors to fight a developer taking over some property in the neighborhood. They might be as unusual as the person who leaps into a river to save a drowning child, or as commonplace as parents working hard at jobs they hate to provide for their children.

Everyday family life is an important locus of struggle against capitalism. The contemporary American family creates a positive environment for its children only through active struggle against capitalist culture, however little people may consciously identify that culture with the capitalist class. The competitiveness and inequality which are fundamental to capitalism exert great pressures on the relations between husbands and wives. Economic hardship or unemployment can subject a marriage to terrible tests. The attacks on their self-esteem which most people experience at work can have poisonous effects at home. The consumer culture hammers away at people's sense of values. Drugs and alcohol are constantly promoted as an escape from struggle and commitment to each other. And their children are surrounded by all the snares and pressures of capitalist culture which the parents themselves experience.

Yet in the face of these intense pressures, most parents work to provide for their children and to protect and shape them in a positive direction. They try to make their marriage a healthy environment in which their children can grow. They investigate what influences at school, in the neighborhood, in the rest of society have good or bad effects on their children and, to the extent they think they can, try to change them. They try to explain the world to their children and give them values and personal resources which will help them to shape their own lives. In all these acts, they are trying to counter the logic, the values, the relationships of capitalism as it is experienced in everyday life.

The alliance which emerged between white and black working class parents of Dorchester (see Chapter One) was rooted in their everyday struggle against capitalism. The ruling elite of Boston was trying to get white working parents to line up with the white elite against black working people, and to get black parents to line up with black politicians and federal and state authorities against whites. What at first may have seemed like a surprising step, for white and black parents to ally with each other, was really a natural outgrowth of cooperative relations they had already created in their own comunities and of values which they already shared—belief in solidarity with other working people and contempt for elites. Once the black and white parents were able to sit in somebody's living room and talk about their children together, they recognized in each other the shared feelings and values that the system was attempting to hide.

Especially in working class communities, people are linked to one another by all the dependencies and strengths which arise out of the effort to survive and to create human society in the face of tremendous obstacles. They are linked by the relations of solidarity which they create in defiance of the official culture of competition and the "me-first" approach. The powerful collective relationships upon which strikes like those of the British miners or Local P-9 depend do not drop from thin air. They are a stronger and more fully realized version of the relationships which are already part of people's lives and communities.

The values which the British miners and Hormel meatpackers expressed in interviews did not grow out of their strikes: the strikes

grew out of their values. The strikes were more dramatic and collective expressions of goals they pursued every day—for their children
and for each other. In collective struggle people discovered how deeply their values were shared by others. They found that the things they
valued most in everyday life became more real; the strikes "fetched
them closer," they "became a real community," now they "really
were brothers and sisters." These vast collective struggles crystallized
the meaning of lives spent in daily struggle in the pit or the kitchen
or on the killing floor. Their sense of triumph came from finding that
the source of the things they valued was each other.

The home and community are not the only arena where people's
anti-capitalist values come into play. The workplace is a key focal
point of everyday struggle over the direction of society.

What most struck Barbara Garson as she interviewed workers for
her book, *All The Livelong Day: The Meaning and Demeaning of
Routine Work*, was people's passionate desire to work well, in spite
of a century of Taylorism, and their resilience and creativity in cop-
ing with demeaning jobs. Garson found that people resisted the dehumanizing nature of their jobs in a multitude of ways. Their resistance
ranged from doing routine assembly work with their eyes closed—to
make it more challenging—to a wildcat strike to shut down an auto
assembly line that had been speeded up past what workers' would
tolerate:

> I wasn't particularly surprised by the negative things I saw in
> factories: speed, heat, humiliation, monotony....It was the posi-
> tive things I saw that touched me the most.

> In factories and offices around this country work is systematically
> reduced to the most minute and repetitious tasks. Supervision
> ranges from counting bones, raising hands to use the bathroom,
> issuing "report cards" with number and letter grades for quantity,
> quality, co-operation, dependability, attendance, etc.

> Through all this workers make a constant effort, sometimes crea-
> tive, sometimes pathetic, sometimes violent, to put meaning and
> dignity back into their daily activity.

> [These are] the men and women who renewed my faith that while
> capitalism stinks, people are something else.[12]

Struggle in the workplace is often invisible, because it has been forced underground. In his study, *Cultures of Solidarity*, Rick Fantasia says that, "Because the overall system [of industrial relations] is designed to channel and derail worker solidarity, independent activity and initiative will not likely appear on the surface of that system, nor will it likely appear in recognizable forms."[13] Class solidarity has to be found rather in the relationships which workers maintain with each other outside the routinized collective bargaining system, and in the "cultures of solidarity" which they develop and draw upon in conflicts with the system.

Workers on the job confront a vast array of forces, all concentrated to suppress militance and solidarity. The most important form of working class struggle in this context is the wildcat (unauthorized) strike, which represents an attack by workers on both the company and the union leadership. The best estimate is that "the majority of all strikes in the post-war period have been wildcats." Wildcats occur far more frequently than official statistics suggest. Bureau of Labor Statistics data only record strikes of greater than eight hours duration; most wildcat strikes are settled in less time.[14]

But "cultures of solidarity" do not involve only militant actions like wildcat strikes. Fantasia describes the day-to-day relationships among workers at a steel alloy castings plant where he worked. At lunch and on breaks, or over a few beers after work, workers created relationships which they were then able to draw upon in struggles with the boss and the union leaders. By swapping stories about their backgrounds, talking about racial matters and swapping ethnic foods, and making jokes and roughhousing, workers learned more about each other, expressed appreciation for each others' backgrounds, and smoothed over areas of potential division. They exchanged opinions about the union leadership and about different pay scales in the plant. They got a clearer sense of what each other thought about things, and they firmed up a consensus about some immediate problems at the plant. "The sharing, affability, and social intercourse among the workers provided a collective means of overcoming the sheer drudgery" of the work, and also created what was "essentially a class cohesion within the plant."[15]

Asserting that people are already engaged in a struggle against capitalist values does not mean closing one's eyes to real problems. It is true that every day we can observe—or at least read about or see on the news—people acting in ways that are competitive and selfish. We can read about parents abusing their children, husbands brutalizing their wives, people robbing or killing or committing any number of terrible acts. But this is not how most people act, and we are shocked by these stories precisely because they violate powerful shared ideas about how people should treat each other.

People are constantly pulled in opposite directions—by their best instincts in one direction, and by their survival training in capitalist culture in the other. The key point is that, when people act in ways that are selfish and egotistical and exploitative and competitive, they are acting according to the cultural ideals of capitalism. When they act in ways that are supportive and cooperative and caring, they are acting in defiance of capitalist culture and the terrible pressures on them to conform to it.

Though they go on around us all the time, people's everyday struggles against capitalism mostly pass unnoticed. They usually involve things that people do so naturally, with their children or co-workers or wives or husbands, that people themselves do not recognize their significance.

These everyday struggles pass unnoticed for another reason: because we are trained *not* to see them. The paradigm through which we are trained to view the world—a paradigm in which only elites have goals of their own which they pursue self-consciously, and in which the fate of the society is to be found in reports on the Gross National Product—makes them invisible. Like data which do not fit the model which scientists have been trained to expect, people's everyday struggles do not fit the "box" of the economic model of society.

The Real Meaning of Everyday Life

The key question is, What is the significance of these struggles at the heart of everyday life?

I believe that in these struggles lies a new model for understanding the role of ordinary people in society, and a new vision of the possibilities for revolutionary change.

Capitalist culture is an exceedingly dynamic force. Its fundamental principle is "dog-eat-dog" competition. The logic of this culture is that people's lives should be loveless and savage.

But most people's lives are not devoid of love or human sympathy. In important parts of their lives—at work and at home, with their husbands or wives and children, with their fellow workers and their neighbors and their friends—most people struggle to create relationships based on anti-capitalist values, on cooperation and sharing, on solidarity and trust and mutual respect.

These qualities cannot come from the brutal and inhuman system which is designed precisely to stifle them. They come rather from the people themselves. The efforts of ordinary people in their everyday lives create whatever measure of equality and solidarity and human dignity exist in their lives and in the world. To the extent that people have these things, they have them because they have fought to make the world as they think it should be. They have created them by struggling to transform capitalist relations into their opposite.

People are daily engaged in a struggle over what it means to be human, asserting their own ideas about human relations and values against the relations and values of capitalism. They are engaged in a constant struggle of creation: creating themselves as human beings, and creating the human world to which they wish to belong.

These struggles often may not get very far, because they are under constant attack. But this struggle is the source of whatever successes people achieve in investing their world with humane values and meaning.

This everyday effort to transform capitalist relations means that most people are already engaged in a struggle to create a new society. The everyday struggles of ordinary people's lives have revolutionary meaning. Revolutionary change is the logical outcome and only real fulfillment of values which are at the heart of people's lives, and of struggles which are well under way.

Open class struggle and the most personal acts of kindness and love are on a continuum of struggle to transform the world. When people advance their efforts to change the world from individual efforts to collective struggle, they enlarge the part of the world that they believe they can affect with anti-capitalist values. When people gather sufficient self-consciousness and collective strength in their daily struggles, in a limited environment such as a plant or an industry or in their community, they mount strikes or protest movements. When their sense of the world that they can reshape with their values becomes sufficiently large, they make revolutions.

Beneath the surface of everyday life, a battle is raging over the direction and control of society. Most people struggle to transform the part of the world that they think they can affect, with values and relations rooted in working class life, while capitalists fight to maintain a social organization and culture which embody their own concepts of human life and value against the incursions of the working class. This is the central dynamic of modern society. There is no aspect of life upon which this struggle does not leave its mark.

The key to making revolutionary change is to see the world with new eyes. A new vision of human beings and a new paradigm for the dynamics of society lie in seeing the continuity between everyday life and revolution. The struggle to shape the world to accord with shared ideas of what it should be is the most fundamental and the most pervasive of human activities. It is this fundamental impulse that makes revolutionary change both necessary and possible.

4

EDUCATION FOR DEMOCRACY

A number of years ago, when our daughter entered the third grade, my wife and I were offered the choice of enrolling her in the "Gifted and Talented" (TAG) program at her school, or of keeping her in the regular program. We had some misgivings, disapproving of what we felt was the elitist nature of programs for the "gifted"; at the same time, we wanted our daughter to have the more stimulating, "enriched" curriculum that the program claimed to offer.

Our misgivings grew when my wife attended the first Parents' Day at the school. As the parents entered the classroom, they were separated by the teacher into parents of "the gifted" and parents of "the others." Just like the children, the teacher explained, the parents of the gifted would sit in a group—referred to as the "Goals Group"—and the parents of the other, presumably "goal-less," children would sit in another group. The teacher repeatedly referred to the "Goals" children and the exciting things they were studying. She spoke with considerably less enthusiasm about the "other" children and their studies.

My wife came home shaken and embarrassed by the low esteem with which the parents of the "goal-less" children had been treated and what it suggested about the normal classroom experience of the children.

I visited with the teacher the next day to ask more about the class and the TAG program. I asked what the enriched program of the gifted children was in reading, as an example. She explained with enthusiasm that the "Goals" children were studying "diamentate" poetry. Now, I have a Ph.D. in English, but I had never heard the term before.

"Diamentate poetry—what's that?" I asked. "Well," she explained, "'diamentate' means 'diamond-shaped.' The Goals Group children are studying diamond-shaped poems."

Enlightened on this matter, I asked what else the Goals children were studying different from the others. "Well," she explained, "after the whole class reads a story, I give the Goals Group a sheet with what I call 'Intelligence Questions' on it." She gave me a sheet. The students had just read stories about Mars, volcanoes, and icebergs. The "Intelligence Questions" sheet consisted of three sets of five questions, each of which began with a word like "design," "create," "assess": "Design a machine which would destroy a volcano"; "Create a new language for a Martian who [*sic*] you meet alone on Mars"; "Assess the value of importance of numbers [*sic*]."

I asked the teacher why she did not give the "Intelligence Questions" to the whole class. She replied that the other children would not be able to answer them.

Now, any parent of eight- or nine-year olds—and any teacher, really—knows that if you walked into a class of third graders and said, "What would a machine to stamp out volcanoes look like?" every kid in class could tell you and draw a picture to show how it worked. If you said, "What would a Martian talk like if one walked into the room?" any kid could think up a language for him. If you asked, "Why are numbers important in the story?" they would have an answer.

The teacher in question was hard-working, dedicated, and well-intentioned. Why was the class set up in this way? What was going wrong?

The teacher had been trained to think that real intelligence is something that few children have. If many students can perform a given task with proficiency, then the task does not require intelligence. It is not a task that will separate the "gifted" students from the others.

The teacher was presented with a problem by the nature of the TAG program—how to design tasks that the "gifted" children would respond to and that the other students would not (for if the other students responded, the tasks would not be exercises of superior intelligence). While the tasks that the teacher dreamed up—reading "diamentate" poetry and answering "IQ Questions"—showed some ingenuity on the teacher's part, they did not differentiate the students on the basis of what one would normally call intelligence.

Rather, they differentiated the children on the basis of their willingness to perform essentially meaningless tasks (reading diamentate poetry rather than simply reading poetry) to please the teacher. They differentiated students, in other words, not on the basis of intelligence but on the basis of values. Those most eager to "succeed" and to distinguish themselves from their classmates, or those who had been most trained to seek their self-definition at the hands of authority figures, would most earnestly perform the tasks designed by the teacher to denote intelligence and personal worth.

This tale does not represent an exception to the normal functioning of the education system but an illustration of it. In this system, students are caught between striving to get ahead by jumping through the hoops that authority sets them, or being left behind. The "lucky" parents are faced with the choice of encouraging their children to play the game for the sake of "success," or allowing them to fall behind with the others; the less lucky watch as their children become demoralized and alienated. The teachers are trained and directed by policy and program design into educational practices which undermine all that the teachers had set out to do in their professional lives: to succeed in the education of their students.

The Conflict Over the Goals of Education

If it is true that there is a war in society between two different conceptions of human goals and values—between competitive and hierarchical values on the one hand, and cooperative and egalitarian values on the other—then it should be possible to analyze institutions within society in terms of this conflict.

The underlying question affecting education is its goal: What are we educating our children for? What are appropriate goals for the education system, and what educational policies and practices, what expectations, what public commitments to education follow from these goals?

My purpose in this chapter is to show that, at the heart of the public education system, there is a conflict over the goals of education. On the one side of this conflict are teachers, parents, and students, who share the goal that students be educated to their full potential. On the other side is an elaborate educational system designed not to educate students but to sort them out and to persuade them to accept the lot in life to which the education system assigns them, whether their destiny be the executive suite or the unemployment line. The policies and practices which characterize educational institutions are designed to achieve this sorting and stamping function. To the extent that teachers and students succeed in anything that could truly be called education, they succeed in spite of the system, not because of it.

I also want to show that it is quite possible to build movements which challenge capitalist goals and values as they dominate social institutions.

I should note here that radical critiques of the education system usually see teachers as an enemy—as part of the system, who, like foremen on an assembly line, enforce the demands of the company on the workers. This analysis of the role of teachers fails to appreciate the extent to which the goals of the system and the goals of teachers are in conflict. In addition, it mistakes the *effects* of teachers' actions for their *intent*. Teachers do much that is positive with their students, often at considerable sacrifice. They also do much that has a negative or even disastrous affect. But what they do that is negative is usually a function of their training or of school policy and practice, carried out either against their better judgment, or without an understanding of its negative effects. Teachers do not become teachers because they wish to see children fail. A clear understanding of the conflict between the goals of the system and the goals of teachers is essential to enable teachers to pursue their goals, and to unite the people who can change the schools.

The Goals of the Public Education System

The function of education in any society is the reproduction of that society—that is, the transmission of the values and relationships which characterize it. According to then Secretary of Education William Bennett, "The primordial task of the schools is the transmission of social and political values."[16] In class society, the social and political values which the school system is designed to transmit are the values of the dominant class. In aiming to reproduce capitalist social relations and values, the goal of the education system is to reproduce inequality. As Jerome Winegar, while principal of South Boston High School, succinctly put it, "The purpose of public education is to maintain the class structure."[17]

The role of the schools in American society has been by no means automatic. The public education system reflects more than a hundred years of struggle between capitalist and working class, and among various groups and disciplines—school administrators, local businessmen, Progressive Movement educators, black parents, and others—for influence over the goals and character of schooling. But if the schools have always been a battleground in the contest over life in America, still "the history of twentieth-century education is the history of the imposition on the schools of 'business values' and social relationships reflecting the pyramid of authority and privilege in the burgeoning capitalist system."[18]

In a hierarchical society which cannot possibly fully use the intelligence and talents of millions of young people, the education system must abort enough young aspirations that they will not demand more than the social system can offer.

To succeed, the education system must prepare students to fail, and to accept that failure as their own rather than the fault of the system. It must prepare most students for working lives spent performing boring and fragmented tasks with unquestioning obedience. It must prepare them for a society in which the idea of human development consists largely of competing for the approval of authority figures and the rewards of status and wealth. It must prepare them for a "democracy" in which the goals of society are not a matter for discussion, and in which the idea of people acting collectively and consciously is subversive and threatening.

From the moment they first climb the kindergarten steps, children confront a school culture which attacks their self-confidence and their relationships to their families and to each other. However much students or teachers may rebel against this culture, there are powerful instruments of structure, policy, and practice which legitimize the culture of the school and make resistance to it difficult and suspect.

The means of the education system in pursuing its goals may be separated into three major elements:

*The expectations of the system for the people in it—that is, for both students and for teachers—tend to be low, differential, individualized, and fixed. The system assumes that most people are not very smart, that they vary widely in their ability, that each person has his own specific quantity of intelligence, and that this quantity does not change. These expectations express capitalist assumptions about human ability, and are important ideas legitimizing a fixed and hierarchical social order. Education policies and practices are designed to prove the correctness of these assumptions in many ways. Norm-referenced testing and grading systems, crowded classrooms and demoralized teachers, short-staffing and other shortages of the resources necessary for students and teachers to succeed at their work: all of these play a role in fulfilling and enforcing capital's beliefs about human ability.

*The relationships encouraged by the system tend to be hierarchical and competitive. For students, "education" means competing for approval and advancement. For teachers, the relationships imposed by the system usually vary from an isolated struggle to survive, to pressure to prove their individual worth—rather than encouragement to cooperate in developing their students. Competition for grades and approval conceals the real goals of the system, while it tends to isolate the individuals trapped within it. It thereby undermines their ability to understand and to alter the school environment or the world.

*Course content tends to have only extrinsic value—as a standard against which to measure students' willingness to master it. Much of the content consists either of "facts" with all the life sucked out of them, or a distorted view of reality devised to justify capitalist rule. The courses present to students a sanitized view of reality, without class exploitation or class struggle, in which society's goods and culture flow down from a benevolent elite to an only occasionally deserving public.

Even course content of potential value is robbed of its significance by being taught in the "jug and mug" style, in which the teacher—the jug—fills all the little mugs with information. Paolo Freire describes this method, in which teaching

> ...becomes an act of depositing, in which the students are the depositories and the teacher is the depositor. Instead of communicating, the teacher issues communiques and makes deposits which the students patiently receive, memorize, and repeat. This is the "banking" concept of education....The teacher teaches and the students are taught...The teacher chooses and enforces his choice and the students comply....The teacher acts and the students have the illusion of acting through the action of the teacher.[19]

This type of teaching, by reducing students to passivity, attacks what is human in the learning process. It is the opposite of real knowledge, which "emerges only through invention and re-invention, through the restless, impatient, continuing, hopeful inquiry men pursue in the world, with the world, and with each other." The banking concept of education, Freire continues:

regards men as adaptable, manageable beings. The more students work at storing the deposits entrusted to them, the less they develop the critical consciousness which would result from their intervention in the world as transformers of that world. The more completely they accept the passive role imposed on them, the more they tend simply to adapt to the world as it is and to the fragmented view of reality deposited in them.[20]

Passivity, lack of critical consciousness, and manageability within a system over which one has no control are of course qualities as keenly sought by employers and politicians as they are valued by the education system.

The ability to compete effectively in the school climate is largely a function of how deeply a student has internalized competition as the measure of his own worth and accepted the legitimacy of the school's standards for "making it."

The willingness to accept these standards is largely class-based. Children from upper class or professional families, which tend to identify with social and school elites and to encourage competition, are more likely to accept this measure of their own worth and the legitimacy of this world view than are students from working class families in which solidarity and equality and resistance to authority are valued.

In working class communities, the schools function something like colonial outposts, bringing civilization to the natives. The school attempts to persuade students to accept a culture in which their own success or failure is specifically measured against that of their friends. The values which students bring to the school from their families are to be replaced by the "superior" values of competition.

This clash of values means that to the extent a child has been brought up with strong working class values of commitment to his friends—that is, to the extent that he does not define himself through authority, but instead through his relationships with friends and other people like himself—he will fail. To get ahead he must devalue his friends and his family, and try to win approval by fitting into the school's notion of intelligent—that is, competitive—values. The more powerful his sense of his family and himself, the less willing he will be to demean himself in this way. If he continues on this path, he will be marked a loser. What is really a clash of values will be perceived as a failure of his intelligence.

What is worse, given the power of the culture with which he must contend, and the absence of a fully articulated alternative view, he may come to accept the school's judgment of him. He may become convinced that he is a failure.

The negative effects of this school culture are not limited to the children who do not fare well in the system. To succeed in this culture,, one must to some extent accept its values. The students who "succeed" do so at least in part by seeking their self-definition at the hands of school authorities; to this extent, they have less and less control over their lives even as they are given the illusion of more control. "Straight-A" students can become isolated and personally distorted by their struggle for success, because they have been the least prepared to understand the operation of the system on their lives. They too are being prepared for a place within the system—for managerial or other jobs in which they are isolated from the rest of the workforce, and are completely dependent on the approval of senior management for their livelihood and status.

A study of drop outs from alternative high schools in the South Bronx lends some support to these points. It found that the drop outs were the most critical and politically astute students in the alternative schools: "Much to our collective surprise (and dismay) the drop outs were those students who were most likely to identify injustice in their social lives and at school, and most ready to correct injustice by criticizing or challenging a teacher. The drop outs were least depressed, and had attained academic levels equivalent to students who remained in school."[21]

The Goals of the People in the Education System

Students and teachers and parents are not a passive mass on which the school culture can be stamped. Because they have goals which are opposed to the goals of the school—goals which they struggle to accomplish with more or less clarity and with more or less success—there is always a counterforce in the schools opposed to the dominant school culture. Because of this struggle, most teachers have some positive effects on their students; most students emerge from the system intact, if not unaffected; most parents maintain some confidence in their children's ability, in spite of the schools' characterization of them. The effects of the system are never as bad as they could be, because the people in it are operating toward different goals.

As in other areas of everyday life, the struggle in education takes many different forms—and the significance or even the existence of this struggle is often not clear.

When teachers encourage all their students to learn, or inspire them to think about the world as it really is; when they try to stimulate and challenge; when they encourage cooperation among their students and create a nurturing environment; when they encourage discussion and critical thinking; when they resist standardized, norm-referenced testing of their students or of teachers; when they fight for smaller class sizes; when they offer each other words of support, in spite of the system's attempts to isolate them; when they steal a few minutes to confer on the needs of a particular student; when they spend long nights correcting papers and preparing lessons; when they dig into their own pockets to finance field trips that school authorities cannot seem to find money for: in any number of things that they do every day, teachers resist the official culture of the schools and try to create another. Even when using the methods of the system—the "banking" method of teaching, for example—teachers are working toward different goals, and thereby blunting the effects of the system.

When students form friendships, or help each other, or resist attacks on their number, or question the curriculum, or resist school authorities (often, of course, this means resisting teachers); when they raise critical questions about the conduct of a class or the school, or exercise their curiosity and intelligence, or think about what education should really mean, or refuse to participate in the race for grades and approval; when they hang for hours on the phone, talking together about "life" and the problems of growing up: when they engage in any number of activities that they do every day, they are resisting the school culture and struggling to create another.

When parents resist the attack on their children, or listen sympathetically to their problems, or encourage them, or talk to friends about the school and about raising kids, or any number of other things that parents do every day: when they do these things, parents are resisting the official culture and struggling to create another.

Whatever good exists in the schools, whatever real learning goes on, whatever real cooperation takes place, whatever real success teachers achieve and whatever real self-confidence students develop: all these occur in spite of the system, not because of it. They occur because the people in education are engaged in a constant struggle to accomplish their shared goals, in spite of the obstacles to their success which the system throws up.

The success of teachers and students and parents in this struggle, however, is very limited. While there are many factors which work against them, the chief one is this: that it is not clear to them that the goals of the system are quite different from their own.

To the extent that they do not understand that the system is designed to produce failure, they cannot truly understand the culture of the school or the policies and practices which characterize it. The confusion over goals also explains why it is so easy for teachers to blame students and their families, and parents and students to blame teachers, for problems created by the education system.

Finally, if the conflict over goals is not clear to them, people cannot understand either the nature of needed change or where change must come from.

The Meaning of the Education Reform Movement

The publication in April, 1983 of "A Nation at Risk," the report of the President's Commission on Educational Excellence, marked the beginning of an "education reform movement" led by government and corporate forces. The movement has produced numerous other reports and reform legislation in at least 40 states.

"A Nation at Risk" began with the dramatic declaration that, if the present public education system had been imposed on the American people by a foreign power, "it would be considered an act of war." According to the report, the principal goal of education is to enable the nation to compete effectively for "international standing and markets" in the world economy. "The demand for highly skilled workers in new fields is accelerating rapidly," it declared, and proposed a new emphasis on computer literacy and science and technology lest we raise "a new generation of Americans" that is "scientifically and technologically illiterate."

But the purpose of the official reform movement is not what its corporate and government leaders claim, to produce a more highly skilled workforce enabling the U.S. to compete more effectively in the world economy. The real purpose of the movement is to lower the educational attainment and the expectations of most students, so that they will accept less rewarding jobs and less fulfilling lives in a contracting economy and a more unequal social order.

If we look at the reform proposals in their economic context, we can see that lowering educational attainment and heightened social control are their real goals.

The economic forces shaping the education reform movement include a continuing high unemployment rate; the massive export of jobs overseas; "de-industrialization," with an accompanying change from relatively well-paid manufacturing jobs to less skilled, lower-paid service jobs; and the de-skilling of work through computerization. These forces will continue to be the context of education for the foreseeable future.

Just two of these developments indicate something of the future that awaits young graduates. In their book, *The Deindustrialization of America*, Barry Bluestone and Bennett Harrison estimate that from 32 million to 38 million manufacturing jobs have been lost in the last two decades through the variety of factors which they call "deindustrialization," or the change of the economy from relatively skilled and well-paid manufacturing jobs, to less skilled and more poorly paid service jobs.[22] In a 1982 study, the Bureau of Labor Statistics (BLS) found that the first fifteen most common job categories available in 1980 were for retail salesclerks, cashiers, secretaries, waiters and waitresses, cooks, stockhandlers, janitors, nursing aides, building interior cleaners, and similar categories. Of the 19 million new jobs expected in the economy by 1990, the BLS projected that 7 million would be low-skilled service jobs; only 3.5 million would be classified as "professional and technical." Even this figure overstates the qualifications needed by the workforce to fill these jobs, since under the BLS classification system, dental assistants and other such jobs are classified as professional. Note that the change to a service economy is an issue quite distinct from unemployment, and far less visible. The average autoworker laid off in the 1982 recession was back at work by 1984—but in a job that averaged 43% less pay.[23]

Contrary to the declaration made in "A Nation At Risk," the data available from the Bureau of Labor Statistics and other sources show that the main effect of the computer revolution on the job market is the "de-skilling" of most jobs. Computers reduce highly skilled work to semi-skilled, and semi-skilled to low-skilled. This, after all, is much of the computer's attraction to capitalists: it makes workers more expendable. While there will certainly be some demand in the future for scientific and professional workers in computer-related fields, these jobs amount to a tiny fraction of the work-force in the computer industry, in which the typical worker is not an engineer or programmer, but an assembly worker averaging $12,000 per year. And even many of these assembly jobs are being shipped to low wage areas overseas—joining Atari in the trek from Silicon Valley to South Korea.

The specific proposals of "A Nation at Risk" do not reflect the expanding demand for highly skilled workers of the reform movement's rhetoric, but the contracting social and economic structure around us. Its proposals are calculated to produce a school setting which is more sharply stratified and fiercely competitive, and to reduce access to higher education. The report proposes raising admissions standards for college entrance without at the same time improving school programs. It proposes that standardized achievement tests be administered at each major transition point for students, "particularly from high school to college or work." It proposes merit pay and master teacher schemes, promoting competition rather than cooperation among teachers, even though much research has shown that staff teamwork is critical to effective schools.

The Minnesota Plan

Is it possible to defeat such powerful forces? In my experience, it is—but only if people understand what the fight is really about.

The most sophisticated and comprehensive of the reform plans at the state level was developed for the Minnesota Business Partnership in the fall of 1984.[24] The Minnesota Business Partnership is an association of the 69 largest banks and corporations in Minnesota, and includes Hormel, 3M, Control Data, IBM, Cargill, and others.

In June, 1985 I was hired as a consultant to the Minnesota Education Association (MEA), to help it deal with two problems. Internally, the union and its board of directors were split into warring factions; externally, the MEA and public education in Minnesota were under attack by the media, the Governor, and by the Business Partnership. The MEA came under attack when it resisted the Business Partnership Plan.

The MEA is a state affiliate of the National Education Association. With more than 37,000 teachers as members, it is the largest union in Minnesota. It had won a reputation around the country as one of the most progressive and powerful NEA affiliates. Its members were some of the highest paid teachers in the country.

Like "A Nation at Risk," the Business Partnership Plan came packaged in very appealing rhetoric. The plan proposed moving to a "mastery learning" system, with an Individual Learning Plan for each student, and was based on a "teaching team" approach. It proposed to raise teachers' salaries, and to "redistribute authority," with greater community control.

On further investigation, however, it became clear that the plan was not what it seemed. The plan would have changed Minnesota schools from a kindergarten through twelve (K-12) to a kindergarten through ten (K-10) structure, so that students would have graduated in the 10th grade; specialized schools would have been established for students who chose to go on beyond the 10th grade. Minnesota has the highest school retention rate in the nation: ninety-one percent of the students in the state complete high school, and a high proportion go on to college. The Business Partnership Plan would have solved this "problem"—of a work-force with more education than the jobs available to it demand—by graduating students when they were 16 years old and making the last two years of high school optional.

The authors of the Minnesota Plan emphasized that the plan did not intend to encourage collaborative team teaching "as done in the '60s." Instead it would establish a Master Teacher program. A typical "Teacher Team" would consist of a Lead Teacher, three Teachers, three Teaching Assistants, and one Adjunct Teacher. The "pay raise" would consist essentially of a "one-time 20% Lead Teacher salary increase."

By "redistributing authority," the plan meant that it would establish "school site management" for every school, so that each school would have its own budget and be responsible for its own curriculum and instruction.

School site management, also called "lump-sum budgeting," is a means of taking the "block-grant" approach engineered by the Nixon Administration to the local school level. In centralized budgeting, interested parties—organized teachers, parents, others—can work together to expand the amount of resources available to be budgeted; in school site management, interested parties can only fight over how a lump sum of money already budgeted to a particular school will be spent.

School site management is designed to fragment communities by making each school an island unto itself, narrowing people's perspectives and undermining their ability to work together for system-wide change; it breaks the connections among parents, teachers, and students with people at other schools, while it encourages competition among special interests within each school. School site management, which did not originate with the Minnesota plan, has been widely praised by government officials, and is being widely imitated.

The Minnesota Plan was designed to dovetail with an existing voucher or "open enrollment" plan in Minnesota. Open enrollment allows students to attend any public school of their choice, either in neighboring towns or, in some states, anywhere in the state. The Bush Administration has announced that the so-called "school choice" option would be the centerpiece of Administration school reform. By June, 1989 open enrollment plans had been passed in at least a dozen states.[25]

Open enrollment reduces the relationship between people and their schools to the relations of the marketplace. If you want a better school, don't try to change this one—shop around. People are encouraged to act as consumers who are passive in regard to the system, but who actively compete with each other for the few available slots.

Open enrollment strengthens the tendency of the public education system to reproduce inequality. It tracks students into particular academic and vocational paths by a very sophisticated method. Students with particular racial and class backgrounds and self-estimates are likely to choose or be counseled into particular schools, where the "self-fulfilling prophecy" syndrome will operate with a vengeance. Entire schools become identified with offering a high or low level of education. As resources follow the most successful students into the most "successful" schools, the gaps between schools widen.

Despite its rhetoric, the Minnesota Plan was designed to encourage an essentially passive, technology-based learning model, in which the Individual Learning Plan and the move to a K-10 system would become means for intensive tracking of students, and for encouraging a high proportion of students to end their education at grade 10. The plan would have created a large pool of 16 year-olds in Minnesota, uneducated and unskilled, who were prepared only for butchering hogs or frying hamburgers. They would have fit nicely into Hormel's plan for a two-tier wage level for its workers.

Preparing To Fight Back

In July, 1985 about 55 state and local leaders of the MEA and myself went on a three day retreat, to begin developing a long range plan to strengthen the organization. My role as a consultant was to help the union see its problems in a wider perspective, and to pull some of the best ideas and practices in the organization into a coherent direction. I was hired to design a long range plan for the union, but the plan would not work unless it essentially came from the people in the organization.

The internal situation of the union was complicated, but came down to a few essential points:

*The most obvious problem was the factional conflict. The board of directors was split between the political machine of the then-president, and those opposed to her—the "in-group" and the "out-group." Part of this split was merely personal; part of it had to do with the autocratic style of the "in-group." There was another dimension to the split, however; the "in-group" was determined to oppose the Business Partnership; the "out-group" wanted to seek an accommodation.

*There was a second split, which extended beyond the board of directors, between those teachers who were militant unionists, and those who wanted the organization to be a "professional association," which would focus on educational issues.

*A third split had to do with great salary disparities between teachers in metropolitan areas and those in poorer, rural communities; some teachers thought that erasing this disparity should be the focus of union activity, while others strongly resisted this approach.

*Finally, participation by the membership in the union was very low. The union had a large staff which conducted most of the business of the union on the members' behalf. Members were largely indifferent and uninvolved.

The external climate of the union was not much different from that experienced by other unions around the country:

*The anti-labor climate of the Reagan years, the collapse of the farm economy, and the slow-down of the business economy, had put the MEA on the defensive in terms of collective bargaining issues.

*After years of being told by the media and the politicians that they and the schools had failed, teachers felt isolated and demoralized.

*The MEA had come under heavy attack for opposing the education reform proposals put forward by the Governor and the Business Partnership. While the MEA had come up with an "Agenda For Excellence" of its own, the plan had been developed without much participation of the membership, and did not really address the key problems in the schools or explain what was wrong with the "official" reform proposals it was meant to counter.

The internal and external problems of the organization were in fact closely related. Since the MEA, like other unions, did not question the corporate structure or its domination of American life, it had made no attempt—in fact, did not know how—to locate the situation of teachers and public education in the larger conflict in the society between labor and capital. It did not understand the conflict between the goals of the corporate establishment and the goals and aspirations of the majority of people, and did not understand the reasons behind the Business Partnership reform plan. It did not have an analysis of the goals, policies, and practices of the public education system which would enable teachers to act together to change it. In other words, it did not really understand why it was being attacked, and was at a loss how to deal with it.

In addition, because the union did not question the goals of corporate power or the basic economic paradigm of American life, it did not really articulate the goals of its members. Teachers have goals not just as wage-earners; they also have goals as teachers—concerns about education—and as members of the larger society. The union did not attempt to extend the morality of a collective vision or the power of collective action to these other crucial areas of its members' lives.

The union had operated for years—with apparently great success—with a narrow idea of unionism which limited union concerns to the contract. Since teachers are excluded by law from bargaining over anything but wages and conditions of employment, "unionism" in the MEA had effectively been reduced to conflict over wages. While the organization had been outspoken on educational issues, these were largely treated by the MEA as "professional development" concerns, to be dealt with not by collective action but individually, in terms of the training and skills of teachers. Its annual convention would pass resolutions on social issues beyond education, but the union would undertake no collective action in pursuit of any wider goals.

Since the union did not see itself as engaged in a war over the future of American society, it followed the "business" or "service" model of unionism—a model which tends to make the members unnecessary. The essential role of the members was to pay their dues. In return, they received certain services from the union: it negotiated their contracts, offered them an insurance plan, spoke on their behalf to politicians and the media. In effect, "the union" was reduced to the paid staff and elected leaders. The low participation of the membership in the union was an inevitable consequence of service unionism;

it was, in a way, a function of its "success" during the prosperous years. The profound weakness of this model was only revealed when the union came under attack in hard times.

The failure of the organization to focus on the conflict over the goals of society had left it fragmented and disarmed, without a clear understanding of why it was under attack, and without a powerful sense of common purpose to unite its members.

The Long Range Plan: "Education for Democracy"

The long range plan, the key principles of which were outlined during this retreat, focused on locating the union in the struggle over the future of democracy in America. As a consultant, my approach was to propose an explanation of why teachers were under attack, and to show how an awareness of what was actually happening in the country could give the union a new sense of its mission and could suggest a strategy for accomplishing it.

The education reform movement launched at the national level with the publication of "A Nation At Risk" in 1983 and in Minnesota with the Business Partnership Plan in 1984 could only be understood, I suggested, as part of an overall corporate offensive against working people. Its purpose was to lower expectations and to take back from people everything that had been won in the 'sixties and early 'seventies.

Several things followed from the analysis I was proposing. It meant that:

*Teachers were under attack not because they had failed, but because they had succeeded—at raising expectations which the corporate system could not—or did not want to—fulfill.

*Not only teachers and students were under attack; the whole community—their hopes for their children and the future, and their beliefs in what democratic society should be like—was under assault. Teachers and the MEA need not be isolated from the community.

*Teachers and the MEA had a mission: to inform people of the meaning of the assault on public education, and to lead a struggle for democracy and against corporate power.

There was another issue that had to be dealt with, however. If it was true that the official education reform movement was destructive, did that mean that the schools were not in need of reform? And if they were in need of change, what should the reforms be? The union leaders—all teachers—strongly agreed with the need for change, and had many ideas about it, but no clear agreement on what change should consist of.

The union needed an analysis of education that could be the basis of its own reform program. To develop a useful analysis, the schools too had to be understood in terms of the wider conflict over the goals of society.

The corporate education reforms were designed to intensify the sorting and molding effects of the schools. Positive change from the teachers would have to challenge the goals of education.

The choice of goals comes down to two: the schools can prepare students to fit into a world over which they will have no control, or they can prepare students to understand their world and to change it. The first goal prepares students to meet the needs of capitalism; the second prepares them for democracy. The MEA, I suggested, should propose education for democracy as the new goal for public education, and as the basis on which the schools should be changed.

The union needed to get off the defensive. It needed to develop more ambitious goals, which would reflect the values and concerns of its members, and which would deepen its vision of unionism. Teaching is a collective act, which always depends in one way or another on the understanding and support of associated colleagues. The union needed to extend its notion of collective values and collective activity to education and societal issues as well as to wages. It needed to set its own agenda, and it needed a clear set of goals which could be the basis of a long range plan.

Three days of discussion led to the development of goals for the organization, and an overall strategy for achieving them. The goals came down to these four. The MEA should:

1. *Prevent the enactment of destructive education reform measures,* by mobilizing statewide to stop the Business Partnership Plan from being adopted by the legislature.

2. *Encourage schools to prepare students for democracy,* by building a positive reform movement of its own.

3. *Strengthen the ability of teachers to act together,* by developing a more powerful vision of what it means to belong to a union, and by other means. "Solidarity" should be a moral vision and a code of values with which the union opposes the "me-first," "get ahead" values of capitalist culture.

4. *Build public support for education for democracy,* by going out to the community with information about the corporate attack on edu-

cation, and enlisting parents, students, workers, and others in a struggle to save the schools and to change them.

The organization still needed a strategy to achieve these ambitious
goals. The strategy agreed upon was this: *The Minnesota Education
Association should take leadership in the state for school reform.* It
should be the leading force both in repelling the business attack on
the schools, and in fighting for positive reform.

This strategy would also be the general framework within which
the union would strengthen itself internally, by bringing the membership more fully into the organization, strengthening organizational
unity, and in other ways. By taking the lead for reform, the MEA
would be uniting teachers among themselves and with their communities in a struggle which mattered deeply to them, and in the course of
which they would become part of the union in a wholly different
way.

If the union was going to lead a struggle against corporate power,
it needed to be much stronger. I asked the assembled leaders, "What
level of the organization's potential strength do you believe you are
operating at now?" Estimates ranged from 3% to 33 1/3%, with most
falling in the 'teens. The leaders agreed with the proposition that
"The strength of the union is the people in it," members and staff. It
was clear, however, that the service model of unionism undermined
the strength of the union.

With more ambitious goals, the MEA would need a new model of
unionism—what I called the "organizing model." In the organizing
model, the members are the union, and are its source of strength.
The members elect leaders and hire staff so that they can fight for
their goals more effectively. MEA leaders and staff already used the
organizing approach at their best moments, but the use of this model
was neither systematic nor consciously differentiated from the service
model.

If the source of the union's strength is its members, how fully it
realizes that strength is a function of two things: 1) how fully the
members understand the goals of the organization, the strategy to
reach them, the issues that confront them, and that they, the members, are the source of the organization's strength; and 2) how fully
the members are integrated into the organization, to influence its direction and to achieve its goals.

The consciousness of the membership is the greatest single source
of an organization's power. It was clear that the first task of the elected leaders and staff of the MEA would be to develop a common

understanding among the members of the goals, strategy, issues, and source of strength of the organization. The second task was to a-chieve the purposeful integration of the members into the union. Much of the long range plan which was later developed was devoted to showing how these two tasks could be accomplished.

In the following months, with the help of staff, leaders, and local members, a plan was developed for carrying out the strategy of education for democracy. Teachers would first go out to their communities and to other unions explaining the corporate attack on education and labor. Teachers would then assess the condition of education in every community and every school in the state in which the union had members. Public hearings and other means would be developed for parents, students, and others to contribute to the assessment. On the basis of this assessment, the MEA would develop a statewide plan for education reform. Finally, the MEA would mobilize its own members, and parents, students, and others around the state to fight for the plan.

The planning process initiated at the union leadership retreat continued through about four months of intensive discussions and interviews with a wide range of union members, staff, management, and elected leaders. It resulted in a long range plan entitled, "Education for Democracy." It passed the board of directors by a 47-2 vote, and was received with tremendous enthusiasm by the rank-and-file. A group of staff, leaders, and I designed a training program to acquaint locals with all the analyses and issues involved in the plan. In two and a half months in early 1986, nearly 25,000 of the union's 37,000 members—a phenomenal rate of participation—participated in three- to six-hour long training discussions.

While the analysis of the corporate attack on education and its implications for American society was frightening to many members, almost everyone felt it had the ring of truth. Many teachers said that they had felt something like this to be true, but had never heard it confirmed before. Other leaders and members, who had been reluctant at first to accept such a drastic analysis, after a few months of reading the newspaper with new eyes and discussion with fellow teachers, became convinced.

The long range plan was not without significant opposition. There were two centers of opposition. Many field staff of the union were opposed to the plan, at least in part because it dramatically changed their roles in the organization. The service model of unionism encourages staff to manage the expectations of the members, so that the members will never expect more than the staff can deliver. The organizing model I was proposing changed the roles of staff to enabling the members to act effectively together on their own, and to raising the members' expectations of what they could achieve. The staff was expected not to manage the members or to do things for them, but to help lead a militant social movement. Some staff were not comfortable with this change. Others, however, were enthusiastic about it, and felt it finally satisfied their idea of what a union should be.

The other center of opposition was the "out-group," the group of board members and others who were vying for power in the union. While they did not dare vote against the plan on a recorded board vote—it was much too popular with the members—and while some of them really supported it, the leader of the "out-group" was deadly opposed to "Education for Democracy." The union was in the midst of an election campaign while the long range plan was being developed and voted on. The night before the election, the opposition candidate for president of the union pledged that, if elected, he would commit the full resources of the union to carrying out "Education for Democracy." After he won the election, however, he deep-sixed the long range plan; within a year he had fired the staff who had been most involved in designing and implementing it.

Although the long range plan was never carried out beyond the training program, the mass understanding of its real intent within the MEA led to the defeat of the Business Partnership Plan, at least for the time being.

While all the old problems of the union and the schools are still there in Minnesota, still the whole process showed something of the enormous potential of a movement which responds to the best values of the people in it and enables them to fight for some of the deepest goals of their lives.

Teachers are like most people: they know that something is deeply wrong in the society, but they are not quite clear what is really happening and whether it is possible to do anything about it. They sense the connections between what is happening on their jobs and at home and in their communities and in their children's lives and in the society as a whole, but have trouble drawing a coherent picture out of the connections. Like the rest of us, they are vulnerable to the attacks of the media and of capitalist culture, which tell them that they, not the system, have failed. To learn that they were under attack not because they have failed, but because they have succeeded, was a huge step in making them feel ready to take the offensive. But this understanding could only come from seeing their lives and concerns in terms of the wider struggle over the fate of American society.

The Meaning Of Real School Change

New goals for public education would require a profound transformation of the expectations, relationships, and curricula of the schools, and of the policies and practices which characterize them. Education for democracy would substitute high expectations for low, cooperation and equality for competition and hierarchy, meaningful curricula designed to help students truly understand their world and the serious problems they must confront, rather than hoops to jump through on the path to "success."

A genuine movement for school reform should change the definition of school success. Success cannot mean winning approval by demonstrating meekness and willingness to accept the goals of authority; it must mean acting with others to understand the world and to change it. Reform must be directed toward enabling students and teachers to become active agents of change—beginning with school change. In Freire's words, real education encourages people to become "transformers of their world."

Education for democracy is common sense; that is, it leads in the direction that most people thought the schools were supposed to go in the first place. It is also revolutionary.

Building a movement consists of enabling teachers and students and parents to become more conscious of their shared goals, and more conscious of the conflict between these goals and the goals of the system. It means encouraging people to develop, through discussion and struggle, their own vision of education and ways to fulfill it. It means the people in schools becoming more aware that they are not the problem in the schools but the solution.

The real successes of such a movement—the real education—will come in the struggle to change the schools, rather than from "reforms" handed down from on high. Teachers and students and parents will be learning in this together.

The movement to change education must be part of a movement to revolutionize the whole society. The education system cannot be understood or changed apart from its role in society. John Dewey once called for education reform to make the schools "schools of democracy." But they cannot be schools of democracy until they become schools of revolution.

PART TWO

Part Two examines the history of the '60s, to show that the movements of this period were defeated by their inability to break from capitalist and Marxist models of change. It shows that the history of the past two decades is driven not by competition among rival business economies, but by a struggle between the world elite and most people over the future of human society.

5

A GLIMPSE OF A NEW WORLD: THE U.S., FRANCE, CHINA

The 1960s witnessed an explosion of revolutionary activity around the world. Revolutionary movements developed in Eastern bloc as well as Western countries, in underdeveloped as well as industrialized societies, in countries experiencing record economic growth as well as those with stagnant economies.

East and West, these movements had certain elements in common. They refused to accept the definitions of human life and values imposed by their own societies; they counterposed to them values which went beyond merely economic considerations, and a view of human possibilites which went beyond the limits of capitalism or Soviet-style Communism. They attacked capitalist and Communist hierarchies alike, rejecting the idea of rule by experts and technocrats. They challenged the personal isolation imposed by these societies. They rejected the idea of technological "progress" for its own sake. They attacked the idea that life should be reduced to the passive production and consumption of commodities. To oppose faith in technology, they offered faith in people; to isolation, community; to passive acceptance of capitalist or Communist culture, struggle; to hierarchy, democracy and movement from below; to inequality, equality; to politics as usual, the politics of vision; to pessimism, a belief in the power of people to make a new world.

In several countries—France and China in particular—these movements came close to making revolutions. Mass struggle in the United States ended Jim Crow in the South and changed the character of race relations thoughout the country. It dramatically undercut the ability of the governing elite to wage war in Southeast Asia. It weakened the grip of labor bosses over the rank-and-file. It challenged the power of the corporate and government elite to direct the society at their will.

But in these and other countries, the openly revolutionary movements of the '60s soon disappeared. What led to the defeat and disappearance of these movements, and what have we to learn from them?

THE UNITED STATES: In Search of a Democratic Society

Forces for change in the U.S. in the 1960s took three principal forms: the black movement, the student movement, and the labor movement. While these three intersected at various levels in official and unofficial ways, and to some extent had overlapping memberships, they were usually perceived at the time and are certainly remembered now as very distinct.

The separateness of these movements reflected their failure to develop an explicit alternative to Communism with which to defeat the capitalist view of a society of competing interest groups.

The Civil Rights Movement

The struggle of masses of black people for civil rights in the South broke the silence imposed on the American people in the Eisenhower years. When Rosa Parks was arrested for refusing to give up her seat to a white man on a bus in Montgomery, Alabama in 1955, the ensuing boycott ushered in a period of mass struggle which changed the face of the South and sparked a period of unprecedented political mobilization in American society.

The struggle of black people was driven by deeper ideals than the offical demands of the movement for voting rights and an end to segregationist practices. The movement struck a responsive chord among a wide range of people, as it embodied a vision of society of human equality and community—a society which in fact could not be realized within capitalism. The mass civil rights movement was implicitly revolutionary.

The civil rights movement had two aspects, however: one as an authentic mass movement from the bottom up, embodying an implicitly revolutionary vision; the other as a campaign stage-managed and directed from the top of U.S. society. The federal government and the corporate establishment encouraged and guided the movement in certain directions by use of the huge resources at their disposal—media coverage of some elements of the movement and not others; grants from the Ford and Rockefeller and other foundations which underwrote some leaders and some aspects of the movement and not others; training workshops and support services from religious and labor groups tied to the corporate establishment; active intervention of the FBI and federalized troops; and other interventions which influenced both the direction of the movement and how it was perceived by the public, North and South.

The ruling class had important goals for potentially so explosive a movement. These came down chiefly to two: one was to keep the movement within the bounds of race and Constitutional rights; the other was to use the movement to modernize the South, bringing the region more fully under the control of corporate capital.

The civil rights movement took place in the context of the most dynamic economic growth in U.S. history. The South had been relatively untouched by the huge modernizing changes in U.S. society in the wake of World War II. Rapidly expanding U.S. corporations wanted to break local control of the Southern economy and its tightly-bound political system, to make it available for corporate expansion. The big corporations wanted the American South to become part of the national market for their goods. They wanted control of Southern farmlands, to replace the inefficient and locally-held sharecropping system with nationally-owned agribusiness. They wanted to drive black and white sharecroppers off the land, to make them available as cheap labor in an increasingly tight national labor market.

Of these two purposes, the need to keep the movement from becoming a class movement uniting black and white in a struggle against capitalism was always the more important. Government officials and corporate leaders could achieve their purposes as long as they could persuade blacks and sympathetic whites that the fundamental cause of inequality was not capitalism but white attitudes. For corporate purposes, the struggle had to be presented as one of downtrodden blacks demanding simple justice from an intransigent and homogeneous population of racist "rednecks," with the only black allies a somewhat reluctant federal government, plus Northern churches and liberals. This is how the struggle was presented to the public, and largely how it is remembered today. (Television presentations like *Eyes On The Prize* and movies like *Mississippi Burning* continue to promote this view.)

From the start, the movement was confronted with a set of related questions: What should be its demands? Who were its friends? Who were its enemies? Should it criticize the structure of inequality and

power in American society—the controlling and deadly grip of capitalism—or simply demand a better place in the society for blacks?
Should it aim to destroy inequality—which would have implied attempting to build a movement from the bottom up, allying with white
workers and sharecroppers—or should it ally with the liberal establishment and build a movement for Constitutional rights?

Segregation in the South had a specific context: it was one of the
devices of a local landowning and business class which kept the great
bulk of Southerners, white and black alike, in poverty and subjuga-
tion: a power structure which crushed sharecroppers, white as well as
black, under a mountain of debt; which used the Klan against white
union organizers and militant workers as well as against black people.
It was a closed and static system, not economically or politically ex-
pansive. It was the opposite of the dynamic system of modern corporate capitalism, from which it served to protect Southern businessmen and politicians.

While they had always met with ferocious opposition, there was a
history in the South dating back to the 1890s of class-based movements uniting white and black workers and sharecroppers. In the
'thirties, movements were organized of black and white sharecroppers
in a number of states, textile mill operatives in North Carolina, miners and steelworkers in Alabama and elsewhere. The Southern Tenant
Farmers' Union began in 1934 when "eleven white men and seven
black men met in a one-room schoolhouse on the Arkansas Delta and
organized themselves into a 'tenants' union." After organizing a successful strike of 5,000 cottonpickers in 1935, the union grew to
25,000 members in four states.[26] In the 1920s and '30s, black and
white coal miners fought organizing wars alongside each other. In
1943, black women led black and white workers in the largest tobacco workers' strike in history at the R.J. Reynolds Tobacco Company
in Winston-Salem, and organized a union there.[27]

A movement led by the black working class could have defined
itself in terms of the struggles of workers of all colors. It could have
identified the local and national capitalist establishment as the enemy,
and exposed racial inequality as a key weapon of the rulers against all
workers. Such a movement would have been very different from what
developed: more powerful, more able to draw on the accumulated
passion of the great majority of people, more prepared fully to articulate the vision of human equality which lay behind the black movement.

The way to a working class movement was blocked, however, in no small measure because the only systematic ideology for understanding racial inequality in the context of class oppression was communism. Not only had communist organizations, such as the Communist Party USA, long since abandoned a class-struggle approach to social change. Communism itself—witness the Soviet Union—had clearly not worked as an alternative.

The civil rights movement of the late '50's-early '60's was led by middle-class preachers who rejected militance and class struggle. They encouraged the movement to rely on the Eastern liberal establishment and the federal government. They strove mightily to keep the black masses in check: to keep their demands within the bounds of Constitutional rights, their actions limited to nonviolent civil disobedience, and their movement in isolation from potential allies in the white working class.

The official civil rights movement won what seemed significant victories—desegregation of Southern schools, the Civil Rights Act of 1964, the Voting Rights Act of 1964, the Elementary and Secondary Education Act of 1965. These and other achievements, however, had limited impact on the fundamental oppression of the masses of black people. Conceived and implemented within the framework of the existing social structure, they were designed to regulate inequality within that structure, giving it more sophisticated forms and more lasting legitimacy than the old Jim Crow laws could ever have done.

As the mobilization of black people and their demands for substantive change grew, another, nationalist leadership developed, calling for "Black Power," and using a militant anti-white rhetoric. Black nationalism did not attack capitalism or question the structure of power in the whole society, which it identified not as "capitalist" but simply as "white." On the contrary, its avowed goal was black political power within that structure.

Black nationalism was ideally suited to give a militant cover to capitalist politics and to serve as an instrument for the black elite, and through them the corporate rulers, to justify their increasingly shaky power over the insurgent black masses. "The major enemy is not your brother [that is, the black elite], flesh of your flesh and blood of your blood," black nationalist leader Stokely Carmichael cautioned. "The major enemy is the honky [white man] and his institutions of racism."[28] Both of these approaches—the liberal integrationist and the militant nationalist—were well suited to the needs of the corporate rulers.

The mass movement for equality continued to grow among black people. In 1965 Watts rebelled, as the rapidly rising expectations of black people crashed with explosive force against the reality in which they were contained. Mass uprisings took place in Detroit, Cincinnati, Newark, and 161 other cities in 1967.[29] The National Advisory Commission On Civil Disorders' profile of the "rioter" showed him to be "somewhat better educated than the average inner-city Negro....He feels strongly that he deserves a better job and that he is barred from achieving it...because of discrimination by employers....He is extremely hostile to whites, but his hostility is more apt to be a product of social and economic class than of race; he is almost equally hostile toward middle-class Negroes. He is substantially better informed about politics than Negroes who were not involved in the riots. He is more likely to be engaged in civil rights efforts, but is extremely distrustful of the political system and political leaders."[30] Black persons surveyed in cities in which disturbances took place listed (in order of importance) unemployment and underemployment, police practices, inadequate housing, and inadequate education as their most important grievances.[31]

The civil rights movement strengthened the numbers and power of the black middle class, but it left the black working class behind. In the '70s, various former civil rights leaders became politically prominent. Andrew Young, former aide to Martin Luther King, joined the Rockefeller-led Trilateral Commission—an organization which played a prominent role in planning international capitalism's counterattack against the movements of the 1960's. Charles Evers, brother of slain civil rights leader Medgar Evers and himself a civil rights leader, became nationally famous as the union-busting mayor of Fayette, Mississippi. Another black leader, Maynard Jackson, was elected mayor of Atlanta; in 1978, when 264 black sanitation workers in Atlanta went on strike to organize a union, Jackson fired them all.[32]

The fundamental problems facing the masses of black people remained untouched. A 1988 study by the Center on Budget and Policy Priorities reported, "In 1987, the income of the typical black family equalled just 56.1% of the typical white family's income, a lower percentage of any year in the 1970s or late 1960s."[33] According to the Children's Defense Fund, black babies in 1987 were more likely than white babies to die in infancy than in any year since 1940.[34]

Comparisons like these, of course, do not illuminate the problems which white and black workers and their families share, or the common strengths on which a revolutionary movement could be built.

The integrationist and the nationalist leadership succeeded in preventing the movement from questioning the fundamental forces which underlay the attacks on black people's lives and from raising questions which could have laid the basis of a broader and more powerful movement.

The New Left

When the student movement, inspired by the dramatic events in the South, began to stir in the early 1960s, it was confronted by a world in which the old ideas of social change had clearly failed. Soviet society was closed and rigid, unequal and unfree. The old left organizations—the Communist Party USA, the Socialist Party, and others—had become ossified and marginal sects, which had long since lost any revolutionary ardor they might once have had. The once-militant labor movement had come under the control of union bureaucrats, who cooperated with management to control the workforce and with the government to "keep the economy moving."

The New Left had its origins in disgust with the old. It sought to break out of the moribund organizational hierarchies and empty debates of the old left to create a movement which would be fresh, vibrant, and in touch with the reality of life in modern corporate society.

There was much that was positive in the New Left. It proposed "participatory democracy" against the anti-democratic nature both of the old left and corporate society. It proclaimed that "the personal is political," to oppose old left ideas of social change which dealt only with economic structures and left the pervasive inequities of everyday life unchanged. It pointed in outrage at the gap between the democratic rhetoric of American society and the reality of the American empire at home and abroad. It called for a politics of commitment and struggle, and rejected the roles in corporate society which students were being trained to fill.

What distinguished the New Left as a body of ideas, however, and eventually sealed its fate, was its view of people, especially working people. The old left saw the working class as the historic agent of change in capitalist society. The New Left declared that U.S. workers, or at least white workers, were "bought off" by capitalism and the consumer economy; "young intellectuals"—students—and "the dispossessed" of the world were the new revolutionary classes.

The student movement was much broader than that part of the movement which held explicitly New Left ideas. Still, the ideas of the New Left formed the conceptual framework which defined much of the student movement's analysis of American society and its sense of political strategy and possibility. New Left ideas exerted profound influence over the growing mass movement. It is not possible to understand the collapse of the movement for change in the U.S. without understanding the role that New Left ideas played in its defeat.

Two prominent academics, C. Wright Mills and Herbert Marcuse, were especially influential in defining the outlook of the student left. In the view of sociologist C. Wright Mills, writing in 1958, the American people "are rapidly being transformed into masses; and these masses are becoming morally as well as politically insensible." Their psychology is "the moral insensibility of people who are selected, molded, and honored in the mass society...If we accept the Greek definition of the idiot as an altogether private man, then we must conclude that many American and many Soviet citizens are now idiots."

In his "Letter to the New Left," Mills said that defining the "historical agency of change" is the most important political issue of our time. The traditional agency of change, the working class, has "collapsed." This leaves "the intellectuals, as a possible agent of change." After all, Mills asked, "who is it that is getting fed up? Who is it that is getting disgusted with what Marx called 'all the old crap.'? Who is it that is thinking and acting in rádical ways? All over the world...the answer is the same: it is the young intelligentsia."[35]

Herbert Marcuse further systematized a view of society in which "'the people,' previously the ferment of social change, have 'moved up' to become the ferment of social cohesion."[36] Modern man, Marcuse declared, has been integrated into capitalism so thoroughly that capitalism has become his "second nature": "The so-called consumer economy and the politics of corporate capitalism have created a second nature of man which ties him libidinally and aggressively to the commodity form. The need for possessing, consuming, and constantly renewing the gadgets, devices, instruments, engines, offered to and imposed upon the people, for using these wares even at the danger of one's own destruction, has become a 'biological' need....The second nature of man thus militates against any change that would disrupt and perhaps even abolish this dependence of man on a market ever more densely filled with merchandise—abolish his existence as a consumer consuming himself in buying and selling. The needs generated by this system are thus eminently stabilizing, conservative needs: the counterrevolution anchored in the instinctual structure."[37]

According to Marcuse, people live in a state of "voluntary servitude." They have reached a stage "where they cannot reject the system of domination without rejecting themselves, their own repressive instinctual needs and values." Liberation would thus be "against the will and against the prevailing interests of the great majority of people," whom Marcuse characterized as "the hostile majority."[38] Marcuse's analysis thus converged with the rhetoric of Richard Nixon at the time, who claimed to speak for a "silent majority" of American people in support of the war.

Marcuse went further than Mills in his attack on the working class. "By virtue of its basic position in the production process, by virtue of its numerical weight and the weight of exploitation, the working class is still the historical agent of change; by virtue of its sharing the stabilizing needs of the system, it has become a conservative, even counterrevolutionary force."[39] According to Marcuse, exploited white workers in the industrialized countries are "partners and beneficiaries of the global crime" of imperialism.[40]

Marcuse viewed human motivation—except the motivation of the intelligentsia, who, it seems, have higher goals—in economic terms; thus revolutionary possibilities exist only "where the consumer gap is still wide."[41] While the working class continues to produce the basis of society, according to Marcuse, it is among the nonconformist intelligentsia that political consciousness resides, and in the ghetto where the need for revolutionary change exists. In Marcuse's analysis, possibilities for revolutionary change exist only outside corporate capitalist society. This can occur most readily in the Third World, where movements take the form of National Liberation Fronts.[42] Within industrialized countries, revolutionary change can only come from "the outcasts and outsiders, the exploited and persecuted of other races and other colors, the unemployed and unemployable....their opposition is revolutionary, even if their consciousness is not."[43]

Marcuse's vision of the people as the enemy of change could hardly have presented the New Left with a more systematic recipe for political isolation and despair. His views perfectly captured the worst of both capitalist and Communist ideology. He gave systematic expression to the elitist contempt of the academic for workers, at the same time as he took further the Leninist view that revolutionary ideas come to the working class only from middle class intellectuals. He expressed better than any corporate leader could the idea that capitalism is human nature and that consumerism expresses the values and needs of the people.

The premise that ordinary people are the enemy of change had enormous practical implications, which made themselves felt at every turn. To the extent that it saw ordinary people as the enemy rather than as the source of strength and revolutionary values, the New Left was doomed to lead the movement to isolation and self-destruction.

The New Left encouraged the idea of a "youth counterculture," in which the idea of revolution was reduced to "personal liberation." In the counterculture, taking drugs was viewed as a revolutionary act, since it was tantamount to "dropping out" of corporate society. Thus two fundamental capitalist values—individualism and freedom from commitment to other people—were tricked out in new clothes by the New Left as revolutionary. The counterculture was quickly and easily incorporated into the capitalist marketplace as a fashion trend. "Revolution" became good business.

The New Left encouraged student activists to see themselves as a moral and intellectual elite. It encouraged activists not to approach people with respect and humility—as if they had something to learn from them—but with arrogance, or not at all. Ordinary people were increasingly opposed to the war, to racism, to many other aspects of their society; they were increasingly active themselves, on the job and elsewhere, in confronting these issues. But they needed the tools that a movement could furnish them: information to dispel the lies of the media; explanations of why these things were happening; analysis of how these particular issues related to the rest of their lives. They needed connections with other active people: a movement that would encourage their participation, solicit their ideas and insights, enable them to act with other people to change their society. The good sense and positive values of thousands of students led them to reach out to other people, including working people, to build a movement; when they did so, however, they were acting in spite of New Left ideology, not because of it.

New Left ideology distorted the meaning and source of the fundamental aspects of capitalist society. To the extent that the New Left depicted the working class as "partners and beneficiaries in global crime," it was carrying out the most important of tasks for the ruling class: convincing the growing movement that ordinary people were the problem in society rather than the solution. Rather than encouraging activists to talk with people and invite their participation in a broad-based movement for fundamental change, the New Left focused on increasingly desperate tactics for attracting media attention or confronting the police.

The New Left and the Old

The fatal flaw of the old left was not, as Mills and Marcuse claimed, that it saw the working class as the historic agent of change. The flaw was that it saw workers as a passive mass, motivated only by economic interests, in a world driven by economic development.

The New Left threw out what was positive in the old left and kept what was bad: its elitism and its anti-democratic nature. Marcuse and Lenin envisioned the same role for the intelligentsia, and their view of people led them to the same anti-democratic positions. Marcuse declared, "the general will is always wrong"—not a happy premise on which to build a democratic movement.[44] While the New Left made much of the idea of "participatory democracy" early on, as the New Left developed it became increasingly undemocratic, finally embracing the Marxist-Leninist conception of organization.

As confrontation with capitalist institutions over the Vietnam War and other issues grew sharper, New Left and Marxist-Leninist ideas increasingly converged. Marcuse's idea that workers in the industrialized countries benefit from imperialism echoed Lenin's 1916 work, *Imperialism, The Highest Stage of Capitalism*—as well as every capitalist politician's speeches. The New Left's focus on Third World nationalist revolutions was a direct development of Lenin, Stalin, and Mao. The New Left's heroes—Fidel, Ho Chi Minh, Mao—were chairmen of Marxist-Leninist parties.

In 1966, New Left and old came together when Huey Newton and Bobby Seale, two black community college students in Oakland, California, founded the Black Panther Party. The B.P.P. combined Black Power rhetoric with military posturing and the organizational structure of a Marxist-Leninist party. It espoused a nationalist ideology borrowed from Frantz Fanon and from Mao, and a program borrowed from the Communist Party USA. It saw blacks in the U.S. as a colony, and called for a U.N.-conducted plebiscite of all black individuals in the U.S. to establish a "Black Nation," whose territory would include the "Black Belt" states of South Carolina, Mississippi, Alabama, Georgia, and Louisiana. It called for "armed self-defense" of black communities and "community control of police." The Black Panthers' analysis of U.S. society was similar to Marcuse's. They saw "white society" as a racist whole. The revolutionary elements were the "excluded" from the society: the black "lumpenproletariat"—by which they meant street people, the unemployed, welfare recipients, and others—and white college students.

The Black Panthers received a huge amount of media coverage. They conveyed perfectly the image of black militance which the ruling class wished to convey to whites. At the same time, their ideas and their methods dampened mass struggle by blacks. The Panthers condemned mass ghetto rebellions, which they called counter-productive, and called instead for urban guerrilla war. Appearing armed on the street or on camera, they presented an image of struggle that dramatically discouraged mass black activity—for it immediately upped the ante by saying that to get involved in political struggle meant to confront the state directly with a weapon; at the same time, it suggested that an armed "vanguard" would act on behalf of the masses of people: beneath the militant posture and rhetoric, the Panthers were budding bureaucrats. The Panthers in many communities divided their time between "armed self-defense"—which usually meant holding out against ferocious police attacks—and running school breakfast programs with government grants.

The Panthers' posturing and nationalist rhetoric played to the worst side of white New Leftists. Many white leftists simply suspended all critical judgment in the presence of Black Panthers or representatives of any other nationalist group which called itself revolutionary.

This mindless and patronizing attitude led to absurd results. When a Black Panther leader, addressing the 1969 SDS convention, announced that "The only position of women in the revolution is prone," the New Left leaders gasped, but they did not object.

The New Left and the Rebirth of Feminism

As SDS and other organizations grew, it seemed increasingly to women in the New Left that there was a substantial division of labor in the meetings: the men spoke and the women listened. Feeling like second-class citizens in the movement, and feeling that the movement had failed to address sexual inequality in the society, women organized groups focused on "women's issues." The movement for women's equality was more than a century old. It was injected with a new surge of life by a generation of feminists from the student movement.

Unfortunately, feminist women used the same model of analysis which the New Left brought to other problems. The New Left accepted the view that sees people in terms of competing interest groups. In addition, for all its rhetorical rejection of hierarchy, the New Left accepted a belief in inequality—seeing itself as morally and intellectually superior to the mass of American people. Inequality within the New Left, including the unequal role allotted to women, was a reflection of the extent to which the New Left mirrored rather than fought against capitalist ideology.

The exposure of the inferior role of women in the New Left hierarchy should have been used to expose the hierarchical ideas about human beings—not just women—which the New Left was bringing to the whole movement. Instead, feminists dissociated "sexism" from the general ideology of inequality in capitalist society. They made it seem a thing in itself, inherent in men, which either could not be solved at all (at least, not in the company of men) or could be solved without attacking the whole capitalist view of human life. In other words, it did not require a revolutionary view of people to understand, or a revolution finally to solve. Feminists saw women as a special interest group, whose interests should be pursued in competition with all other groups. Feminism, like black nationalism and other aspects of the New Left, mirrored capitalist ideology, and was easily coopted by it, to become a means of social control for corporate and government leaders and of career advancement for feminists.

The Collapse of the Student Movement

The New Left was not the only activist leadership on the scene in the '60s. In 1962, Progressive Labor Party (PL) was formed by former members of the Communist Party USA. PL was a disciplined Marxist-Leninist party, which became a critical force in SDS in 1967. PLers were short-haired, clean-cut, anti-drug, and serious; they made rapid headway among SDSers eager for a clear and coherent analysis of what was happening in U.S. society.

Progressive Labor saw the working class, white and black, as the agent of revolution, and rejected the claim that white workers benefit from imperialism. It saw racism as a capitalist tool to attack both white and black workers, rather than a benefit to white workers; it attacked nationalism as a tool of capitalists as well. It opposed the Black Panther Party's idea of revolution made by the "lumpenproletariat," and said instead that the vast majority of black people—working or unemployed or on welfare—are workers, who form the leading edge of the U.S. working class.

The 1968 general strike in France and other events gave fresh credibility to PL's belief in the working class; in addition, PL's leading role in student strikes at Harvard and several other campuses strengthened the organization's role in SDS. The National Office of SDS was still in the hands of New Left leaders, who called themselves the Revolutionary Youth Movement (RYM). At the June, 1969 SDS convention in Chicago, the showdown came between RYM and PL. The PL forces outnumbered the New Leftists, and the New Left leadership split from the meeting.

Progressive Labor then led the organization to destruction by its own path. PL's strategy for students was that they should link up with workers. While this could have been a promising strategy, it was confounded by all that PL brought from the old left to the situation. It had a narrowly economic conception of what motivates workers, at the same time as it disdained the real concerns of students. PL took SDS out of the business of leading the anti-war movement, to try to organize students to support whatever strikes and other struggles workers might be involved in. With its Communist ideology and organizational structure, PL soon devolved into hysterical sectarianism.

A few months after leaving SDS, Revolutionary Youth Movement activists adopted the name "Weathermen," after Bob Dylan's song. The New Left leaders had joined with the Black Panther Party in denouncing "white racist America," had joined with feminists in denouncing men, had joined with Marcuse and others in denouncing the working class. This left them with a very small portion of humanity with which to make a revolution. They believed they could ignite a youth rebellion through "exemplary action," and organized what they called their "Days of Rage" on October 8, 1969, in which a few hundred of them smashed car windows on Chicago's Gold Coast. Soon after, about three hundred of the Weathermen went underground. The New Leftists finally fulfilled the logic of their political position—in which everyone is the enemy—by becoming terrorists.

Nixon's invasion of Cambodia in May, 1970, and the National Guard murder of students at Kent State and Jackson State, sparked the most massive wave of student strikes in U.S. history. Students went on strike at one-third of the nation's nearly 3,000 campuses; in the first week of May, ROTC buildings were burned or bombed at 30 campuses.[45] Everyone expected that when the students returned in the fall, things would really heat up. But the campuses returned to quiet in the fall of 1970.

The movement had run its course. It could not translate its anguish at the continuing slaughter in Vietnam or the continuing inequalities in American society into action, because it saw as an enemy the only people who could act to change these things—the American people. Rather than reaching out to them, learning from them, developing with them a more profound analysis of what was wrong with the society and what could be done to change it, the New Left retreated into increasingly violent actions by ever smaller circles of people.

The surviving mass movement, deprived of radical leadership, fell into the hands of liberal politicians and old left groups like the Socialist Workers Party, which insisted that the war be pursued as a single issue, wrenched free from its context in U.S. society. Thus the idea of radical change in the U.S. receded—not only the idea that fundamental change was possible, but the idea that it was necessary.

The capture of the movement by liberals was not the only reason that the idea of fundamental change ceased to be articulated. As we have seen, there is an intimate connection between our view of people and the degree of change that we believe possible. The left's revolutionary analysis of capitalism could not long survive in the company of its counterrevolutionary view of people.

While some small Marxist-Leninist sects were organized in the 1970s, for the most part the left which survived the '60s concluded that revolutionary change is not possible in the United States. The left adjusted its analysis and its goals in light of what it thought possible, and thus decided—at least implicitly—that capitalism is the best possible system in the United States. It restricted its program to liberal reforms designed to insure that capitalist exploitation is administered fairly—that is, among whites, blacks, Hispanics, Orientals, men, women, the young, the old, the heterosexual and the homosexual, etc., etc.—and that the inequality of capitalist society is perfectly unequal, without regard to "race, gender, or sexual preference."

The mass movement had grown in spite of, not because of, New Left ideas. The point is not that New Leftists were bad people or insincere. They were for the most part good people trying sincerely to accomplish good things. They were trying to solve the problem presented to them by the counterrevolutionary nature of the old left. They misunderstood the basis of counterrevolution in the old left, however, and they remained trapped in the negative view of people which justifies the old order everywhere, whether Communist or capitalist.

Those aspects of the student movement which were peculiar to the young—drugs, the "counterculture," rock 'n' roll—were the least revolutionary. Those things which students had in common with other people—rage against the war and against inequality in American society, disgust with lying politicians and puffed-up "leaders," despair at boring and meaningless jobs, contempt for the consumer economy—were potentially revolutionary. But anger at the system could only be revolutionary when joined with a view of people which saw people as distinct from the system and in struggle against it. It could only become revolutionary when it saw the revolutionary transformation of American society as really *possible*, and began to work for it.

Labor in the Sixties

Workers in the U.S. in the '60s engaged in levels of open struggle not seen since 1946. Struggles on the shop floor intensified, as workers fought with managers over the day-to-day control of work. Previously unorganized sectors of the workforce—teachers, public employees, hospital workers, and others—joined unions, and fought for change with an unaccustomed militance, often in defiance of the law. Increasingly, these and other unions included large proportions of black and other workers previously underrepresented in the union movement. Strike activity, after relative quiet in the 'fifties, broke out in every sector of the economy and in every part of the country from 1965 on. More and more, these strikes were wildcat strikes, waged not only against the company but also against union leaders perceived to function as part of the management apparatus.

But the labor movement was caught in the same bind as the black and student movements. It was trapped between accepting the corporate system and all that it represented or building a movement which explicitly challenged capitalism—in the name of Communism. Workers in the '60s fought hard against many aspects of capitalism, as they experienced them in their lives or saw their effects in the wider society. But there was no analysis available to them which revealed the shared values behind their everyday struggles. No movement spoke of the conflict between their values and the values of the system. No coherent view went beyond capitalist and leftist ideas of people as passive consumers. No vision showed masses of people to be already in motion in a struggle to humanize the world. In short, there was no vision of people and social change which articulated the meaning of working class struggles and showed the potential for revolutionary transformation.

Working people had no interest in emulating the "workers' paradise" in the Soviet Union. As long as Communism seemed to be the only alternative to capitalism, the road to a revolutionary challenge to the corporate system was blocked.

Workers in the 1960s were in a double bind—caught not only between two systems, but also between their bosses and their own union leaders. In the decades since the birth of industrial unionism in the US, workers had lost control of their own organizations. Bureaucratic leadership had siphoned power in the unions out of the hands of rank-and-filers and militants. Elaborate grievance procedures took struggle from the shop floor to the bargaining table. In this "business unionism," union officials cooperated with management to keep workers in line and to insure production.

While labor-management collaboration dampened struggle, it could by no means wipe it out. Autoworkers wildcatted around the country in 1955, and again in 1957 and 1961. In 1959, steelworkers went on strike for 116 days. One measure of increasing worker restiveness was the extent of corporate effort at shop-floor control; from 1948-1966, there was a 75% rise in the ratio of supervisory to non-supervisory personnel in the private sector.[46]

From the mid-sixties, the pace of strike activity rapidly advanced, and included more and more sectors of the workforce—not only autoworkers, electrical workers, steelworkers, textile workers, and others, but newly-unionized teachers, hospital workers, and municipal employees. As the composition of the industrial workforce included larger numbers of black and other minorities, these strikes witnessed increasing class unity. More and more, these strikes were wildcat strikes.

Union members were active in the civil rights movement, and they participated in huge numbers in the famous civil rights March on Washington of 1963; but the official AFL-CIO presence there was part of the means by which corporate capital kept the working class movement within acceptable bounds.

The AFL-CIO leadership—consistent with its close cooperation with government and corporate leaders—supported the war in Vietnam, as well as other anti-labor measures. But many workers and local leaders were actively opposed to the war, and individual unions began taking an explicitly anti-war stand. At a conference on November 11, 1967, 500 delegates representing fifty unions from thirty-eight states voted unanimously for an immediate end to the bombing of North Vietnam and recognition of the National Liberation Front in South Vietnam. In 1968 the United Auto Workers left the AFL-CIO because of its continued support for the war.[47]

At the same time as the liberal UAW leadership opposed the war, however, it continued to cooperate with the automakers and the corporate rulers. Neither the UAW nor the other liberal unions explained the war to its members as a function of U.S. capitalism. They did not relate the war to other aspects of the society or seek to mobilize workers against it. The unions' function was to contain struggle, not to ignite it. In 1968, with even the *Wall Street Journal* calling for an end to the Vietnam War, to oppose the war was not necessarily a radical step.

In spite of the roadblocks to unity thrown up by union officials and New Left ideology, some continuing alliances were created between students and workers during the '60s. In 1969, for example, students striking at San Francisco State and workers at the Standard Oil plant in Richmond, California built an alliance which was announced at a news conference, where Jake Jacobs, secretary-treasurer of Local 1-561 of the Oil, Chemical, and Atomic Workers said: "It is not just police brutality that united us. We are all exploited, black workers more than whites, but we all have the same enemy, the big corporations. And it is corporations like our enemy, Standard Oil, that control the Boards of Trustees of the state college the students are fighting."[48]

It was young workers, black and white, who were on the front lines in Vietnam. As GIs became more opposed to the war, their resistance led to the eventual collapse of the military as a fighting force. In 1971, desertions reached nearly 100,000. David Cortright, author of *Soldiers in Revolt,* reported that "Soldier antiwar committees and underground newspapers began to appear everywhere." Black rebellions broke out at Long Binh Jail in Vietnam, at Camp Lejeune in North Carolina, at Travis Air Force base in California, and elsewhere. Soldiers began to "frag" unpopular officers; the Army admitted to 551 incidents of "fragging" in the years 1969-72, resulting in 86 deaths and over 700 injuries—numbers which do not include officers shot by their own men with firearms. After the bloody battle of Hamburger Hill in May, 1969, "embittered troops placed a notice in their underground newspaper offering a $10,000 reward for fragging the officers in charge." More and more troops refused to go into action.[49] U.S. intelligence estimated that as many as 60 GIs a week were crossing over to the Viet Cong.[50]

U.S. troops were withdrawn from Vietnam in large part because they could no longer be relied upon. (They were also needed to guard against insurrection at home. Over 15,000 troops, including lead battalions of the 82nd and 101st Airborne, were needed to put down the 1967 uprising in Detroit. Virtually all the regular troop formations in the United States at the time were deployed to put down the rebellions which followed in the wake of the assassination of Martin Luther King in 1968.[51]) Returning GIs formed "Vietnam Veterans Against the War" and other antiwar organizations.

1970 marked the biggest strike wave since the post-war explosion of 1946. The strikes, both wildcat and authorized, showed a deepening of the working class movement to unite key elements of the revolutionary upsurge of the '60s: mass mobilization from the bottom-up, unified struggle of white and black workers, and increasingly bitter contestation of the conditions of work.

In spite of New Left ideas about "bourgeoisified workers" and the "disappearance of the working class," U.S. society was increasingly torn by open class war. Teamsters rejected a settlement between their leaders and the trucking bosses with the first nationwide wildcat Teamsters strike, in what the New York Times called "a revolt against the national union leadership and a $1.10-an-hour raise that has been accepted in a national contract."[52] A bitter twelve week strike ensued, in which 4100 National Guardsmen were called up in Ohio to protect scabs. It was these same Guardsmen who went onto the Kent State University campus, after a student strike had broken out in the wake of the invasion of Cambodia, and murdered four students. In August of 1970, the first strike of U.S. postal employees, also a wildcat strike, broke out in New York, and quickly spread around the nation. It was led by black rank-and-filers from the New York local.

The leadership of the major unions for decades had bargained away workers' control over the pace and conditions of work in exchange for higher wages; rank-and-filers and many local leaders had for years fought this trend. The struggle over working conditions had its most famous outbreak in Lordstown, Ohio, where General Motors had put the plant in charge of the General Motors Assembly Division (GMAD), known as "the Marine Corps of GM divisions." Line speed was increased from 60 cars per hour to 102 cars. Supervision and discipline were intensified. In February, 1972 workers voted by a 97 percent majority to strike over working conditions. Said GM's director of labor relations: "the story of industrial life in the twentieth century will single out the Lordstown strike of 1972 as marking the explosion of youth and its rebellion against the management and union establishment."[53]

The Power of the Vision

In spite of the organizational and ideological constraints by which each of them were hemmed in, the popular movements of the '60s in the U.S. had achieved great things. They had challenged the power, the plans, the policies of the most powerful ruling class in history and had forced major changes in American society. They had stood up for justice, for equality, for democracy. They had faced police clubs and dogs, had gone to jail, had gone on strike. They had shown that the good in society comes not from the top of society, from the war-planners and mystifiers and hypocrites, the corporate and government and labor and educational and religious elite, but from the ordinary people who have built it. They had raised fundamental questions about the direction of U.S. society, and held up as never before a mirror to the society, demanding that the reality of America be examined in light of its professed ideals. They had constructed from the insights, the dreams and hopes, the ideas and values of millions of ordinary people, a vision of life as it should be, and they had invested millions of people with real hope and real determination that this dream come true.

If this vision never found its full articulation, if it never was able to emerge clear and coherent out of the tangle of capitalist and Marxist ideas in which the movements were trapped, still it made its power felt. The power of the vision was felt in the hearts of those who participated in it and acted to fulfill it. Its power was felt also by the elite whom it threatened.

These movements cut deeply into ruling class control of the society. They undermined its freedom of action in maintaining the business empire abroad. They dramatically reduced its profits. Before the '60s were over, the rulers had already begun planning a counterattack; in 1971 they began to implement it.

FRANCE: The May Revolt

In May, 1968 the world was electrified by events in France. In response to brutal police repression of a student demonstration, two, then three, then seven, then nearly ten million French workers occupied their factories in the "largest general strike that ever stopped the economy of an advanced industrial country, and the first *wildcat general strike* in history,"[54] in a movement which brought France to the brink of revolution. After fifty years of counterrevolution, the European proletariat had stepped back onto the stage of history. Revolution was once again on the agenda.

The May Revolution was not about wages or what reformist unions generally present as the "economic issues." The standard of living—measured in refrigerators and cars and TV sets—of French workers at the time of the strike was at an historic high; French workers contemptuously rejected the unprecedented pay increases with which government and union leaders tried to lure them back to work.

Rather than an uprising against economic deprivation, the revolt was a movement of the whole working class against the totality of capitalist alienation: boring jobs, mindless consumerism, powerlessness. The French May showed that the alienation characteristic of modern society is not necessary or permanent—that beneath the calm surface of capitalist control lie forces capable of springing the whole structure into oblivion.

The Revolution of Everyday Life

Of the several revolutionary groups active in the May events, a group calling itself the Situationist International (SI) developed the most penetrating analysis of modern society. The Situationists were a handful of people who, beginning in 1957, set out to reintroduce the idea of revolution to modern society. Through widely-circulated pamphlets, books, and journals, they had an influence entirely out of proportion to their numbers. To the extent that any one group can be identified with such a huge event, the spirit of the Situationists was the spirit of the French May. In the Situationists' ideas one can see germs both of the successes and the ultimate failure of the May revolution.

The starting point of SI analysis was the counterrevolutionary nature of Bolshevism and the left: "Admitting that there is no revolu-

tionary movement is the first precondition for developing such a
movement."[55] The similarity between Soviet and Western societies
consists essentially in the fact that people's everyday lives are managed from above by a small group of specialized rulers, who manipulate appearances to give people the illusion of freedom while maintaining the reality of control.

The Situationists understood that the whole project of revolution
had to be thought out anew. If revolution seems ridiculous now, they
declared, it is only because an organized revolutionary movement no
longer exists in the advanced industrial countries. Revolution simply
has to be "reinvented." Anything else implies acceptance of the existing order.[56]

The Situationists focused on the lived experience of modern reality
as the basis of reconceiving the idea of revolution. "Everyday life is
the measure of all things," they declared: "of the fulfillment or rather
the nonfulfillment of human relations; of the use of lived time; of
artistic experimentation; of revolutionary politics."[57] Everyday life is
"the battlefield where the war between power and the totality [of
human desires] takes place, with power using all its strength to control the totality."[58]

The Situationists analyzed the extraordinary means which modern
elites have developed for dominating society. They maintained that,
"In societies where modern conditions of production prevail, all of
life presents itself as an immense accumulation of *spectacles*."[59] The
spectacle is the organization of appearances by the ruling class, to
make people believe that their lives are humanly satisfying—lives
which in fact are impoverished and unfree, where their jobs have
been dehumanized and their only activity consists in the passive consumption of commodities which seem endlessly produced by economic forces with the appearance of natural laws. The spectacle replaces
religion in its function of concealing man from himself: "Docility is
no longer ensured by means of priestly magic, it results from a mass
of minor hypnoses: news, culture, city planning, advertising, mechanisms of conditioning and suggestion ready to serve any order, established or to come."[60]

The Situationist critique was uniquely attuned to modern societies
in which people are trapped by an abundance of material goods rather
than by material deprivation. Modern capitalist society "tends to
atomize people into isolated consumers." In this society, "the abundance of consumer goods [is] nothing but the flip side of alienation in
production."[61] The society is characterized by a new kind of poverty.

People do not lack material goods; they lack human fulfillment. People are trapped in repetitive, isolated, specialized activities, in which they are "as deprived as possible of communication and self-realization."[62]

The Situationists were acutely aware that reformism is a means of social control—that "partial demands are essentially contrary to a total change."[63] The goal of a movement must be "the revolutionary transformation of everyday life, which is not reserved for some vague future but is placed immediately before us by the development of capitalism and its unbearable demands."[64]

Why Was The Revolution Defeated?

The French Communist Party controlled the Confederation Generale du Travail (CGT), the largest federation of industrial unions in France. Though it had long since followed a policy of collaboration with capital, the party still employed the rhetoric of class struggle and to some extent had been able to maintain its reputation as the revolutionary party of the working class. It still had a disciplined membership among workers in key industries.

The occupations movement was undertaken in defiance of the CGT leadership. After it had spontaneously spread countrywide, however, the CGT leaders sanctioned the strike, to try to put themselves back at its head. The CGT leadership used all the means at their disposal to weaken the strike. By controlling the factory gates, Communist leaders managed to a large extent to isolate one factory from another and to keep workers apart from students. They discouraged political discussion in the factories, and encouraged individual workers to drift home. They inveighed against "international elements" stirring up trouble and called on the police and the capitalist state to "maintain order."[65]

The mass movement in the streets and factories and offices was impelled by ideas and aspirations which threatened both the capitalists and the Communists. In spite of the their combined efforts to quell it, the movement continued to gain momentum. Both the DeGaulle government and the Communist leadership were stunned by the onrushing mass mobilization, and seemed powerless to keep up with events. For a time, power in the society was up for grabs: "it is precisely because the occupations movement was objectively at several moments *only an hour away*" from revolution that it struck such terror in the state and the Communist Party.[66]

But no alternative leadership came forth from the ranks of workers or students with the credibility and vision to fill the void and to lead the movement forward. The Situationists later wrote that, "The majority of [the workers] had not recognized the total significance of their own movement; and nobody could do it in their place."[67] When DeGaulle called for new elections, the Communist Party and CGT leadership supported him. In the vacuum of revolutionary leadership, the trade union leaders were able finally to persuade the workers to go back to work.

This massive movement was brought under control and defeated because it was unable to create a revolutionary alternative to capitalism and Communism. People needed a new vision based on a new paradigm of society to reveal the significance of the revolutionary actions which they had already taken, and to give them the self-confidence to take their movement to its conclusion. No leadership emerged which articulated as a revolutionary vision the implicitly revolutionary actions and values and goals of the people.

While there were a number of small revolutionary groups which attempted to lead the movement forward, they too, like the Communist Party, were Marxist organizations. The Situationist International itself remained locked thoroughly within the Marxism on which these other parties were based. The SI mistakenly thought that the counterrevolutionary nature of Marxist-Leninist parties was a function of their concept of organization. In fact, the problem was more fundamental. It was a function of their view of people—a view which the Situationists shared. While the Situationists rejected the idea of many contemporary Marxists of a "bourgeoisified" proletariat which had been integrated into capitalism, still they believed that most people—most workers, most students—participate in the "general passivity." According to the SI, most people are caught up in "the spectacle" and cannot see beyond it. The working class is always potentially active, the SI thought, but its normal condition is to be "a passive object."[68]

The Situationists found the *reason* for revolution in people's everyday lives, but they did not find the *source* of it there; for the Situationists as for Marx, the source of revolution lay in the economy, in the contradiction between social production and private appropriation. The Situationists did not talk about people in everyday life as real actors; they talked about the operation of capitalism, as if it stands above society and unfolds according to its own laws.

There was a huge gap between human reality as the Situationists and other Marxists described it—a passive working class dominated by economic forces—and the possibilities of human society which they set forth—"the conscious domination of history by the people who make it." It was a gap which people found finally unbridgeable.

There was nothing in what the Situationists or the other groups said which could assure workers and others that the new world which they seemed to be creating was real or could be made to last. With no idea of revolution being put forward which showed the working class to be an already active force in everyday life, there was nothing to show that ordinary people were capable of taking history in their hands. The idea that people are passive in everyday life dramatically undermined the confidence of people that they could create a new world—that they could get there from here. It was too great a leap, too radical a break.

With no new view of human life and struggle which broke free of the Marxist paradigm of history, the workers reluctantly gave in to their Marxist union leaders. Without a sure bridge into the future—an idea of people already engaged in creating it—the workers stepped back into the past.

CHINA: The Meaning of the Cultural Revolution

No other event in recent history has elicited such universal condemnation as the "Great Proletarian Cultural Revolution" in China. Capitalists and socialists, Chinese Communist Party leaders and Soviet apparatchiks, U.S. officials and their leftist critics have raised a global chorus against it. What is the cause of this inspiring unity?

In a decade of worldwide revolutionary struggles, events in China of the 1960s represented the furthest development of revolutionary ideas and mass revolutionary mobilization, challenging both capitalist and Communist concepts of society. Some of the most important lessons of the revolutionary movements of the '60s are to be learned from the Cultural Revolution. Now, with the spring 1989 uprising in China, understanding this period is all the more urgent. The historic developments in China over the past two decades, including the "economic reforms" and the spring uprising, can only be understood against the backdrop of the Cultural Revolution.

The Cultural Revolution began in late 1965 with a power struggle in the Chinese ruling elite. One faction of the Communist Party lead-

ership wanted to pursue a model of economic development similar to
the Soviet model, emphasizing heavy industry and using economic
incentives—pay differentials based on productivity, piece-work,
etc.—to spur production. The other faction, led by Mao, emphasized
a mix of agricultural and industrial development and the lessening of
differentials between the countryside and the city. Moreover, Mao's
faction stressed mobilization of the peasantry and working-class,
based on egalitarianism and political commitment, to increase production.

Both sides in this conflict were committed to the supremacy of the
Chinese Communist Party (CCP); their disagreement lay in how best
to secure that power. Beneath the disagreements about economic development lay a debate which could not be conducted openly: how to
harness the huge and unruly Chinese masses in a way that would
consolidate the power of the Communist elite.

Factional disputes among Communist leaders have been frequent
enough in the past. What distinguished the dispute among the Chinese
elite was that Mao's faction calculated that it could not prevail except
by mobilizing the population on its side. The Cultural Revolution
began as Mao's attempt to rouse the masses of people to crush the
opposition among the ruling elite to his strategy for development in
China. But, as one ex-Red Guard wrote, "Mao Tse-tung ignited the
revolution but he could not control it....The genuine revolution was
born from the pseudo-revolution."[69]

The genuine Cultural Revolution represents the most ambitious and
sustained attempt in history of a revolutionary movement to overthrow the new ruling class which a revolution based on Marxism-Leninism had brought forth.

Background to the Cultural Revolution:
The Chinese Revolution, 1927-1949

The Cultural Revolution must be understood in the context of decades of revolutionary struggle in China. The revolution which Mao
and the Communists led had two aspects. On the one hand it was an
authentic mass revolutionary movement, which articulated the struggles and aspirations of the vast Chinese peasantry and others. On the
other hand it was a movement tightly controlled and directed by a
Marxist-Leninist hierarchy, which channelled the revolutionary energy

of the people according to its own interpretation of the needs and possibilities of social change in China.

Mao had written prophetically in 1927:

> In a very short time, in China's central, southern, and northern provinces, several hundred million peasants will rise like a mighty storm, a force so swift and violent that no power, however great, will be able to hold it back....Every revolutionary party and every revolutionary comrade will be put to the test, to be accepted or rejected as they decide. There are three alternatives. To march at their head and lead them? To trail behind them, gesticulating and criticizing? Or to stand in their way and oppose them? Every Chinese is free to choose, but events will force you to make the choice quickly.[70]

The party strove to harness the huge forces of the peasant revolution to achieve the goals of Chinese Marxism.

Consistent with Marxist-Leninist doctrine, the party believed that revolution in China should take place in two stages: a democratic revolution and a socialist revolution. By democratic revolution, Mao meant the destruction of feudalism and warlordism, and breaking the grip of foreign capital on the Chinese economy. It would be a "people's revolution," to include not only workers and poor peasants but also rich peasants and the "national bourgeoisie," Chinese capitalists not tied to foreign capital. These two groups were seen by the party as integral to the democratic revolution because of their role in economic development; consistent with Marxist theory, capitalist development would create the material basis for socialism. By "socialist revolution," Mao meant state ownership of the means of production under "the dictatorship of the proletariat," which in practice meant the dictatorship of the Communist Party ruling on behalf of the working class.

The twists and turns of Communist policy reflected the contradictory nature of the revolution. The party was constantly confronted with the problem of both mobilizing the masses to achieve its goals, and keeping them in check, so that they not rebel against the inequality being maintained in their lives by the party. The party strove to keep the peasant revolution within the bounds of capitalist models of development. For example, party policy in liberated areas during the war with Japan, which invaded China in 1937, was to suppress peasant struggles for land reform, which would have threatened rich and some middle peasants; the party limited reform to strict enforcement of rent and tax reductions which were the official, though unenforced, policy of the Kuomintang, the Nationalist Party of Chiang Kai-shek. Only when civil war broke out with Chiang Kai-shek in 1946—that is, not until the Communists needed the revolutionary energy of the peasant masses—did the Communists proceed with land reform.

The party used the idea that economic development is the basis of social progress to define and justify its unequal role in relation to the masses. That relationship was one of dictatorship—a dictatorship which, if essentially benign in the period of revolutionary struggle (if dictatorship can ever be benign), became increasingly oppressive after Liberation in 1949, as the party consolidated its power and developed the administrative machinery to rule a huge country.

As the party gathered into its hands all the economic and political power of the country, it became an increasingly alienated ruling apparatus. The stage was set for another revolution.

The Outbreak of Cultural Revolution, 1965-1966

There had been serious policy disputes among the Chinese elite throughout the revolutionary period. These disputes intensified after Liberation. The beginning of the Cultural Revolution in 1965 brought these differences into the open, and marked the beginning of Mao's explicit attempt to enlist the masses on his side in a contest over the nature of Chinese socialism and the direction of its development.

The message which Mao and his allies used to mobilize the masses was twofold. The Sixteen Point Program of August, 1966, issued by the Central Committee of the Communist Party but expressing Mao's viewpoint, declared that the Chinese Revolution was in danger of following the course of the Soviet revolution, becoming one more "revisionist" state. (By "revisionist" Mao meant betraying the principles of Marxism-Leninism. He was not here calling for a truly democratic society; Mao admired Stalin, and felt that the Soviet Union had gone wrong *after* Stalin's death.) The party, according to the program, contained some bureaucrats who "had wormed their way in" and who wanted to restore capitalism in China. These "capitalist-roaders" had distanced themselves from the people. Members of the governing apparatus had begun to lord it over people and to take special privileges for themselves, while the people had grown apathetic and accepted these privileges as unavoidable.

The problem went deeper than just a few bad party members; the problem, Mao contended, was that, as revolutionary struggles receded from people's memories, the tendency for traditional ways of thinking and old inequalities to reappear also grew. According to Mao, the cultural "superstructure" of the society had not yet been changed by the revolution in the economic "base" of society, and still reflected many bourgeois habits of thought from China's pre-revolutionary past. Thus a revolution was needed at the level of culture as well.

This revolution, Mao declared through the program, should strive to bring about an end to divisions between mental and physical labor, an end to rule by experts and bureaucrats, a simplification of all governmental and administrative tasks so that anyone could take part in them, the destruction of elitism in education. It should establish cooperation and equality as the bases of economic development, and mass democracy as the basis of political life. Mao called on the masses to create a "Chinese People's Commune" modeled on the Paris Commune of 1871. This model implied the destruction of the party bureaucracy and creation of a revolutionary government based on mass democracy, with popularly elected officials subject to immediate recall, who, unlike the privileged Communist cadre, would receive no higher compensation than a workman's average wage. Property should be redistributed in an egalitarian fashion.[71]

A French Maoist who participated in it described the Cultural Revolution in this way:

> What it amounted to, really, was that the population was mobilized to comment on anything and everything in the society which had been subjected to the influence of tradition, including teaching, art, and literature. It was also necessary for the people to be able to criticize the workings of the state, since the distance between the rulers and the ruled was one of the crucial problems. This led to a movement of critical comment on the people in positions of authority whose purpose was to bring the rulers and the masses closer together. It was an effort to recast the structure of power...[72]

The first stage of the Cultural Revolution thus presented the Chinese masses with an historic opening. Up to this time, they had been under strict and repressive party control. Now they were being encouraged by the leader of the party to criticize the party openly, and to express two decades of pent-up resentment.

The Second Stage: Power Seizure

Unfortunately for Mao and his allies, "the masses" took the revolutionary process very seriously—enough so that Mao was forced to use the army to intervene at several points to contain and finally to destroy the movement which he had unleashed.

There were three main organized forces in the Cultural Revolution: Mao and a handful of Party leaders loyal to him; forces loyal to another Communist leader named Liu Shao Ch'i (the "capitalist roaders"), which included the party apparatus; and a third force, which over time developed a radical critique of Communist rule of Chinese society. As the Cultural Revolution proceeded, this mass revolutionary force came to be attacked by both Mao and the "capitalist roaders" as the "ultra-left." According to some figures, the ultra-left comprised organizations with some 30 to 40 million followers.[73]

In the spring and summer of 1966, Red Guard organizations were created with Mao's encouragement at several universities in Beijing and elsewhere. Membership in these first Red Guard organizations was largely restricted to students from families of Communist Party cadre, and they were essentially a conservative force. Much under the influence of party leaders, they deflected criticism from party cadre, and instead focused their attack on the "bourgeois" consciousness of students and other people as the main problem in Chinese society. These conservative Red Guards "attacked anything even slightly related to bourgeois culture: they cut off long hair on the street, burned books which they considered to be at odds with Mao-Tse-Tung-Thought, destroyed art treasures, and so forth." They imposed a "red terror," attacking the houses of the bourgeoisie, teachers, and professional people, and subjecting "class enemies" to torture and detainment in private jails. Leaders of these Red Guards were accorded the privilege of standing beside Mao and pinning on his Red Guard armband at a mass rally in August.[74]

At the same time, radical students began to form rebel Red Guard organizations. The members of these new groups were not attached by blood to the party, and were prepared to attack it. The conservative Red Guards had been organized from the top down by party leaders. The rebels began to organize a movement from the bottom up. They denounced the activities of the conservative Red Guards, and engaged in pitched battles with them. Presumably because he had found the conservative Red Guards unsuitable for his purposes of attacking the party apparatus, Mao and the informal leadership group which he created to circumvent the party—the Cultural Revolution Small Group—in October, 1966 came out in support of the radicals. The rebel Red Guards had by then grown into mass student organizations. In November, 1966 they reached out to contract workers (temporary workers, among the most exploited in China), factory workers, and peasants. Thus was born a popular revolutionary movement prepared to challenge the Communist bureaucracy.

In January, 1967, beginning with a power seizure by rebel workers in Shanghai, this mass revolutionary movement seized control of government ministries, factories, and transportation apparatus over much of China and drove out Communist officials at every level. In seizing power, the masses thought they were carrying out Mao's directive to establish a Chinese People's Commune on the model of the Paris Commune.

After the party officials had been driven out, Mao stepped in to reverse the "January Storm." Mao's goal had not really been to destroy the Communist Party, but to force members of the ruling bureaucracy to stand aside, so that he could reconstitute it according to his own wishes. He announced that the time was not ripe for the establishment of the "People's Commune," and persuaded the people—who still believed in his leadership—to give up their new power to "Revolutionary Committees," to include representatives of the party, the People's Liberation Army (PLA), and the masses. To the radicals' demand that "90% of the cadres step aside," Mao reiterated his dictum of the Sixteen Point Program that "95% of the cadres are good"—thus preserving intact the party apparatus. He then directed the army to suppress the mass organizations. According to a big character poster put up in Canton [Guangzhou] in 1974, 40,000 revolutionaries were killed and one million people imprisoned in Kwantung Province alone by the PLA.[75]

The Cultural Revolution continued for two more years, alternating between periods in which the radical masses or the party apparatus and conservative mass organizations closely linked to the party were in ascendancy. Mao stayed largely in the background, intervening only when one side or the other seemed to be gaining too much power. The radicals learned more about the nature and depth of change necessary, and came to see the People's Liberation Army as an instrument of the Red bourgeoisie. This convinced them that armed struggle was necessary to wage the revolution. In July and August, 1967 the radical mass organizations seized weapons from the PLA all over the country, and fought pitched battles with the army in "The

August Local Civil Revolutionary War." In "The September Set-back," Mao persuaded people to surrender their weapons, though the radical mass organizations organized resistance which was bloodily suppressed over a six-month period.[76]

Armed struggle continued to break out. In the spring of '68, peasants in Kiangsi Province seized trains loaded with weapons bound for Vietnam and used them to attack the People's Liberation Army, and strikes broke out throughout the country. At Ji Shui in Hupeh Province, peasants armed themselves and set up their own communal economy. In August of '68, masses of people again broke into the arsenals of the army and seized weapons.

Now the struggle reached a climax. Up to this time, Mao had not been openly attacked by the ultra-left, and most people still did not clearly understand him to be their enemy. For the first time, Mao was forced openly to declare himself the enemy of the ultra-left. He declared Sheng-wu-lien, the North Star Study Group, and other mass ultra-left organizations to be counterrevolutionary, and ruthlessly suppressed them. With his open crushing of the rebel movement, Mao's role was finally exposed. He succeeded at destroying the ultra-left, but his attempt at controlled revolution had failed. Maoism was exposed to millions of people as a fraud.[77]

To the party, Maoism was exposed as inevitably in conflict with its ability to rule. On the basis of its experience during the Cultural Revolution, the party concluded that it could not continue to control a population collectivized and mobilized for avowedly socialist goals. It began to seek ways to demobilize the masses and to privatize Chinese life. Its search for a new basis for its rule led to the economic reforms of the 1970s and '80s.

While resistance to the restoration of party control continued—in Kiangsi Province, for example, in the spring of 1969, rebel forces organized mass strikes of peasants and workers; in September, 1969 mass struggle was re-ignited in Hupeh by a big character poster entitled "When Mankind Is Liberated, I Am Liberated"—the Cultural Revolution was brought to an official end in April, 1969 with the commencement of the Ninth Congress of the Chinese Communist Party, "thus enabling the Maoist leaders to maintain the fictitious posture that the Cultural Revolution had been carried out under the leadership of Chairman Mao and the Chinese Communist Party."[78]

The "Ultra-Left" In The Cultural Revolution

While information concerning the ultra-left is fragmentary, several documents produced by ultra-left groups were smuggled out of China or were written by members of the ultra-left who escaped to Hong Kong after their defeat. These documents suggest some of the significance of the real revolution which Mao ignited with his "pseudo-revolution." At the same time, they convey the confusion of the ultra-left over the role of Mao Tse-tung and over the validity of Marxism-Leninism as a revolutionary ideology.

The most important of these documents is "Whither China?," produced in early 1968 by Sheng-wu-lien, a coalition of 20 radical Red Guard and rebel-worker groups formed in October, 1967 in Hunan province. Sheng-wu-lien numbered between two and three million followers.[79]

"Whither China?" expresses the contradictions of the radical movement: a slavish devotion to Mao Tse-tung, and a determination to destroy the Red bureaucracy of which he was the chief representative. Because of Mao's enormous prestige in China at the time, each of the conflicting sides in the Cultural Revolution claimed to be carrying out Mao's line. It is difficult to judge just how much of the "Maoism" in "Whither China" reflects the real sentiments of the authors; it seems, however, that at the time of its writing the ultra-left still had profound illusions about Mao.

Sheng-wu-lien believed that the ruling Communist Party had become a "Red bourgeoisie." The goal of Sheng-wu-lien was "overthrow of the rule of the new bureaucratic bourgeoisie, complete smashing of the old state machinery, realization of social revolution, carrying out the redistribution of property and power, and the establishment of a new society—the 'People's Commune of China.'"[80] Sheng-wu-lien likened its mass organization to the revolutionary soviets established in Russia in 1917. It cited Mao's directives as authority for its call for revolution.

Why Was The Cultural Revolution Defeated?

Beneath the ultra-left's confusion over the role of Mao lay a more profound weakness. "Whither China?" accepted Marxism-Leninism as the keystone of revolutionary thought, as if the Chinese Communist Party could be adequately analyzed—and the party itself overthrown—without moving outside the theory of social change on which the party's birth and development were based.

According to "Whither China?" there were some steps taken by members of Sheng-wu-lien to organize revolutionary cells at the lowest levels of the Communist Party and also to set up a new Marxist-Leninist party to replace the existing Communist Party. But these efforts were doomed to failure, because they were based on the premise that the Red bureaucracy had betrayed Communism. In fact, the Chinese Communist Party had not betrayed Marxism-Leninism or Maoism, but fulfilled them.

The revolutionary left could have overthrown the party only if it had challenged the ideological basis of the party's exploitative relationship to the people. The ultra-left was defeated because it stayed trapped within the Marxist conception of people and change which had brought forth the Red bureaucracy it was up against. The ultra-left did not have a revolutionary theory which could adequately articulate the meaning of the massive revolutionary struggle which was underway; it could not adequately explain how the party had developed its oppressive role, or show how a new revolution could be different. It could not enable the Chinese masses to realize their ability to make a revolution of a new type, without the party and without Mao.

The lack of an alternative theory of revolution also explained why the revolutionaries remained unclear about Mao's role until he destroyed them; their illusions about Mao were rooted in their illusions about the Communist movement whose contradictions he embodied.

There is a later document, written in 1974 by a member of the ultra-left who had escaped to Hong Kong, which challenges the Marxist framework of the Chinese Revolution. Even this document, however, does not really escape the Marxist view of people and history.

In "The Dusk of Rationality," Yu Shuet links Sheng-wu-lien and the May Revolution in France. In both, she says, "...advanced elements of the masses appear and they reject all the 'parties' and 'sects' which seek to monopolise revolution." In both revolutions, man is seeking to cast off the alienation and emptiness which are results of being dominated by material things. "Now the masses have risen and sought to establish a new relatedness to the world in which man will truly be man...In the new relatedness, man rediscovers his own existence."[81]

"Revolutions in the past," Yu Shuet asserts, "yielded results contradictory to beliefs." This, she says, has also been the outcome of rev-

olutions based upon Marxism-Leninism. The reasons for this lie in
the nature of Marxist philosophy, which shares the fatal flaw of traditional rationalist philosophy. In rationalist philosophy, man is assigned
an insignificant role; he is merely a "rational animal" in a world dominated by material forces. Marxism continues this view of man subordinate to material forces. Marxism holds that "freedom is the recognition of necessity"—that is, that freedom for man lies in recognizing the pre-eminence of economic forces. In this "theory of necessity," Marxism establishes "the philosophical foundation of an authoritarian dictatorial society."[82]

In China and the USSR, says Yu Shuet, Communist parties "made
use of proletarian uprisings or civil wars to realise nationalisation of
capital" in the hands of the party-controlled state. The result is "totalitarian state economies" which are still capitalist, and in which
"The ruling party itself becomes the ruling class and is above the
masses." This is not the function of the outlook of individual leaders.
There is no difference in this regard between Stalinists and Trotsky-
ists: "It is inevitable for a Leninist party which attains political power
in a country through the revolutionary strength of workers and peasants to follow totalitarian state capitalism."

In totalitarian state economies, state capital, in the possession of a
small handful of leaders, "nakedly and endlessly" exploits the workers. State controlled economies like that of China and the USSR are
not planned economies but controlled economies. "Undoubtedly," Yu
Shuet comments, "the existing world is still a capitalist world."[83]

Although she attacks Marxism, Yu Shuet's views retain fundamental elements of the Marxist outlook: a belief in economic development
as the basis of history, a belief in the "backwardness" of working
people, and a belief in capitalism as a progressive stage in history.

These beliefs are not only the fundamental elements of the Marxist
paradigm; they are also the basis of the Chinese Communist Party's
exploitative relationship to the "backward" masses as it directed capitalist development in China in their name. It was precisely these beliefs that underlay and legitimized the Communist Party's domination
of Chinese society.

It seems clear that the ultra-left did not develop a theory which
adequately expressed the goals and values which the revolutionary
movement embodied and for which it fought. It stayed within the
Marxist paradigm because it did not see clearly how the Marxist conception contradicted its own aspirations, and because it saw no alternative.

Thomas Kuhn shows that people do not abandon one way of explaining the world, however much it may seem to contradict their experience, until there is an alternative explanation available to take its place; he explains also that, without an alternative model of society with which to compare it, people cannot fully understand the flaws of the existing model. The ultra-left in the Cultural Revolution saw no alternative to the Marxist paradigm, and therefore remained trapped within it, unaware of how deeply it contradicted the goals of the revolutionary movement.

The Cultural Revolution represents the exhaustion of Marxism as a theory of revolution. It shows that the great historical task at this time is the construction of a new paradigm of social change which, because it sees the masses of people as active makers of history, can lead to the society which it envisions.

6

THE EMPIRE STRIKES BACK

The leaders of post-World War II society had believed revolution in industrialized societies to be a threat of the past. The events of the late '60s changed that assumption.

In the early '70s, the international ruling elite began a worldwide counteroffensive against popular rebellion. The key focus of their efforts was the economy. If the full-employment economy of the 1960's had provided the context for a "revolution of rising expectations," they reasoned, then expansion had to give way to contraction. In the '70s and '80s, governments in the U.S. and elsewhere promoted slow growth and recession, unemployment, the massive destruction of income maintenance programs (welfare, food stamps, unemployment compensation, and the like), and other measures to lower people's expectations and to tame popular resistance.

To strengthen their long-term control, world leaders undertook a massive restructuring of world society. The key to this restructuring was a huge leap in the integration of the world economy. Millions of jobs were shipped from the developed countries to low-wage areas overseas, leading to "deindustrialization" on a massive scale. Work was deskilled through the use of computers, and millions of workers were displaced by new technologies. Permanently high rates of unemployment were built into the industrial economies.

My purpose in this chapter is to show that the "economic crisis" of the 1970s and '80s is not economic but political. High unemployment, deindustrialization, and other developments which have transformed American and world society in these years are not problems which the rulers are attempting to solve but weapons which they are using in a war to crush the revolutionary aspirations of the world's people.

Contrary to the opinions of most mainstream and Marxist commentators, the closing decades of the twentieth century are not driven by rivalry among the business elites of the U.S. and Japan and Germany for markets or control of resources, but by a struggle between revolution and counterrevolution: a war between an international elite acting in concert on the one hand and the vast majority of the world's people on the other. The war is over the future of human society.

Preparing the Way: The Story of the 1970s

As the movements of the '60s gained momentum, the explosion of militant labor struggle sent shock waves through the business establishment. Profits began to slide as workers won wage and benefits gains, and as struggles for safety on the job and protection of the environment added to costs. Profits of non-financial corporations fell from 15.5 percent in the period of 1963-66 to 12.7 percent in 1967-70. In spite of corporate efforts, profits continued their slide throughout the '70s: from 10.1 percent in 1971-74 to only 9.7 percent through 1978.[84]

In addition to undermining profits, mass struggle was undermining elite control. Black ghettoes were exploding in rage. The armed forces in Vietnam were collapsing as a fighting force. Labor officials were losing control of the rank-and-file, as the wave of wildcat strikes continued to build. 1969 saw 2,000 wildcat strikes—twice the number of 1960.[85] The *Wall Street Journal* reported in 1970:

> Observers of the labor-management scene...almost unanimously assert that the present situation is the worst within memory....Morale in many operations is sagging badly, international work slow-downs are cropping up more frequently and absenteeism is soaring.[86]

Business leaders began clamoring for a recession in 1967, to restore "discipline" to the labor force. Richard Nixon's election in 1968 led almost immediately to an engineered recession, as the government cut the federal budget to slow the economy. Unemployment rose sharply in 1969 and early 1970. Business leaders began to take heart as the government put the brakes on the economy:

> "Corporate executives I've checked with are cautiously optimistic," insurance executive W. Clement Stone concluded in a 1970 interview. "There is what I call a wholesome recession....As for employees, with a fear of losing their jobs, they're really putting

their heart into their work. Formerly, it was, 'What's the difference.'"[87]

The recession of 1969-70, however, proved inadequate to the task of taming discontent. Teamsters and postal workers went out on nationwide wildcat strikes in 1970, and other strikes continued to erupt. Over 66 million work days were lost due to strike activity in 1970, "a record exceeded only by 1946 and 1959 in the postwar era."[88] Campuses exploded in an unprecedented strike wave after the invasion of Cambodia and the murder of students at Kent State. The recession was also shortlived, as Nixon shifted gears and began to stimulate the economy to insure his victory in the 1972 election.

Many government and business leaders recognized the need for a strategic counteroffensive against workers and popular movements. They began the planning and organizing necessary to undertake what the authors of one book call "The Great Repression."[89] To plan the counteroffensive on the U.S. domestic front, the chief executives of the two hundred largest corporations organized the Business Roundtable. The Business Roundtable planned and coordinated massive campaigns to roll back wages and benefits, and to weaken the power of organized labor, directing its earliest efforts at the construction industry; at the same time, it began a wide-ranging public relations and lobbying campaign to gut the Clean Air Act and to promote the deregulation of business. The campaign for deregulation of industry gained steam as the '70s progressed; "deregulation" became the watchword of corporate leaders and politicians of both parties.[90]

To coordinate economic policies on the international level, David Rockefeller and others organized the Trilateral Commission, which included corporate, government, and labor leaders from the U.S., Western Europe, and Japan. A report of the Commission said that "The international system which depended for its leadership in the past on the United States alone now requires a truly common management." It recommended formation of a supranational advisory commission of three heads of state to set policy for the Trilateral nations. Annual economic summits and other forums were used to coordinate internal economic and political policies of the Trilateral countries.[91]

Corporate and government leaders undertook a massive public relations effort, to convince the public that the gains working people had made in the '60s were having a negative effect on the competitive position of the U.S. in the world economy. An often-cited *Business Week* editorial declared in 1974:

It will be a bitter pill for people to swallow—the idea of doing with less so that big business can have more. Nothing that this nation or any other nation has done in modern history compares with the selling job that must be done to make people accept the new reality.[92]

Corporate and government leaders pressed their counteroffensive on many fronts. Corporations went on the attack against their employees, with sharply intensified supervision and disciplinary practices, speed-up, and other measures. They began to spend millions on union-busting consulting firms. Business, Doug Fraser, then president of the UAW, said in 1978, had declared "a new class war."

From 1973 to 1979, the Federal Reserve Board restricted the money supply in an effort to slow the economy.[93] In 1974, the Ford Administration severely cut the federal budget, to produce the deepest recession since the Great Depression. "We need a sharp recession," one business leader had declared. Another said, "This recession will bring about the healthy respect for economic values that the Depression did."[94]

The results of the 1974-75 recession, however, were not as anticipated. The Administration had purposely created a recession because the high unemployment rates associated with recessions are supposed to make workers hungry enough that they will accept lower wages to get or keep a job. But a study conducted by the President's Council of Economic Advisors reported with dismay that, while the pace of wage growth slackened during the recession, the rate of price increases slowed even further, with the disturbing result that real wages actually rose during this period.[95]

The recession had backfired. Corporate and government leaders learned a hard lesson: "As it was with the Vietnamese, however, so it was with U.S. workers: a short quick war could not be won....With no swift and decisive victory for business in sight, the macroeconomic decision makers prepared for a prolonged period of programmed economic stagnation, hoping at least that high levels of unemployment in the long run would bring labor to heel."[96]

Throughout the rest of the '70s, neither business nor labor was strong enough to win a decisive victory against the other. The nation entered a period of "stagflation." Stagflation was the name devised to describe the historically unprecedented combination of high unemployment and rising inflation. Economists and politicians declared the phenomenon a mystery. In fact, stagflation was a result of the combination of two factors: economic stagnation and political stalemate. Economic stagnation was a conscious policy of the government, intended to increase unemployment and to weaken labor; inflation was a function of corporations' efforts to recoup through higher prices the profits that high wages made so elusive.

When the Carter Administration took over the reins of power from the Ford Administration, it took the effort to break the back of popular resistance to new levels of international coordination. The Carter Administration had the distinction of including twenty-five members of the Trilateral Commission among its highest officials. They included, in addition to Jimmy Carter himself, Vice-President Walter Mondale and National Security Advisor Zbigniew Brzezinski, Secretary of State Cyrus Vance, Ambassador to the United Nations Andrew Young, Secretary of Defense Harold Brown, Chairman of the Federal Reserve Board Paul Volcker, and eighteen other officials.[97]

Democrat Jimmy Carter was presented by the media as a well-intentioned if ineffectual leader, with "populist" policies which did not quite succeed. In fact, Carter's policies were as much the conscious weapons of capital as those of Republican Presidents Ford before him and Reagan after him. Carter was a loyal Trilateralist who took the war on working people further than any previous president.

The Carter Administration's contribution to the corporate counteroffensive included:

*"voluntary" wage and price controls, during which prices were allowed to creep up while wage gains were suppressed;

*dramatic cuts in the corporate tax rate, which shifted even more of the federal tax burden from corporations and the rich onto the shoulders of working families;

*21% interest rates, designed to "zap" labor by slowing expansion and rapidly increasing unemployment;

*cuts in federal aid to the cities, which threw great numbers of public service employees out of work, while cutting public services to working class families;

*cuts in job training funds for unemployed youth, which magnified the increasing desperation, particularly among black youth, who were experiencing unemployment rates in excess of 40% at the time;

*a vast leap in arms expenditures, which took funds out of the productive economy while pouring public funds into the coffers of defense contractors; and

*the decontrol of oil prices, which enriched oil companies at the expense of ordinary people, at the same time as they slowed the economy by soaking up available resources.

Despite its zealous efforts, however, the Carter Administration was not able to break people's resistance to the forces of capital. It remained for the Reagan Administration to bring to fruition efforts well-begun by President Carter and others.

The Meaning of the Reagan Administration

The Reagan Administration was ushered in with a fanfare of theories about how to "revive" the economy, some of them more harebrained than others. Supply-side economists used the Laffer Curve to demonstrate that deep tax cuts would lead to increased government revenues and wipe out the deficit. Monetarists like Milton Friedman claimed that shrinking the size of government and controlling the money supply would "unleash the private sector" to produce more jobs and also cut inflation. Cold warriors and "neo-liberals" called for massive increases in defense spending to defeat "the Evil Empire," while the radical right demanded dramatic cuts in social welfare programs "to protect the family."

The policies based upon these theories had what were, according to some observers, entirely predictable results. Two years after Reagan's election, the country was plunged into its deepest recession since the Great Depression. Twelve million were unemployed. Millions were added to the rosters of the poor, and millions of families on welfare suffered new deprivations. In two short years the Administration created more federal debt than had the previous two hundred years of American government.

Despite appearances, however, the seemingly contradictory policies of the Reagan Administration formed a coherent whole. Far from being the schemes of crackpot ideologues, or the conflicting programs of rival schools of economic thought, these policies were sophisticated weapons of class war. They were the culmination of policy developments initiated in the Nixon years, nurtured through the Ford Administration, and brought to near maturity by President Carter.

To understand Reagan's policies, it is necessary to distinguish between his public agenda and his real agenda. His real agenda was revealed more clearly in what he did rather than in what he said—in the effects of his policies rather than in the claims with which he justified them.

What was the real agenda behind cuts in social programs, for example? Cutting these programs was obviously not meant to balance the budget, as he claimed. If that had been the President's real intent, he would have done it—by taking money from the arms buildup, for example.

The real purpose of cuts in income maintenance programs was to complement the high unemployment rate in attacking working people. As we have seen, the recession of 1974-75 did not achieve its intended effect of cutting the rate of wage raises. Barry Bosworth, head of President Carter's Council on Wage and Price Stability, concluded that the problem lay in the substantial level of income maintenance programs built up over the years since Roosevelt's New Deal and Johnson's Great Society. Because of these programs, workers had something to fall back on when they were laid off. As one economist complained, "the unemployed of today are subject to less economic pain than used to be the case, because of the development of more generous income-maintenance programs."[98]

The Reagan Administration's purpose in slashing social programs was to solve the problem which the Carter Administration had identified. The purpose was to increase the pain and to make people desperate enough to accept wage and benefit cuts.

What was the purpose of huge military expenditures if they were not intended for "national security"? In addition to preparing the military for deployment against popular movements overseas which threaten U.S. business interests, these expenditures had important domestic functions. They were a way of transferring enormous amounts of public wealth to private corporations, without creating many new jobs. Because of inflated Pentagon costing practices and the large capital expenditures involved in highly-specialized arms manufacturing, a dollar spent on arms yields many fewer jobs than a dollar spent on, say, education or public health. Investment in military hardware was attractive to policymakers precisely because it took dollars out of the productive economy and still transferred them to big business. The arms buildup was a way of strengthening the corporate sector while weakening labor.

The Pentagon budget, the federal deficit, and the resulting high interest rates were coordinated elements of the corporate strategy for undermining the power of working people. The defense buildup served to create the federal deficit, which was needed to justify cutting social programs.[99] The deficit was also useful as a means of driving up interest rates, as the federal government competed for available capital to finance the deficit. The high interest rates acted as a brake on economic growth, making possible a tightly controlled expansion while maintaining a high level of unemployment.

If we distinguish between the rhetoric and the reality of Reagan's policies, they made a great deal of sense:

*"balanced budget" rhetoric justified attacks on social programs, while

*"supply-side" rhetoric justified tax breaks and other giveaways to corporations and the rich.

*The huge budget deficit justified continued high interest rates necessary to sustain high unemployment and to enrich the banks, while

*enormous military expenditures made it possible to transfer public wealth to the private sector without producing many new jobs.

*Great emphasis on "defense" justified military expenditures, turned people's attention away from problems at home, and helped prepare for the use of military force abroad to crush popular movements which threatened U.S. business interests.

President Reagan did not fail at his real agenda. He succeeded at the job he set out to do. His policies yielded important results in the 1981-82 recession:

*The 1982 return on high-quality corporate bonds—usually held by banks and wealthy investors—was 44%, the highest return in history.[100]

*Chrysler Corporation's stock rose a spectacular 426% in 1982. American Motors and Ford's stock more than doubled, while GM's rose 62%.[101] All this while over 200,000 auto workers lost their jobs, many of them to be permanently replaced by automation.

*The Department of Labor reported that contract bargaining in 1982 resulted in first-year wage increases of 3.8%, the lowest in the fourteen years that the department had kept such records. And this was for unionized workers who had kept their jobs.[102]

The downward trend for workers has accelerated since 1982. In 1986, first-year wage increases in contract bargaining had fallen to 1.2%. In manufacturing, first year wage gains fell from 7.2% in 1981 to -1.2% in 1986.[103]

The impact of the corporate counteroffensive on wages from the early '70s to the present is startling. Average weekly earnings adjusted for inflation declined 7.4% from 1973 through 1979, mainly through the effects of inflation; from 1979 through 1985, they declined an additional 7.6%, mainly through the effects of bargaining concessions, for a total decline of 14.4%.[104] The real wages of the average non-supervisory worker in the U.S. are continuing to fall at about one percent a year.[105]

Government policies have wrought enormous destruction in the lives of ordinary Americans during these years. Health care and nutrition have so deteriorated in some American communities that, according to a 1989 report of the United Nations, a child born in Romania had a better chance of surviving its first year than a child born Roxbury, a black neighborhood in Boston.[106]

The Reagan Administration cut federal housing expenditures by more than 80%; this reduction, coupled with inflated housing costs and reduced wages, has resulted in a huge population of homeless people in the U.S., the majority of them families with children. A 1989 Rutgers University study estimated that there may be as many as 14 million homeless people in America, with from 655,000 to 4 million homeless on the streets or in shelters in any one night, and twice that number "hidden homeless," who are doubling up with family or friends.[107] The message intended by the capitalists to working people as the homeless line the city streets is loud and clear: "Stay in line, or you'll be out there with them."

At the same time, these policies contributed to a huge transfer of wealth from ordinary Americans to the richest. According to the Joint Economic Committee of Congress, the net worth of the richest one-half of one percent of U.S. households grew by 90% from 1962 to 1983; for the next richest one-half of one percent, the growth rate was 72%. A small class of very rich people—less than ten percent of the U.S. population—own 78% of all U.S. business assets and 72% of its stock. This class—the capitalist class—increased its share of all wealth in the U.S. from 65.1% in 1962 to 68.8% in 1983. According to the Joint Economic Committee study, "the dramatic increase in the share of national wealth held by the richest Americans...did not begin until late in the 20-year period between the two surveys (1962 and 1983).[108]

The victory of the corporate counteroffensive allowed capitalists to begin a new period of sustained, carefully-controlled economic expansion and higher profits. A newspaper headline in early 1987 summarized the story of the period—"Economy slow, profits jump": "The nation's economy slowed sharply in 1986," the article reported, "but corporate profits posted their biggest rise in three years as businesses held down labor costs, according to separate government reports yesterday."[109]

Capital had—for a while, at least—solved its problem. With a carefully planned attack on working people, using unemployment and recession and budget cuts and other measures as weapons, it had finally made people desperate enough to give back much of what they had won in the 1960s and '70s. It had lowered their expectations of life in America.

Restructuring World Society

Government policy has been only one element in a many-sided business counteroffensive. The rulers of the U.S. and their international colleagues have decided that the successful maintenance of their control requires the restructuring of world society, so as to give maximum strategic advantage to their class.

This restructuring is based upon an unprecedented globalization of capital. Some of its major elements include:

1. **The export of jobs**. Capitalists have always used the threat of runaway shops as a weapon against workers. Kim Moody describes the earlier migration of U.S. industry which took place in the 1950s:

> The memory of confrontations with tens of thousands of workers in cities like Detroit, Flint, Toledo, Akron, Gary, South Chicago, and Pittsburgh haunted capitalists and managers alike in the years following the decade of class confrontation that climaxed in the 1946 strike wave. Beginning in the early 1950s, industry began to move away from those centers in search of areas without strong union traditions."[110]

The strike wave of the 1960s and '70s brought new levels of industry relocation, this time overseas. From 1950 to 1980, direct U.S. investment overseas increased by 16 times, while domestic investment increased only by a factor of 8.[111] In terms of jobs, this meant, for example, that General Electric during the 1970s added 30,000 foreign jobs to its workforce and reduced its American force by 25,000. RCA cut its U.S. force by 14,000 and added 19,000 abroad.[112]

According to a congressional report, by 1970 "close to three-quarters of total U.S. exports and upwards of one-half of all imports [were] transactions between the domestic and foreign subsidiaries of the same [U.S. and foreign] multinational conglomerate corporations." [113] From 1970 to 1980, U.S. private assets located abroad rose from $118.8 billion to $579 billion, an increase of 335%.[114] Ford Motor Company now has more than 65 percent of its assets and 58 percent of its workforce overseas. In 1979, 94 percent of Ford's profits came from its overseas operations. 63 percent of Coca-Cola's profits and 83 percent of Citicorp's profits came from overseas in 1979.[115] By 1989, 80 percent of Coca-Cola's profits came from overseas.[116]

The figures which quantify the shipment of jobs to low-wage areas overseas understate the usefulness of this weapon for corporations; for every company which has actually moved its operations, there are others which have used the threat of plant-closings to blackmail their workforce into making concessions.

But moving overseas in itself is not enough to escape class struggle. A wave of strikes hit Western European business in 1968-69. Ford Motor Company's Belgium plant was struck in 1968; a 1969 strike against Ford of England prevented shipment of needed assemblies to its plants in Belgium and Germany. Companies sought new ways to undermine labor's growing power. They found new tactics in "outsourcing" and "parallel production."

In 1976, after years of planning, Ford introduced the Fiesta, its first "world car." The Fiesta was produced in parallel manufacturing facilities in a number of countries, with each plant highly specialized to produce specific parts. As Bluestone and Harrison describe it, "The engines were manufactured in two parallel plants located in Almusafes (Valencia), Spain, and in Dagenham, England. Final assembly was located in Spain, England, and in Saarlouis, Germany. Each plant was designed to operate normally below potential capacity, in order to be able to absorb additional orders in case of a work stoppage elsewhere."[117]

The Ford Fiesta, in the words of a Ford executive, "began a new chapter in multinational business cooperation with management implications far beyond the European continent or Ford."[118]

2. **"Deindustrialization,"** or the change of the economy from relatively well-paid manufacturing jobs to poorly-paid, non-union service jobs (See Chapter Four). A study of the Joint Economic Committee found that nearly three-fifths of the new jobs created from 1979 to 1984 were low-wage jobs paying less than $7,012 per year measured in 1984 dollars.

Deindustrialization can occur through a variety of causes: by relocating manufacturing facilities to low-wage areas overseas, shutting older plants as productivity improves through newer technology, diverting corporate resources into more profitable activities, "milking" corporate merger acquisitions—called "cash cows" in industry—by selling off plant and equipment.

Deindustrialization is occurring in all the industrialized countries, not just the U.S. While it devastates workers and their families and communities, deindustrialization represents new profit opportunities for the wealthiest capitalists, as well as a weapon to use against working people.

3. **The deskilling of work through computerization.** The driving force behind technological advances in capitalist society has always been capitalist efforts to control the workforce. Marx wrote more than a hundred years ago, "It would be possible to write a whole history of the inventions made since 1830, for the sole purpose of providing capital with weapons against working-class revolts. We

would mention, above all, the self-acting mule, because it opened up a new epoch in the automatic system."[119]

Computerization marks a new stage in the struggle of management to wrest knowledge of the work process away from workers, and to encode their knowledge in machinery. The new technology is intended to make the individual worker more expendable and to give management significantly more control over the pace of work.

Computerization is also being used to degrade work in new ways. In her book, *The Electronic Sweatshop*, Barbara Garson details "how computers are transforming the office of the future into the factory of the past." When welfare offices in Boston were computerized, the job classification of professional social workers was changed to "Financial Assistance Workers." Their work is no longer defined in terms of case loads, in which they have responsibility for providing a range of services to individual clients. Instead, each Financial Assistance Worker performs a specific task for a large number of clients. Their work is measured in the number of keystrokes they make each month. The worker loses the freedom to make decisions about particular cases, as well as losing status and pay. In this way, a formerly professional job is reduced essentially to a clerical position.[120]

4. A permanently high unemployment rate. A high unemployment rate was a critical element of the frontal attack on working people during the Reagan years. The government was able to prolong the business expansion which began in 1982 by keeping unemployment high; in this way it was able to keep labor weak, minimizing inflationary pressures and allowing the slow expansion to proceed. A high federal deficit, high interest rates relative to inflation, and defense spending sustained at high levels, all enabled the government to "fine-tune" the slow expansion at a pace which kept the labor supply plentiful.

Government and private economists declared during the Reagan years that 7 percent reflected the new "natural rate of unemployment" in the economy; any lower rate would be inflationary. They meant that a lower rate would allow workers sufficient bargaining power to drive up wages—which in turn would lead companies, if profits were to be maintained, to raise price levels.

From 1986 on, the unemployment rate began to edge into a range between 5.3% and 6.5%, without substantial inflationary effects. The reason for the fact that workers did not seem to gain much in bargaining power may be a function of the devastation which the capitalists had wrought in the social safety net. In the mid-'70s, more than 75% of unemployed workers received unemployment insurance benefits; during the Reagan years, eligibility requirements were rewritten to limit worker access to benefits. As a result, "more than two-thirds of all U.S. workers who were out of work in 1988—more than 4.5 million—received no benefits at all."[121] Being unemployed is a much more serious matter today than it was in the '70s. The "whip of hunger," the traditional tool of capitalist discipline, is back firmly in the bosses' hands.

5. Other elements of the restructuring include the **casualization of labor** (maintaining a substantial part of the workforce as temporary or contract employees), and **two-tier wage structures** (in which new hires advance on a lower wage path than other employees). The purpose of these measures is to build divisions into the structure of the workforce, making unified action by workers more difficult. According to the Bureau of Labor Statistics, temporary work accounted for more than one out of 13 jobs in 1985.[122] From 1984 to 1986, more than 1.7 million workers were brought under contracts containing two-tier pay systems.[123]

The restructuring of society is by no means limited to economic measures.

6. **The attack on public education** has been an important element in the corporate strategy to lower people's expectations, and to redefine the goals of human development in terms of the needs of the economy. (See Chapter Four.) Similar education reforms have been promoted in Great Britain and other Trilateral countries. They have been the occasion of general strikes in France, Spain, and Portugal.

7. **Government terror campaigns in Third World countries.** The U.S. developed the modern use of mass terror as an instrument of political control in its counterinsurgency campaigns in Vietnam and Latin America in the 1960s and '70s. From its initial use in these campaigns, the U.S. developed the widespread use of torture and government terror in the societies under its control. In their carefully--documented study, *The Washington Connection and Third World Fascism*, Noam Chomsky and Edward S. Herman demonstrate that "Hideous torture has become standard practice in the U.S. client states."[124] Death squads accounted for over 70,000 deaths in El Sal-

vador from 1982-88. Death squads and official government action led to the slaughter of over 100,000 peasants and workers in Guatemala from 1979-85. The "people power" government of Corey Aquino is now promoting the growth of death squads in the Philippines.[125]

Mass terror in the U.S. business empire is not random or uncontrolled but planned and purposeful. As Chomsky and Herman put it, "Torture, death squads, and freedom of investment are positively related. Terror in these states is functional, improving the 'investment climate,' at least in the short-run..."[126] Government terror, in Chomsky and Herman's words, is intended to keep people "atomized and passive." Its purpose is to destroy labor unions, peasant associations, teacher and other professional associations—any means or forms of popular organization that would give people a measure of political power, and would thus interfere with the freedom of U.S. capital to exploit the population.

While the forms of capitalist control in these overseas low-wage areas are more savage than the means of control in the U.S., they are not different in their purpose or in their nature. The purpose of torture and the purpose of imposing high unemployment rates while destroying income maintenance programs is the same—to frighten people and to keep them atomized and passive. At home and abroad, the investment climate is positively related to human desperation.

The Significance of the Trade Deficit

The historic reversal of the U.S. role from net exporter to net importer of goods—the well-known U.S. trade deficit—is the principal evidence used to support the notion that contemporary economic developments are results of international competition and the supposed decline of the U.S. economy. But the trade deficit—to the extent that it is real—is better understood as a conscious instrument of capitalist policy, rather than the unintended effect of economic decline:

*The trade deficit is largely a fiction, caused by the relocation of U.S. industries offshore. By 1975, more than 30 percent of "foreign" imports were actually from U.S. companies which have set up production facilities overseas.[127] U.S. multinational corporations located offshore now constitute the third largest economy in the world, after the U.S. and the Soviet Union. As the President of the Bulova Watch Corporation, which manufactures watch movements in Switzerland, assembles them in Pago Pago, and sells them in the United States, said, "We are able to beat the foreign competition because we ARE the foreign competition."[128]

*Many imports involve another aspect of the integrated world economy: co-production by supposedly rival companies to their mutual advantage. GM, Ford, and Chrysler own large parts of Toyota, Nissan, and other "foreign" auto makers. While U.S. Steel was loudly complaining that foreign steel manufacturers were "dumping" steel below cost, to secure price supports from the Carter Administration, it was financing its "competition" in South Africa and Japan.[129]

*Large trade deficits are not evidence of a weak U.S. economy; in fact, something like the reverse is true. From late 1985 to late 1987, the volume of U.S. *exports* rose by over 20 percent, while the trade deficit continued. "The trade deficit persists," explained economics reporter Robert J. Samuelson, "because imports haven't yet declined":

> The rhetoric and reality of the U.S. trade deficit are sharply at odds. Listen to the rhetoric, and the United States is slowly becoming an economic has-been....Look at the reality, and another story emerges. The trade deficit doesn't reflect lack of competitiveness so much as the huge pulling power of the U.S. market. It's the world's richest, most accessible market: an enormous global bazaar where everyone wants to sell.[130]

*Most of the apparent decline in the U.S. competitive position occurred while the U.S. economy was at its most prosperous—so that economic "problems" of the late '70s and early '80s can hardly be attributed to this decline. As one analyst reports, "almost two-thirds of the reduction in United States' manufacturing production and export shares occurred in the 1950s, with almost half taking place between 1955 and 1960." In the late seventies, the very period when the outcry about American manufacturing export shares was loudest, they had actually stabilized or even increased.[131]

*Imports have been an important weapon for disciplining workers in the corporate counteroffensive. The flood of imports encouraged by the strong dollar and other policies from the early '70s weakened U.S. workers' bargaining power, and gave credibility to the threat that, "If you don't accept this pay cut for the good of the company, you'll be out of a job." Auto imports, for example, have been a useful tool for U.S. car manufacturers in rolling back the power of autoworkers; what U.S. manufacturers have lost in market share to the Japanese and Germans, they have more than made up for in reduced worker wages and bargaining power and increased company profits. In addition, imports play a significant ideological role, lending credence to capitalist attempts to push nationalism among workers. U.S. workers are encouraged—by their bosses, and often by their unions—to join the "company team" in the competition with Japan and other countries, while the Japanese are pitted against workers of other lands.

*The trade deficit allows the U.S. economy to play its role as locomotive of the international economy. By keeping up a steady flow of imports, the U.S. ruling class has been able to prop up the dangerously fragile economies of deeply indebted Third World nations. In this period of world low-growth, these economies desperately need the market which the U.S. provides.

The principal means of the U.S. government for encouraging high imports has been to keep the value of the dollar high relative to other currencies. The strength of the dollar has had other important uses in coordinating the economic policies of the Trilateral countries; these uses provide further evidence that these developments were matters of policy coordinated at the highest international levels rather than the unintended effects of economic competition.

For example, as the dollar was strengthened in the early 1980s, the British pound was devalued. The Thatcher regime used the resulting record unemployment to break the back of British trade unions; at the same time, British manufacturers experienced record profits as their exports soared. High U.S. interest rates, which were instrumental in driving up the value of the dollar, provided a profitable outlet for German capital, while creating an economic slowdown of historic proportions in West Germany—a slowdown much desired by German business leaders. During much of 1984 and 1985, German metallurgical and auto workers had been on strike. In December 1985, with massive amounts of German capital pulled out of Germany to be invested in the U.S., unemployment surpassed 10% in West Germany for the first time since 1948, and allowed German capital to restore some discipline to a restive working class. In 1987, the value of the dollar was allowed to decline sharply; while this decline was often presented as a "problem" in the popular press, it was a policy of the Administration and its international allies, aimed at stimulating the U.S. economy in anticipation of the 1988 elections.

The 1987 Stock Market Crash

From the end of the 1981-82 recession until the fall of 1990, the U.S. experienced the longest period of uninterrupted economic growth in its history—a measure of the success of policymakers' efforts at slow expansion in an environment of high unemployment. There were some economic shocks in this period, notably the stock market crash of 1987. The market crash was not evidence, however, as some Marxist analysts claimed, that the economy was in crisis or out of control.[132] On the contrary, it was further evidence of the extraordinary ability of ruling circles to manipulate economic events to suit the needs of the overall system of capitalist relations.

The stock market began its most sustained rise in history in 1982, setting historic highs over fifty times in 1987 alone, until it came crashing down in October of that year. The crash of 508 points represented a drop of 22.7 percent of the value of the market, compared with a 12.5 percent drop in 1929: a collapse of truly historic proportions.

The collapse of stock prices appeared to be the immediate effect of a policy decision to rein in the runaway speculation which had characterized the market in its heady climb preceding the crash. As David Warsh, Business Editor for the *Boston Globe*, put it:

> The bubble burst because policy-makers set out to prick it: As central bankers watched the gap between the expected rate of return on stocks and bonds widen over the course of 1987, they instinctively did what they are supposed to do. They tightened up on money before the party got too wild. Their refusal to supply liquidity put the kibosh on the runaway bull market, just as surely as a similar tightening had smashed the silver speculation in 1980.[133]

Paul Volcker, former chairman of the Federal Reserve Board, commented that the stock market crash "is not necessarily bad" if it stimulates reductions in the budget deficit.[134] Indeed, this may have been part of the purpose of the central bankers. Reductions in the deficit—by raising taxes or cutting the budget—would apply the brakes to the global expansion, and would hack away further at social programs.

In fact the Federal Reserve did not respond to the '87 crash with deflationary policies. Instead it eased restrictions on the money supply, thus signalling to investors that it did not intend to bring the economy into recession at that time. By the summer of 1989, the stock market had returned to its pre-crash level. The Fed succeeded in providing a "soft landing" to the economy in 1989—slowing growth without resorting to recession.

In 1990 workers' total compensation rose by 4.9 percent. While, in the face of 6.1 percent inflation, workers still lost ground, the rise in wages was enough to persuade the Fed that a recession was needed.[135]

Competition or Counterrevolution?

Using an economic model of history, most Marxist and mainstream analysts see the key developments of the '70s and '80s as part of an economic crisis brought on by increased competition in the world economy. America moved from a position of world dominance to one of competition with Japan and other business economies, they explain. This led to "the economic crisis of world capitalism: overcapacity, intensification of competition, heightening interimperialist rivalry, economic stagnation, rampant inflation, and high unemployment."[136] Most Marxists acknowledge that unemployment and recession, government cutbacks and deindustrialization, at least in part are policies intended to weaken labor. Still they believe that the overall process is driven by international competition—by factors, that is, internal to capitalism as an economic system.

But as we saw in reviewing the much-vaunted trade deficit, the evidence contradicts the economic model. Bowles, Gordon, and Weisskopf demonstrate that virtually all the slowdown in the American economy during the 'seventies "can be statistically accounted for" in terms of a conscious capitalist strategy to attack working people.[137] They concur with a study by Brookings Institution economist Robert Z. Lawrence which found that, "on balance, domestic demand factors [that is, decreased demand for goods caused by recessionary policies] account for nearly 100 percent of the changes in U.S. manufacturing

during the 1970s."[138] In other words, government and corporate policies designed to attack workers for reasons other than international
competition are the reason for the plant closings, the wage cutting,
the unemployment, the pain suffered by American working people in
these years.

The driving force of economic policy and development in the last
two decades has been class war. Those things which working people
around the world have experienced as painful problems, and which
have been explained both by capitalist apologists and most Marxist
analysts as the symptoms of economic crisis, are weapons of class
war, wielded by the international elite for the purpose of consolidating their control.

It is true that the U.S. domination of the world economy which
characterized the '50s and '60s has been brought to an end. This
domination, however, has not been replaced by unbridled competition, but by a level of international elite cooperation unmatched in
history. The extent of that cooperation is itself a measure of how
threatened the world elite feel by the dangers of a renewed revolutionary upsurge.

Within the framework of international elite cooperation, the competition which has been allowed to take place has been functional for
international capitalism, in much the same way that the competition
encouraged within the U.S. airline industry was functional—for breaking unions and weeding out weaker airlines. Capitalism has emerged
strengthened, not weakened, by this competition, even though individual companies, or even whole industries in some countries, may
have lost.

In this era of global corporations operating in a world economy,
the competition of national economies is a useful fiction to disguise
the real source of the problems people face, and the real solution. As
one analyst has put it, "The nation-state is the jurisdiction through
which capital disciplines labor and plays off groups of workers
against each other."[139]

I am not suggesting that there is no crisis in the world economy.
This crisis does not arise, however, from competition among business
economies, or from some inherent "laws of capitalism." The crisis
arises from growing class struggle around the globe, and from the
limited ability of the ruling class to suppress people's drive to rebel.
The problem of capitalists is not each other; their problem is their
inability to subdue the working population. Capital is in crisis because
it cannot win the class war.

The real force driving the history of the twentieth century is the worldwide struggle of people to destroy capitalist and Communist control and create a new world. As the century moves to a close, the revolutionary crisis in world society is deepening, and the possibilities of revolutionary transformation become ever greater. More than ever, the forward movement toward world revolution depends upon understanding the real human aspirations which are driving history, and developing a model of social change which can bring them to fulfillment.

PART THREE

Part Three reviews the role of Communism in the working class movements of the twentieth century, to show that it has been consistently counterrevolutionary, and that the Communist betrayal of working class struggle is the logical fulfillment of Marx's theory of history and his view of people. It explains that trade unions and the left, to the extent that they accept the legitimacy of capitalism, function as instruments of capitalist control. It examines the collapse of world Communism at the end of the '80s, and shows that the way has been prepared for world revolution as never before.

7

COMMUNISM
AND COUNTERREVOLUTION

For most of the twentieth century, Communism has defined the possibilities of opposition to capitalism. But the Communist alternative to capitalism has proved to be disastrous: unequal, exploitative, oppressive, unfree. Rather than a revolutionary path to working class democracy, it has proved to be another form of elite control.

What explains the reality beneath the rhetoric of Communism? What has been its real role in the tumultuous history of this century? These are the questions I will take up in this chapter.

The left typically explains the failure of Communism as not intrinsic to the Communist idea of change itself, but the result of some extrinsic event or circumstance: the backwardness of the Russian economy at the time of the Russian Revolution, or Allied intervention in the Russian Civil War, or the failure of Western European workers to come to the aid of the Russian working class. In this view, Communist ideas need not be re-examined or rejected, because they have never been tried in appropriate circumstances.

My purpose in this chapter is to show that the outcome of Communist revolutions was an inevitable function of Communist ideas about people and change. I want also to show that Communism has played a consistently counterrevolutionary role. Capitalism has survived the twentieth century only with the active intervention of Communism.

There is another reason for examining the history of Communism. Communism represents the fullest development of revolutionary theory and practice in history, as well as the most perverse distortion of revolutionary ideals. Within its history lies the real experience of millions who have fought to change the world. The October Revolution in Russia, the Chinese Revolution, the Vietnamese triumph in the face of the armed might of France and the United States: all these represent stunning historic achievements as well as stark perversions of the goals of most of the people who accomplished them. We cannot learn from this history unless we can understand its profoundly contradictory character.

To recover all that has been inspiring and instructive in these revolutionary movements, it is necessary to separate the revolutionary aspirations that drove them from the particular theoretical constructs which led to their distorted and ugly reality. A new paradigm of history can provide the perspective to enable us to understand the hidden history of the revolutionary tradition.

The Russian Revolution—From February to October, 1917

The Russian Revolution of October, 1917 marked the first time in history that a revolution of the working class—of workers in their factories and peasants in their fields, soldiers at the front and sailors in their fleets—succeeded. The regime of the Czar had collapsed before the aroused populace in February; it was replaced by a reform government of industrialists, big landowners, and liberal aristocrats, led by Alexander Kerensky. This government of a more modern elite kept in place the basic structures of elite control of Russian society, and continued Russia's involvement in World War I, then in its fourth year.

In October the Kerensky government was overthrown in a virtually bloodless uprising of workers and soldiers, led by the Bolshevik Party. Millions of working people around the world took hope. Capitalists and kings trembled. The age of modern revolution had begun.

At the time of the February Revolution, the Bolsheviks were just one of several small revolutionary parties in Russia. From February to October, however, the Bolshevik Party won the contest for leadership of the revolutionary masses. The strengths of Bolshevism proved decisive in leading the October revolution to victory; its weaknesses led swiftly and inescapably to the revolution's distortion into a new class society.

Alone among the Social Democratic parties of Europe, the Bolsheviks had refused to support the great slaughter of World War I, instead calling on workers of all countries to turn their guns on their masters. Alone among the parties, the Bolsheviks came to believe that working class revolution was necessary and possible in Russia at that

time. After the fall of the Czar, they relentlessly attacked the Kerensky government and called for workers' revolution against capitalism.
They had a disciplined organization of tremendous energy, which, in
the words of an anti-Bolshevik commentator, "seemed to be everywhere" with posters, literature, meetings, speeches, rallies, all expressing the demands of the people: "The land to the peasants! The
factories to the workers! All power to the Soviets!"[140]

The Communists not only had revolutionary slogans. They also had
a coherent theory of social change. Fifteen years before the revolution, Lenin had declared that, "Without a revolutionary theory, there
can be no revolutionary movement," and had set about developing a
coherent theory of how revolutionaries can intervene in history.

Lenin's Contribution To Marxism

Lenin's great contribution to Marxism was to show that political
consciousness, developed and disseminated through a disciplined party
of professional revolutionaries, is the decisive factor in Marxist revolution. The other, more orthodox Marxist parties of the time were
mass parties; they believed that economic developments determine
historical events, and that economic conditions would eventually develop to a point at which the working class would spontaneously take
revolutionary action. While they espoused socialism as their long-term
goal, these parties confined themselves in practice to economic demands to improve the living standards of workers; they refused to
challenge the political ideas and power of the existing regimes. The
mainstream and much larger Marxist party in Russia, the Mensheviks, believed that workers' revolution was impossible in backwards
Russia—since economic conditions in the accepted Marxist sense were
not ripe—and opposed it.

With his creation of a vanguard party dedicated to the task of revolution, Lenin supplied to Marxism the vital element it was missing:
conscious human subjects who by their own actions could create the
conditions for revolutionary change. In Marxism-Leninism, the name
given to Lenin's development of Marxist theory, the Bolsheviks possessed clearly developed principles of political action joined with a
theory of organization. Together, these became powerful instruments
of revolutionary practice. They gave the Bolshevik approach a unique
strategic coherence, and invested Bolshevik cadre with "revolutionary

optimism"—a confidence in the eventual triumph of their cause which was to prove of inestimable importance.

But Lenin's coherent theory had a fatal flaw. Lenin was right about the central role played by consciousness in human affairs, and about the need for a party dedicated to the task of building revolutionary consciousness. He was wrong about what political consciousness is and where it comes from. Lenin's view of revolutionary conscious- ness turned the revolutionary party into a device for elite control of the working class.

As we have already seen, revolutionary goals and values come from ordinary working people. Revolutionary consciousness consists of working people's consciousness of themselves as the source of the values and vision to create a new world. Lenin, however, believed that workers have no goals or vision but their own self-interest. With other prominent Marxists, he believed that revolutionary ideas come not from workers but from intellectuals.

Political consciousness, Lenin thought, consists of knowledge of capitalism, its laws of development, and its effects on every element of society; it is essentially technical knowledge, beyond workers' ex- perience. Workers of themselves are capable only of "trade-union consciousness"—consciousness of the economic relations between themselves and their employers, and of the need for collective strug- gle to improve the conditions of their exploitation by capital.

If revolutionary ideas and goals come from the theories of bour- geois intellectuals, then the command and control of the revolutionary party must be in the hands of top leaders most expert in these theo- ries. Lenin's idea of revolutionary consciousness led him to a concept of revolutionary organization in which the goals, tactics, vision and possibilities of revolutionary transformation were all controlled from the top down. Rather than being the lifeblood of revolution, ideas and initiative from below were seen as a threat to party control.

In this way, what had been conceived as the center of organized revolutionary consciousness turned into its opposite—a device for sup- pressing the consciousness of workers. Lenin's view of the source and content of revolutionary consciousness ensured that the relation- ship of the Bolsheviks to the masses would be essentially technocra- tic: party "experts," rather than the people, would determine the scope and direction of the revolution. The goal of the revolution would be economic development, within a framework which the party would control.

This theoretical relationship between the party and the working class was to be of critical practical importance. While the Bolsheviks helped to lead the revolutionary struggle forward, they simultaneously confined that struggle within increasingly narrow and technocratic bounds, sucked the vital democratic element from it, and turned it into its opposite: a device for a new elite to control the economic and political life of the country.

From Lenin To Stalin

The relationship of party to workers established in Leninist theory was the decisive factor shaping the subsequent history of the Soviet regime. There was, as Maurice Brinton maintains in *The Bolsheviks and Workers' Control*, a "clear-cut and incontrovertible link between what happened under Lenin and Trotsky and the later practices of Stalin." After reviewing the history, says Brinton, it is impossible to accept the view—as do many on the left—"that the whole course of events was 'historically inevitable' and 'objectively determined' by the difficult circumstances of the Revolution. Bolshevik ideology and practice were themselves important and sometimes decisive factors in the equation, at every critical stage of this critical period."[141]

Under the leadership of the Bolsheviks, the Russian Revolution smashed the power of the bourgeoisie and the property relations of private ownership on which their power rested. It did not alter "the authoritarian relations of production characteristic of all class societies."[142] The effect of Bolshevik leadership on the workers' revolution was that the Russian workers exchanged new masters for old—Communists for capitalists—within a set of productive relations which were essentially unchanged.

Brinton focuses on the crucial years from 1917 to 1921, when Lenin and Trotsky were leading the Bolsheviks. In this period the question of who would make decisions regarding production was the primary focus of conflict over the shaping of the new social order.[143] "Thousands of revolutionaries were to be killed and hundreds of thousands incarcerated" by the Bolsheviks in the struggle over this question.[144]

The Bolsheviks did not believe in "workers' management"—in workers' power at the point of production. They believed rather in a socialism which consisted of the nationalization of industry in the hands of a State which supposedly would be in the hands of workers, but which in fact would be dominated by the force that understood the interests of workers better than they knew themselves—the party.

The principal form of workers' struggle to manage production in the revolution was the Factory Committee Movement. Beginning in March, 1917 Factory and Shop Committees sprang up "in every industrial center in European Russia." From the start they challenged managerial prerogatives.

Before the October Revolution, the Bolsheviks supported the Factory Committees as the most effective "battering ram" against the old order. Immediately after the revolution, however—that is, as soon as they were in possession of the State—the Bolsheviks sought to suppress the committees, by subordinating them to unions and other higher administrative bodies under Bolshevik control.

In the Factory Committees was a fighting instrument of workers at the point of production, prepared to develop a truly national coordinative and directive capability. But this would have put power in the hands of the workers, rather than in the hands of the Bolsheviks:

> Underlying the controversies, what was at stake was the whole concept of socialism: workers' power or the power of the Party acting 'on behalf of' the working class. 'If workers succeeded in maintaining their ownership of the factories they had seized, if they ran these factories for themselves, if they considered the revolution to be at an end, if they considered socialism to have been established—then there would have been no need for the revolutionary leadership of the Bolsheviks.'[145]

The Factory Committees had to be suppressed because they would have made rule by the Bolshevik elite unnecessary.

Many Bolshevik supporters attribute the most repressive features of Communist rule to intervention and civil war, and the failure of revolution in Germany. But the struggle of the Bolsheviks to snuff out workers' power at the point of production represented the approach of the Bolsheviks *before* the revolution was subjected to shocks from outside. They took place *before* Allied intervention or civil war had broken out; they took place a full twelve months *before* the attempt at revolution in Germany.

In the early months of 1918, the Bolsheviks began to build a national administrative apparatus based upon the technical and managerial staffs of the old industrialists. Lenin defended this step on the grounds of economic necessity. This step, however, was undertaken mainly on political grounds. Leninist ideology had long since established the basis for rule by "experts." The bourgeoisie, former officials, managers and technicians were the principal elements of the population who stood in the same essential relation to the workers as did the Bolsheviks; their inclusion in the ruling apparatus was essential if the Bolsheviks were to enforce party rule over the society. The only other source of technical knowledge would have been the workers themselves, acting collectively and democratically at the point of production—for the Bolsheviks, an inadmissible solution to the "economic" problems of the revolution.

In the early spring of 1918, Trotsky, as Commissar of Military Affairs, reorganized the Red Army, restoring saluting and special forms of address, special living quarters and privileges for officers, and the death penalty for disobedience under fire. He did away with the election of officers and other democratic forms of organization which revolutionary soldiers committees had established.[146]

At the same time, the Bolsheviks undertook vigorous steps to restore labor discipline, using the "scientific management" methods of the capitalists.[147] In addition Lenin called for collective leadership at the factory level to be replaced by one-man management.[148] Managers with dictatorial powers—often the previous owners themselves—were installed in the factories.[149]

In late May, 1918, widespread civil war broke out. It had the effect of hastening the extension of party control to all economic and social life. Labor was militarized under Trotsky. Trotsky explicitly denied that Bolshevik policies were a function of the civil war: "I consider that if the civil war had not plundered our economic organs of all that was strongest, most independent, most endowed with initiative, we should undoubtedly have entered the path of one-man management in the sphere of economic administration much sooner and much less painfully."[150]

There is no need to furnish further details here. The record makes clear that the Bolsheviks pursued relentlessly, in every sphere of life, policies which were entirely consistent with their view of workers and of social change. The foundations of Stalinism were well-laid by Lenin and Trotsky in the immediate wake of the revolution.

The "Third Revolution"

Workers and others struggled against the stifling of the Revolution both inside and outside the party. There were important factors working against them, however. The Mensheviks, the other large Marxist party, were consistently hostile to workers' power. The Bolsheviks initially had wide support among the most advanced workers as the most firmly and consistently revolutionary party; when the party switched its position in the first weeks after the revolution from support of the Factory Committee Movement to bringing the committees increasingly under the control of party-dominated bodies, the significance was not at first clear. By the time it was, workers had already lost control of production, and with it their most important base for resistance. During the civil war and Allied intervention, workers rallied to the Communists to put down these threats to the revolution—thus further strengthening Communist control.

Nevertheless, as the civil war drew to a close in 1920, resistance to party domination became widespread. Peasant uprisings, against grain requisitions and for other causes, became commonplace in the winter of 1920-21, with more than 118 risings reported in February, 1921.[151]

Resistance reached a high pitch in the two places which more than any others were the birthplaces of the Russian Revolution. Strikes broke out in Petrograd at the end of February. On March 2, the sailors, soldiers, and workers of Kronstadt, a fortified island city and home base of the Baltic Fleet a few miles across the ice from Petrograd, rose in revolt.

The rebels, disillusioned with Bolshevik rule, established a revolutionary commune. They took up the slogan of the October Revolution, "All power to the Soviets," but they demanded "free soviets"—free, that is, of Bolshevik domination. The rebels "appealed to the entire Russian population to join them in a 'third revolution' to finish the job begun in February and October 1917"—a revolution to overthrow "the dictatorship of the Communist Party, with its Cheka and its state capitalism..."[152]

But the Kronstadt rebels made the fatal mistake of not seizing the initiative, failing to march across the frozen Baltic to join forces with the striking workers of Petrograd. Given sufficient time to recover itself, the Communist regime went on the attack. On March 17, 1921, Revolutionary Kronstadt fell. Once inside the city, the Communist forces indulged in "an orgy of bloodletting." Several hundred prisoners were shot on the spot; hundreds others were taken back to Petrograd, where for the next few months they were taken out in small batches and shot.[153]

If Russia had by 1921 become, as the Kronstadt rebels claimed, "a vast concentration camp," in the wake of the rebellion it became even more grim. Lenin vigorously suppressed what little freedom of debate had remained in the party. In 1924, Lenin died. In 1926, Stalin suppressed the opposition which had grown up around Trotsky. "One by one, the revolution devoured its makers," as more and more leading party figures, along with millions of peasants and workers, were murdered or disappeared in Stalin's forced labor camps.[154]

The horrors which developed under Communism are often attributed to the failure of the revolution to spread to Western Europe. It is true that Lenin expected the working class of Germany and elsewhere to come to the aid of the Bolsheviks by making their own revolutions.

Voline, a Russian anarchist who was active in the revolution, comments that Lenin was correct in expecting that successful revolution in one country would "set fire to the world." His mistake was in believing that *Communist* revolution would spread in this way. Lenin could not see that Communist revolution was sterile: "it could set fire to nothing, for it had ceased to 'burn' itself;...it had lost the power of spreading, a character of great causes, because it had ceased to be a great cause....[Lenin] believed that the ultimate fate of the Russian Revolution depended upon its extension to other countries. Exactly the opposite was true: extension of the Revolution depended upon the results of the revolution in Russia."[155]

The Role of Communism in the Twentieth Century

The history of Communism subsequent to 1917-1921 was true to its beginnings. As the Soviet state consolidated its power and recruited former members of the bourgeoisie into its fold, its distance from the ordinary people of Russia increased, along with its need to crush any authentic revolutionary aspirations among party members or workers. Though they had begun as sincere revolutionaries, Marxist-Leninist doctrine led the Communists to constitute themselves as a new ruling class, which ruthlessly exploited the working people and peasants, and with growing cynicism used the prestige of this first "socialist" revolution to mask their real role in Soviet and world society.

After their original fear and hostility, the capitalist powers began to see the Soviet government not only as permanent, but as one with which they might usefully deal. The United States recognized the Soviet government in 1933. In 1935, the Soviets signed major trade agreements with France and Great Britain, and the Soviet Union and France signed the first military pact between the Soviet state and a capitalist power.[156] The Bolsheviks were on their way to becoming fully accepted partners in world management.

Apologists for the Soviets argue that the alliances formed by the Bolshevik government with capitalist and Fascist states, culminating in the Hitler-Stalin Pact in 1939, was born of a desire to protect socialism in the Soviet Union—a claim which, when the true history is considered, is preposterous. It was the character of the Bolshevik regime itself, as a new ruling class which implacably maintained capitalist productive relations within Russia, which primarily determined its relationships with the capitalist regimes. It was to protect themselves and their own interests, not the working people of Russia or the world, that the Soviet rulers governed.

In 1935 the Communist movement dramatically changed its political direction. No longer would the Communist parties of the world encourage working class revolution, even on the Marxist-Leninist model; rather they would create Popular Fronts with so-called "progressive capitalists" in their respective countries to oppose Fascism and to stabilize capitalism. In the name of anti-Fascism, the world Communist movement became officially and openly an ally of the capitalist "democracies."

While the alliance with capital was justified by Communist leaders as a temporary tactic to forestall the Fascist advance, in fact it too was a function of the nature of the Soviet regime as much as of the international situation. In 1934 Stalin had begun the great terror to purge the remaining revolutionary elements from the party.[157] The Soviets were on the eve of the Moscow trials, in the course of which Stalin executed or imprisoned many thousands of opponents, including most of the surviving Old Bolsheviks who had participated in the Revolution. The Communists were liquidating the remnants of the October Revolution at home; it only made sense that they liquidate their nominally revolutionary policies abroad as well.

Nevertheless, the real nature of the Communist regime was not at all clear to many millions of people both inside and outside the Soviet

Union's borders. The Soviet Communist Party and the Communist parties in various countries around the world had the most revolutionary reputations of any existing parties. The Communists had been the only Marxist party to oppose World War I consistently. The Soviet Union was surrounded by aggressive capitalist powers which had intervened once already to put down the revolution, and the country had suffered inestimable devastation from German invasion in World War I, from Allied invasion after the war, and from civil war—facts which seemed to justify draconian measures. Finally, the Communists were the first and only party which had discovered how to practice Marxism as a theory of modern revolution—and there was no other.

For all these reasons, millions of ordinary people saw the Soviet Union as a beacon of hope in a dark and threatening world.

With their revolutionary reputation largely intact, the Soviets began to play a critical role in supporting capitalism and preventing the outbreak of working class revolution.

Revolution and Counterrevolution in Spain

The first real test for the Soviet Communist leaders as allies of world capital came with the outbreak of civil war and social revolution in Spain. The Soviet and Spanish Communist parties played a crucial role for international capitalism in Spain, undermining the revolution and assuring the Fascist victory.

The 1936 revolt of General Franco against the bourgeois Republican government ignited social revolution in Spain. The government, "fearing the revolution more than it feared Franco," refused to arm the workers and peasants against the imminent Fascist revolt.[158] With no other recourse, workers armed themselves—with clubs and kitchen knives, sticks of dynamite brought from mines and construction sites, rifles seized from sporting goods stores, and a few racks of government rifles brought over by sympathetic soldiers—and began the fight against the Fascist takeover.

While the Fascist army had vastly superior arms and training, the workers and peasants had the aspirations of the people on their side. The workers' militias beat back the Fascist armies, spreading the social revolution as they went. Workers in Catalonia and in some other regions seized factories and began to run them collectively, producing war materiel for the front and supplies for the cities; they elected workers' committees to organize workers' militias and to carry the revolution forward in the areas under their control. Peasants seized Church lands and large estates and turned them into cooperatives; they elected peasant committees to oversee the tasks of provisioning the front and the cities.

The capitalist powers had a great stake in preventing the spread of revolution in Spain. Not only did France and Great Britain have huge investments there in mining and other industries; they were afraid that revolution in Spain might spread into France and beyond.

France, Great Britain, and the United States declared their "neutrality" in the Spanish struggle; they refused to sell munitions to the Republican forces, while Nazi Germany and Fascist Italy poured arms, planes, and elite forces into Spain to assist Franco.

After several months, the workers' militias ran out of arms and ammunition. The Soviet Union agreed to sell arms to the Republicans, but only on one condition: that they abandon the revolution. The Communists demanded that the workers' militias be disbanded, and that factories and lands be returned to the bourgeoisie.

Betrayed by the leaders of the trade unions and other organizations, and without a strong revolutionary leadership of their own, the workers and peasants were finally forced to return the factories and land to their former owners. With the disbanding of the workers' militias, the government police and the regular army were re-established, and with them the authority of the bourgeoisie.

Politics is the chief factor in civil war. With the abandonment of the revolution, the civil war was lost. The war became a conventional war, in which all the advantages of arms and equipment were Franco's. Soviet secret police, sent by Stalin into Spain for the purpose, began rounding up and executing revolutionary leaders. Government forces invaded villages which refused to disband their cooperatives and shot recalcitrant peasants. Peasants and workers in areas held by Franco, seeing no difference between the Fascists and the Communist-bourgeois coalition government, stopped challenging the Fascist troops.

In May, 1937 workers in Barcelona rose against the Popular Front goverment; they erected barricades and fought the Republican/Communist troops. After several days, however, the leaders of the leftist and anarchist organizations persuaded the workers to give up the fight. The last chance at re-igniting the revolution was lost, and with it the war against the Fascists.

Whatever turns of Marxist reasoning or Popular Frontism the party used to justify it, the Communist role in Spain was consistent with the savagely reactionary Stalin regime which was directing it. The Communists did their dirty work, and the world was made safer for the power of elites.

World War II and the "Grand Alliance"

World War II represented the greatest crisis of the world capitalist system since World War I. The Great War had triggered revolution in Russia and social upheaval throughout Europe; the fear of world capital was that the Second World War would bring with it socialist revolution in Europe. The Allies thus had two primary goals in waging the war: to defeat German imperialism, and to prevent the outbreak of socialist revolution on the continent as Fascist forces fell to indigenous resistance movements chiefly made up of workers and led by Communists. Of these two, the prevention of revolution was the more important goal. It governed Allied war planning on such key matters as the opening of a Second Front, and conditioned the relationships between Churchill, Roosevelt, and Stalin.

As the war drew to a close, the forces of working class revolution in Europe were immeasurably stronger than ever before. Fascism had provided the backbone of capitalist ruling structures in the occupied countries; now, as Fascism was smashed, capitalist structures collapsed. As Fernando Claudin puts it, "The war tended to turn into a revolutionary war once the movement of the struggle against Fascism led to conflict with the ruling classes which had used Fascism to maintain their domination, once the war brought into action the proletarian classes or they acquired arms and a consciousness of their power."[159] The great fear of the allies seemed on the verge of being realized.

In four European countries—in France, Italy, Greece, and Yugoslavia—Communist-led resistance forces liberated large sections of the country from the Fascists before the arrival of Allied troops. In each of these countries, the Communists were the leading political and organizational force within the working class, and the working class in each was in a position to create socialist revolution at the time, or to lay the foundations for settling the question of political power with the weakened capitalists in the near future. As Claudin explains, "...in 1944-45 only the Communist parties could halt the revolutionary movement of the proletariat, and in practice this is what they did."[160]

The national uprising of the French resistance took place before the Allied landing at Normandy; the greater part of France, including Paris, was liberated by the armed forces of the Communist-led resistance, with the active support of the population at large. Liberation committees were established everywhere as organs of popular control.[161]

At the direction of Moscow, when the Allies arrived, the resistance forces gave over their weapons and their political power to them. In a word, "the party liquidated the popular armed forces built up during the resistance."[162]

French capital had collaborated with the Nazis through the Vichy regime and had been devastated by the Nazi defeat. In the years immediately following liberation, the French Communist Party energetically set about restoring capitalist power in France, suppressing strike activity and calling upon the people to "steel themselves for the battle of production as they steeled themselves for the battle of liberation."[163]

In Italy as in France, the Communists led the resistance. By 1945, there were over 300,000 armed partisans organized into combat units in the north of Italy.[164] As Claudin points out, "the greatest worry of the Italian ruling classes and the Allies was the possibility of a revolutionary explosion in the north after the defeat of the Germans."[165]

In the fall of 1944, the Allies halted their advance up the Italian peninsula, to allow the German and Italian Fascist troops freedom to smash the growing power of the partisans. The Allies maintained this truce until mid-April, 1945 when, with Germany already practically defeated, and in fear of partisan victory throughout the north, they again went over to the offensive.[166]

The partisan army and the workers of the north had already begun a general uprising. Ten days before the Allies arrived, the partisans liberated Bologna, Modena, Parma, Piacenza, Genoa, Turin, Milan, Verona, Padua and the whole region of Venice, and placed them under the control of national liberation committees.[167]

But at the direction of the Italian Communist Party (PCI), the partisans surrendered their arms to the Allies and returned confiscated lands and goods to the capitalists and big landowners. The national liberation committees were dissolved and former officials were appointed by the Allies to administer the towns—all with the cooperation, even at the insistence, of the Communist leadership.[168]

The Greek resistance had the same revolutionary character as the Italian and French resistance. In 1944, with over 1,500,000 men and women organized in its ranks and in control of most of the country, it was "within a hairsbreadth of victory," not only over the Nazis, but also over the monarchy and British imperialism, which stood behind it.[169] But the Greek Communist leadership acceded to Stalin's demands to give over power to the British-backed royalist forces. After eighteen months of fierce repression at the hands of the British, the Greek resistance finally undertook civil war in much less favorable circumstances. The British still were unable to prevail, and gave over the fight to the United States. U.S. forces, in the first exercise of the "Truman Doctrine," intervened in the civil war on the side of the royalists. In August, 1949 the revolutionary forces, in internal disarray because of Stalin's continued interference, were finally defeated.

Only the Yugoslav Communist Party under Tito resisted the pressure from Moscow to surrender the arms and power of the partisan forces to the bourgeoisie. As the revolutionary forces liberated areas from the Germans, they carried forward social reform and agrarian reform based on popular democratic power. As it progressed, "the war of liberation inevitably took on the form of a civil war against the bourgeoisie and the big landowners." [170]

Stalin did all that he could to stop the advance of the Yugoslav revolution. He offered military supplies to the bourgeois-royalist forces at the same time as he refused arms and ammunition to the Yugoslav Communists.[171] He expelled the Yugoslav party from the international Communist movement, and organized vituperative attacks on them from every quarter. He arrested and executed a number of Yugoslav Communist leaders who had accepted an offer of safe passage to Moscow in an attempt at compromise. He attempted to organize a *coup d'etat* against the party leadership.[172] The Yugoslav party, however, persisted in its aim and completed the revolution.

Stalin also attempted to put the brakes on another Communist-led revolution in these years. As late as 1947, after the civil war in China had already turned irreversibly in favor of the revolutionary forces led by the Chinese Communist Party, Stalin tried to force Mao and the Chinese party into surrendering their forces and weapons to Chiang Kai-shek—an act which would likely have led to a repetition of Chiang's 1927 slaughter of Communists in Shanghai. The Chinese party resisted Stalin's pressure; in 1949, the revolution was victorious.

What explains the role played by Stalin and, under the influence of the Soviet party, most of the Communist parties of the world in this period of capitalism's greatest crisis? Why did the Communist parties of the world rush forward to save capitalism?

The answer to this question is complicated, but the factors come down chiefly to two. One is that, at a series of conferences during the war, culminating in Yalta, the Soviet Union had agreed with Great Britain and the United States to divide the post-war world into "spheres of influence," dominated by one power or another. The revolutions in France, Italy, Greece, and Yugoslavia had to be put down, because Stalin had already agreed that these countries would remain in the Western bloc.

Stalin had no such hesitations in those areas which it had been agreed would be in the Russian sphere. Soviet troops imposed "socialism" in the countries of Eastern Europe which Roosevelt and Churchill had agreed would be Stalin's to control. Soviet encroachment into Eastern Europe, like Soviet discouragement of revolution elsewhere, was a part of the division of world into spheres of influence.

The second factor in the counterrevolutionary role played by the Communist parties had to do with the nature of the Soviet regime at home. Paraphrasing Isaac Deutscher's detailed study of the question, Claudin says:

> The foreign policy of the Soviet bureaucracy could not do other than reflect, in some form, its domestic policy....The victory of a socialist revolution throughout Europe would have meant the end of the isolation of the Russian revolution, but....this would endanger the political and ideological basis of the bureaucratic and totalitarian system built on the basis of isolation. From being an objective influence on the system, isolation had become a necessary condition for its survival and for the privileges of its ruling class.[173]

In other words, the Soviet Communists' fear was that revolution from below in Europe would lead to revolution from below in Russia, and the end of the Soviet ruling class.

The "Cold War": 1947-1989

I have reviewed the hidden, counterrevolutionary history of Communism at some length, because the relationship of the United States and the Soviet Union during the period of the Cold War—not to mention the present period of perestroika—cannot be fully understood apart from it.

As the immediate post-war years drew to a close, the world divided into two apparently hostile camps, which, however, had a deep and abiding common interest: the prevention of working class revolution anywhere in the world.

While it still declared itself the world center of socialist revolution, the Soviet Union had become a firmly counterrevolutionary power, with as much to fear from authentic revolutions from below as the capitalists. The Communist parties of Western Europe became part of the "loyal opposition," ruthlessly opposing any efforts to create movements to their left. The Communist parties of Eastern Europe became ruling apparatuses closely tied to the Soviet power.

The counterrevolutionary development of the Communist movement had profound implications for the post-war world. It meant that world capital faced a world without revolution—at least in that part of the world about which capital was most concerned, war-ravaged Europe. Capital could undertake the rebuilding of the world it had nearly destroyed secure in the knowledge that no significant organized force would challenge its legitimacy. Competition with the Soviet Union would be within the comfortable mold of interimperialist rivalry—a rivalry which both powers could use to advantage to strengthen their control of their own populations and to justify the projection of military force abroad.

The Cold War between the United States and the Soviet Union was much like what Orwell describes in *1984*: a perpetual state of warfare which fulfilled important needs of the ruling elites of both societies.

The Cold War provided the ruling elites with a much-needed external enemy to justify internal control. Capitalism and "the American way of life" became synonymous; to criticize capitalist domination of American society was to be disloyal, a "dupe" or worse of the Communists. In the Soviet Union, to criticize Communist domination was to be "in the service of the capitalists."

Both the U.S. and the USSR had acquired extensive interests beyond their own borders as an outcome of World War II. The Cold War provided each superpower with a rationale to protect its interests abroad. The United States invaded foreign lands, installed puppet governments, bombed and tortured and starved countless millions of people to save the world from Communism. The USSR, while it never had foreign holdings as extensive as those of the U.S., had similar interests and a matching rationale. Soviet tanks were not in Hungary or Czechoslovakia to crush the aspirations of ordinary people, but "to save them from capitalism."

Through all this long and bloody contest, the elites in control of the Soviet Union and the United States have principally had to fear not each other but the people of the world, against whom they worked in collaboration. The relationship of the Soviet Union to the United States in this working arrangement has been one of what Noam Chomsky calls "junior partner in global management."[174]

Their respective roles have been something like a global "bad cop-good cop" routine. The United States ferociously attacks revolutionary movements. By cutting off all other means of support, the U.S. forces these movements into the waiting arms of the Soviets. The U.S. in this way accomplishes three important purposes. It justifies further attacks on the movement, which is now truly "Soviet-dominated." It makes the movement liable to Soviet control, so that the Soviets may remove any democratic or radical tendencies from it. Finally, the U.S. can thereby demonstrate to people in other countries who may be thinking of revolution that their fate will be the same: to be attacked savagely by the U.S., only to "escape" into the orbit of the Soviet Union.

The USSR, at least until the collapse of Communism at the end of the '80s, was uniquely prepared for the role of guiding Third World revolutions in a "safe" direction. It retained some of the prestige of the October Revolution. In addition, it possessed an admirable ideological rationale for channeling these movements in the desired direction. Using Marxist-Leninist theory, the Soviets could claim that the only type of change appropriate in these countries is "national liberation" from imperialist—i.e., U.S.—domination, in which the party builds up the economy, under its firm control. Thus control is maintained by the party, and the danger of revolution from below is averted.

The Vietnamese and Nicaraguan revolutions, so different in their ways, both represent movements which the United States preferred to see driven into the Soviet camp rather than left to develop as independent and potentially democratic and liberating revolutions. The U.S. went to great lengths to cut tiny Nicaragua off from any other source of support but the Soviet Union. The willingness of the Sandinistas to follow the Soviet line led to absurd results, such as Nicaraguan President Daniel Ortega's public support of martial law in Poland. By accommodating itself to the Soviet line in this and other ways, the

Sandinista revolution increasingly lost its attractiveness for other revolutionaries, and thus its threatening quality. Similarly the Vietnamese revolution, bombed and battered by the United States, was driven to rely on the Soviet bloc as its principal source of support. While the Vietnamese party always had the structural characteristics of Marxist-Leninist parties, it had developed a degree of internal democracy and radicalism unique in the Communist movement.[175] As the American war on Vietnam wore on, Soviet aid and Soviet influence further insinuated themselves into the Vietnamese revolution, and removed those dangerous characteristics which could have ignited democratic revolution throughout Southeast Asia.

The Solidarity movement in Poland in 1980-81 called for elite collaboration of a different type. Here was a mass movement uniting 10 million workers in the industrial heart of Central Europe. If this movement turned revolutionary, it could have swept into the rest of Europe, East and West.

Far from encouraging the Poles to throw off the Communist yoke, Western leaders urged caution. Western media and politicians lavished praise and attention on Lech Walesa and other counterrevolutionary elements in Solidarity, and magnified the threat of Russian intervention in Poland if the movement became openly revolutionary. (1980 was not 1956 or even 1968; a Soviet invasion of Poland, in the unlikely event it was attempted, could have spread revolution throughout the Soviet bloc.) Western leaders did nothing to oppose the imposition of martial law by General Jaruzelski. Instead, they collaborated behind the scenes to stabilize the Communist government. U.S. and West German banks, deeply concerned lest further stress on the Polish economy lead to a radicalization of the mass movement, renegotiated the $28 billion debt incurred during the 1970s by the Polish Communist government.

There are many other instances of capitalist/Communist collusion during the Cold War period. The point is that, while capitalism presents itself as eternal and all-powerful, in fact it is temporary and conditional. It has survived the twentieth century because the opposition to it has been dominated by another system which has had as great a stake in the suppression of authentic revolution as capitalism itself.

8

FROM MARX TO LENIN

Lenin assigned the dominant role in Marxist revolution to the revolutionary party. Leninism has had disastrous results in the modern history of revolution. But what does this say of Marxism itself?

Marx and Engels had declared that "The Communists do not form a separate party opposed to other working-class parties" and that "the emancipation of the working class is the task of the working class itself." Just two years after the publication of *What Is To Be Done?*, Rosa Luxemburg, a revolutionary leader of German Social Democracy, wrote a scathing attack on Lenin's view of the party, later published under the English title, *Leninism or Marxism?*[176] A number of present-day Marxists see Leninism as a fundamental distortion of Marxism.[177] In their view, Marxism has not failed; it simply has never been tried.

My purpose in this chapter is to show that Leninism, or Marxism-Leninism, is not a distortion of Marxism, but follows from the Marxist paradigm of history. Leninism is a consistent development of the internal logic of Marxism, adapting it for practical use. If "there has been no serious and lasting non-Leninist Marxist challenge to Leninism,"[178] it is not because there are no elements of Marxism which contradict Leninism; it is because the particular development of Marxism which Leninism represents is necessary to operationalize Marxism as a theory of revolution. The Soviet Union and other Communist societies represent not a betrayal of Marxism but its fulfillment.

Marx's Model of History and Social Change

In pointing out what was essential to his approach, Marx once commented that others had described the development of class struggle. "What I did that was new was to prove...that the class struggle necessarily leads to the *dictatorship of the proletariat.*"[179] Marx believed that he had discovered the underlying forces which drive history and social change, and that he had constructed a science describing the "laws of motion" of these forces—a science describing where these forces come from, how they develop, and where they inevitably lead. As his collaborator Frederick Engels said at Marx's graveside, "Just as Darwin discovered the law of evolution in organic nature, so Marx discovered the law of evolution in human history."[180]

Marx believed that the study of these laws constitutes a "science of revolution": a system of thought which could examine with scientific accuracy the unfolding of history, and which could serve as a guide to the working class revolutionary movement. Marx was, Engels said, "before all else a revolutionist."[181] Marx and Friedrich Engels were deeply involved, in thought and action, in the revolutionary workers' movement of their time. Behind all of Marx's theoretical investigation of history and economic development lay the goal of revolution.

Marx's writings comprise a vast opus. As some Marxists have pointed out, there are statements in Marx—some of them minor, some of them fundamental—which contradict the positions or the spirit of Leninism. There are also points at which Marx contradicts himself. Even on so fundamental a point as the class dynamics of capitalist society, one can find contradictory statements in Marx, who sometimes suggests that capitalist society will diverge towards two poles, with wealthy capitalists at one and an ever-expanding, ever-poorer proletariat at the other, and at other times states that "the middle class will increase in size and the working proletariat will make up a constantly diminishing proportion of the total population."[182]

To truly understand the relation between Marx and Lenin, one must focus not on individual passages but on the fundamental structure of Marx's thought. Beneath the sometimes conflicting statements of Marx, there lies a consistent and powerful paradigm which attempts to explain the development of human history. It is in this model that lie the power and sweep of Marx's analysis. It is here also that lies the inevitable road to Leninism.

While there may be disagreements among Marxists as to what constitute the sum of fundamental elements of the Marxist paradigm of history, we can list the following as essential:

—The contradiction between the forces of production and the relations of production is the central contradiction in society. (By "forces of production," Marx meant the means of production—factories, tools, machinery, etc., and the labor force, with its skills and other qualities. By "relations of production" he meant "the economic ownership of productive forces"—for example, the bourgeoisie's ownership of the factories under capitalism.[183])

—History proceeds in stages, each of which is characterized by a particular level of technological development. As Marx put it in one striking passage, "The handmill gives you society with the feudal lord; the steam-mill, society with the industrial capitalist."

—Economic development is the driving force of history; each stage of history represents progress in man's domination of nature and the overcoming of economic scarcity.

—Scarcity—the need for economic development—led to the creation of classes in human society; class society—inequality—is the basis of economic development; the creation of a classless society is dependent on the overcoming of scarcity—that is, on the development of the productive forces of society to a point where scarcity is replaced by abundance.

—Capitalism, in spite of the horrors it has wrought, is a necessary and progressive stage in human history, because by its development of economic forces capitalism creates the essential conditions for socialism.

—Capitalism brings into being the class which is the agent of socialist revolution: the industrial proletariat; in the powerful phrase of the *Communist Manifesto*, "What the bourgeoisie...produces, above all, is its own gravediggers."

—Each stage of history is characterized by the dominance of one class, with one primary dominated class; thus feudal society was characterized by lords and serfs, capitalist society by capitalists and workers.

—The ideas and understanding of men reflect their social practice and relations; the dominant ideas of any age are the ideas of its dominant class.

—Revolutions occur when the relations of production pass from developing the forces of production to fettering these forces, and the forces of production break the bonds of these fetters.

—Revolutions do not occur until all the possibilities of the forces of production within the relations of production have been fulfilled.

—Capitalism will inevitably fall of its own internal contradictions: "capitalist production begets, with the inexorability of a law of Nature, its own negation."[184]

Marx characterized his system of thought as "historical materialism," which Engels in his Introduction to *Socialism: Utopian and*

Scientific described as "that view of the course of history which seeks the ultimate cause and the great moving power of all important historic events in the economic development of society, in the changes in the modes of production and exchange, in the consequent division of society into classes, and in the struggle of these classes against one another."[185]

Marx's View of Human Beings

Marxism contends that capitalism contradicts humanity's essence as a species. Historical materialism can be described as Marx's attempt to show that history is moving inevitably in the direction of fulfilling humankind's nature—a nature of which class society, in particular capitalist society, has deprived it. The subject of this history is humanity's "species being."

Marx discusses the dehumanizing nature of capitalism in his early writings in terms of "alienation" or "estrangement," and in his later writings in terms of the division of labor. For Marx, the working class is defined primarily not by what it does but by what is done to it. Workers—"proletarians"—are those men and women who are forced by their circumstances to live by the sale of their own labor power to capital. "Estranged labor"—that is, labor performed not freely but as a means of subsistence, the products of which are taken from the laborer—turns "Man's species being...into a being alien to him." Under capitalism, man is alienated from other men and alienated from himself.[186] The effect of the division of labor on the laborer, Marx quotes Adam Smith, is that "He generally becomes as stupid and ignorant as it is possible for a human creature to become."[187] Man can only overcome alienation by doing away with private property and creating communist society.[188]

Marx saw human nature as an abstract ideal rather than as something present in each human. For Marx, the proletariat does not act out of any qualities of its own which exist in the real individuals who comprise it; it acts rather out of the logic of its nature as a class. According to Marx, proletarians—workers—are dehumanized by capitalism; they revolt against their dehumanization, to fulfill the role of their class in history.[189]

While Marx clearly saw the industrial proletariat as the agent of revolution against capitalism, his view of workers as dehumanized is inconsistent with the idea of workers fighting for revolution as conscious historical subjects. Marx's model of history endows the proletariat with an historic mission at the same time as it deprives the proletariat of the human qualities which would enable it to fulfill this mission.

There is thus a contradiction in Marx between the idea of class struggle, in which the exploited are conscious historical actors, and the economic paradigm of history acting by its own laws which gives rise to that struggle. This contradiction presents itself immediately in the *Communist Manifesto*, which ringingly declares, "The history of all hitherto existing society is the history of class struggles," and then proceeds to explain the struggle between bourgeoisie and proletarians in terms of economic forces which are rendered abstract and inhuman to the extent that Marx and Engels present them "scientifically," operating independent of human will.

The capitalists themselves are compelled to follow the imperatives of the economic system. These imperatives—the need to compete, to expand, to maximize profit—lead to the capitalists' eventual destruction as a class; the "laws of motion" of capitalist development drive the society forward in history to a time when a passive working class will be driven to revolutionary action. The capitalists' pursuit of their own goals leads to an outcome fundamentally different from what the capitalists had sought.

Marx accepted the capitalist view of human motivation: "individuals seek *only* their particular interest," he declared (Marx's emphasis).[190] For Marx, self-interest is fundamental to historical materialism as a science. Only self-interest is scientifically valid as a motivation; the rest is "ideology." Marx's belief that he had discovered a "science" of revolution rests on his notion that the relations of production and the economic forces which they constitute operate independently of men's will. He does not mean by this that individual thought or initiative is not possible or not a real factor in society, but that individual acts often have results contrary to their intent, and that the economic forces constituted by the sum of individual actions act according to their own laws.

Marx finds all the laws of history and economics to be finally derived from the contradiction between the self-interest of the individual and the "general good" of the community. As the individual acts to pursue his particular interest, he sets in motion forces which drive history forward. As Engels expressed it, "...it is precisely the wicked passions of man—greed and the lust for power—which, since the emergence of class antagonisms, serve as levers of historical development."[191] Marx thought his great accomplishment was to find the eventual destruction of capitalism and the creation of a fully human society in the operation of economic forces arising from individual acts based on self-interest.[192]

Workers as individuals in Marx's paradigm do not have any goals beyond their individual interests. They do not act in conscious pursuit of revolutionary goals, and they do not act to fulfill a vision of human life and values fundamentally opposed to the capitalist vision. They have goals larger than their particular interests only as they represent man's "species essence" seeking to fulfill itself—that is, only as abstractions.

Though it is destined to act as the agent of revolution, in Marx's paradigm the working class puts an end to human exploitation not as a conscious goal on behalf of all humanity, but as the inevitable by-product of ending its own exploitation. It accomplishes the general interest of humanity by acting in its own self-interest.[193]

Lenin's Problem

The problem with which Lenin was confronted by Marx's ideas was essentially this: In a world driven by economic forces governed by their own laws, how do human beings consciously intervene in history to make a revolution? If the proletariat has been dehumanized, how can it act as a conscious revolutionary force? How can it become, as Marx put it, "dehumanization conscious of its dehumanization and therefore self-abolishing"?[194] If real individuals—including workers—act only in pursuit of their own interests, who will act on behalf of humanity?

Marx's apocalyptic vision of the working class rising in response to its dehumanization proved not to be of much help from the standpoint of practical revolutionary politics. The mainstream Marxist organizations—the Social Democratic parties of Germany and elsewhere—hewed true to Marx's view of the primacy of economic conditions in human affairs. They were faithful to Marx's prescription of mass parties which do not distinguish themselves from the working class as a whole. By the late nineteenth century, these parties had been well integrated into bourgeois political and economic life. While they paid lip-service to the ideals of working class revolution, they used Marxist economic theory to keep struggle within the bounds of the capitalist economy.[195]

Lenin's conception of the revolutionary party was his attempt to create a revolutionary force which would act on the basis of its own consciousness to fulfill a revolutionary program on behalf of all of society. He was attempting thereby to solve at one stroke the fundamental problems of revolutionary practice which the Marxist paradigm of history presented. If workers have no goals as individuals which rise beyond the capitalist motivation of self-interest, then it is not possible for workers as a class to be the source of revolutionary consciousness. If workers are dehumanized by capitalism, they cannot be the source of the restoration to humanity of its full human nature. If human consciousness is shaped by economic conditions, workers of themselves are in no position to grasp all of human history in order to transform it.

Marx's declarations to the contrary, the logic of the Marxist paradigm is that workers can only be the beasts of burden of the revolution, not its conscious creators. In his conception of the revolutionary party, Lenin was supplying to Marx's science of revolution the historical subject, the conscious creator of a fully human society, which the making of revolutionary history demanded. Historical materialism was based on the contradiction between actions to serve individual interests and effects which serve the general good. In the revolutionary party, Lenin was positing a body which would act consciously and scientifically on behalf of the proletariat and the general good.

Lenin's conception of the nature and role of the party, and of the content of political consciousness—knowledge of the "laws of capitalism" and the effects of their operation on all of society—faithfully reflected Marx's idea of "the science of revolution." Lenin's idea of socialism, fraught with such implications for workers' management and the Factory Committee Movement in Russia, was likewise faithful to a Marxism which equated the "relations of production" with "property relations." Marx and Engels had declared in the *Communist Manifesto*, "...the theory of the Communists may be summed up in a single sentence: Abolition of private property." The first task of the victorious proletariat, they continued, will be "to centralize all the instruments of production in the hands of the state, i.e., of the proletariat organized as the ruling class, and to increase the total of productive forces as rapidly as possible." This is precisely what the Bolsheviks did—with the slight difference that the state was in their hands, acting on behalf of the "dehumanized" proletariat. The subsequent role of the party-state was consistent with a paradigm which sees economic development as the basis of human development and inequality as the basis of economic development.

The power of Marxism to inspire and to mislead derive from the same source: its credibility as a science of history and revolution. By analyzing capitalism and demonstrating its impermanence, Marx convinced people that they could understand and transform human society in its totality. By building his science on a view of people which saw them as dehumanized by capitalism and which denied them motives other than narrow self-interest, Marx created a system of thought in which working class revolution could only be brought about by a party with larger motives—revolutionary goals for all of society—which substituted itself for the working class and acted on its behalf. Marx thus created a science of revolution against capitalism which preserved capitalism's most fundamental characteristic—its view of working people—and which guaranteed that any revolution made in his name would repeat the fundamental characteristics of capitalist society.

Lenin's theoretical achievement was to elevate human consciousness to a plane where it was capable of formulating goals other than those which, according to the Marxist paradigm, economic conditions impose, and where it could act consciously to create the conditions for the revolutionary transformation of social reality. Leninist theory enabled revolutionaries for the first time to break free from the tendency of the Marxist paradigm to trap human actors within the possibilities and movements of larger economic forces. In his concept of the revolutionary party, Lenin created a form in which human actors could assemble and assess every aspect of human experience from the point of view of consciously transforming the conditions within which human experience is created. Revolutionaries would no longer have to depend either on capitalism collapsing from its own internal contradictions, or on man's "species essence" becoming conscious of its violation by capitalism, to make revolution.

It is no mistake that, whatever their distortions of socialist revolution as Marx and others envisioned it, only Marxist-Leninist parties have succeeded in making revolutions based on Marxism. The world-wide influence of the Bolsheviks in the wake of the Russian Revolution was not simply a function of the prestige they enjoyed as the leaders of the first successful workers' revolution. It was a function of the fact that only they had discovered how to practice Marxism as a science of revolution.

For all its disastrous effects, Leninism represents an historic advance in the history of revolutionary thought, and in the ability of human beings to become the conscious makers of history. The very reason that the Bolsheviks, under Lenin's leadership, were able to play a decisive role in the Russian Revolution, is that only Leninist doctrine showed the possibility and the means within Marxism for conscious human subjects to understand and to master the huge unfolding forces of class society in revolutionary change. Marxist-Leninist parties have succeeded in leading revolutions to the extent that they have understood the capacity of human consciousness and initiative to shape history. They have distorted the revolutions which they have led to the extent that they have misunderstood the source and content of that consciousness, and the nature of the social transformation which it makes possible.

However great Lenin's achievement, it consolidated the dehumanized view of workers fundamental to the Marxist paradigm, and gave further impetus to the tradition, already well-established in Marxism, of seeing middle-class intellectuals as the source and guiding force of revolutionary consciousness. It has led to revolutions which are technocratic and dehumanized, and has resulted finally in the widespread discrediting of the idea of revolution itself—until the Marxist paradigm of history is finally overthrown.

9

THE FAILURE OF THE LEFT

Anyone searching the political landscape for a vibrant leftwing movement in the United States today is bound to be disappointed. While the problems in American society have grown more serious, the left movement which was so broad and powerful in the '60s and early '70s has been marginalized.

What explains the fate of the left? What is its present role in U.S. society? What will it take to change it? These are the questions I will take up in this chapter.

The problem, I believe, is not that the left is weak but that it is wrong: wrong about social change and its possibilities, wrong about what is happening in the world, and, most importantly, wrong about people.

The problem of the left can be stated very simply: it does not believe that revolution is possible. The left is thereby forced to believe that capitalism is the best *possible* system in the US. The left accepts capitalism, or some "humanized," liberalized version of it, as defining the limits of political and social possibility. Not seeing a realistic alternative to the system, all the left's thought and work is undertaken within the limits imposed by this one.

The reasons that the left believes fundamental change is impossible come down essentially to two: 1) Communism has failed, and the left can imagine no other alternative to the present system; and 2) the left does not believe that *people*, the American people in particular, are capable of, are interested in, will fight for, or will tolerate, fundamental change. The left believes, in fact, that the great majority of people are deeply imbued with the values and outlook of capitalism, and are content to live within the system as it is.

The old left and New Left of the '60s failed to create an alternative view of human motivation and social possibility to counter capitalism and Communism. As a consequence, the left of today is trapped within a view of people which is essentially negative. The left sees nothing positive in people's lives, and consequently sees no basis in the lives of ordinary people for fundamental social change. It is marginal to society because its characteristic ways of thinking about issues and people are marginal to the realities and meaning of everyday life.

Small as it is, the left is by no means insignificant. In the absence of an alternative movement, the left defines the meaning and possibilities of opposition to the existing order. The left reinforces fundamental capitalist ideas about people and the possibilities of human society. In its own way the left contributes to the capitalist illusion that society cannot change because "this is the way people are."

The Real Existing Left

One difficulty in discussing the left in the U.S. today is defining it. Because of its inability to create a comprehensive vision of change, the left consists of a hodge-podge of small groups, ranging from the liberal to the communist left, with ideas which have much more in common than the various groups realize or would care to admit.

The universal starting point within the left is a refusal to challenge capitalism, even while it attempts to mitigate capitalism's inevitable effects. Because it refuses to challenge the system, the left is always on the defensive, trying to stop some new atrocity from happening—some new budget cut, some new slaughter. It is never engaged in exposing and seeking to change the whole fabric of life—the daily atrocity of working life and political life and social life sucked as free of human content and interest as the ruling class can make them.

Because it does not think that fundamental change is possible, the left shrinks from exposing the systemic nature of the problems which people face. Thus the left does little to explain the connections among issues. It tends instead to view each issue in isolation from its role in U.S. and world capitalism and from its links to people's everyday lives, so that the issue will fit with the left's political practice—which consists largely of appealing to Congress or trying to replace one set of politicians with another.

By refusing to place issues in the wider context of class struggle, the left sanitizes issues and robs them of their significance. For example, the various organizations active against U.S. intervention in Central America, such as CASA, CISPES, and Neighbor to Neighbor, isolate the issue of Central America from other aspects of the savagery of capitalism. They make no attempt to explain the goals of

U.S. capitalism in Central America, or to show that death squads and other means of government terror in Central America have the same goal as unemployment and other capitalist weapons here: to destroy people's relations with one another and render them frightened and passive. They do not link the struggles of the people of Central America with the everyday struggles of working people here, to show that the goals and the meaning of the struggles are the same. These organizations present the workers and peasants of El Salvador and Nicaragua mainly as victims, rather than as people leading the way in a revolutionary struggle to be emulated here. The frequent fundraising letters and appeals for legislative action are filled with atrocity stories, which may move people to pity or horror, but do not do much to deepen their understanding of the meaning of U.S. intervention or to raise their hopes of the possibility of change. The effect, in fact, is the reverse: they make the system seem all-powerful, and real change impossible. They call for negotiations to stop the violence, rather than victory for revolution.

The anti-apartheid movement has largely presented the issue in South Africa as one of race rather than capitalist exploitation, so that the solution is not the destruction of capitalism and the creation of a new society in South Africa, but extending the franchise there to blacks; the solution is to be "democratic"—like the US. Presenting the problem in South Africa as race rather than class exploitation and struggle also diminishes its effect in exposing the nature of U.S. society; it suggests that the only connections to be made with people here are with black people trapped in ghettoes, rather than with working people of all colors trapped in capitalism.

The anti-apartheid university divestment movement isolates that issue so as to sanitize the institutions involved. The American university is a key institution in the structure of capitalist domination of U.S. and world society. It generates the ideas which justify capitalism, does the research which helps sustain it, trains students to fit into it. The anti-apartheid movement has not used the university's stockholdings and other roles in South Africa as a way of opening up a wider examination of the university's role in upholding capitalism at home and abroad. It has not used the divestment struggle to examine the social goals of higher education, or the ideas in which students are being trained, or the roles in U.S. society for which they are being prepared.

By focusing its analysis and demands so narrowly, the anti-apartheid movement encourages the idea that the university plays mainly a positive role in U.S. society—a role which is being tainted by its involvement in South Africa—and that the university can be "purified" by divesting. It makes the apartheid issue a moral issue of racial justice, attainable within capitalist society with some cosmetic changes; it thus marginalizes the apartheid issue and obscures the need for fundamental change.

When the left does attempt to make some connections, the connections it makes are misleading. The Jobs with Peace Campaign, for example, focuses on the U.S. military buildup and its effect on civilian jobs and expenditures, such as education and housing. But rather than showing that the military budget serves a critical function for the ruling class—by rationalizing unemployment and cuts in social programs, transferring public wealth to the private sector, and protecting U.S. investments overseas from working class struggle—Jobs with Peace leaders claim that the military buildup *hurts* the capitalist economy. Thus, they imply, they are trying to *save* American capitalism, and make it more competitive with the Japanese and German economies, while at the same time providing more jobs for American workers. Somehow, the military budget is all a dreadful mistake, not a function of the system but an abuse of it. The enemy is not capitalism, but poor decision-making by the present crop of politicians.

Presenting the military budget as an abuse of capitalism rather than as functional within it isolates the issue from all the other aspects of people's lives which are under attack by the system. It presents people merely as *victims* of a budget process which does not take their needs sufficiently into account, rather than as actors and participants in a class war, whom the military budget is a weapon designed to attack.

The leaders of Jobs with Peace with whom I have talked do not really believe this nonsense. What they do believe, however, is that it is not possible to talk with people about the *real* significance of the Pentagon budget—not only because the organization's financial backers would not like it, but because, they believe, people themselves would reject any explanation which attacked the capitalist system. They believe that their organization's demands—for greater housing expenditures, for example—are "objectively revolutionary," because, according to them, they are demands which it is not possible for the system to fulfill. They reject the notion of raising demands or ideas which are subjectively revolutionary—that is, which would depend on people acting as conscious historical subjects to achieve goals in which they truly believe, in a movement of whose significance they are fully aware.

Since the left is constrained by its view of political possibility from attempting to build a mass movement which challenges the system, it must attempt to build a movement within it. This means that its political practice, apart from occasional demonstrations and speechifying, consists mainly of electoral politics and lobbying and courting of the powerful. The lesson that the left teaches by its political practice is that the important people are those at the top of the hierarchy: Congressmen and Senators and state representatives, labor officials and boards of trustees and leaders of organizations. The important relationships are not those with each other and with the great mass of ordinary people, but with bigshots and the media.

The internal relations of leftist groups are consistent with keeping political debate and action within very narrow bounds: they are top-down and bureaucratic, with no real struggle over how to deepen the organization's grasp of the issues, no real development of the people within the organization, and no real involvement of people in reaching out to the public in a mass and collective way. "Membership" often consists of nothing more than paying dues and receiving a newsletter, or of volunteering one's time on a campaign designed by a small leadership group. It does not include shaping the direction of the organization.

In the seventies, in addition to more traditional leftist approaches, "citizens' action" or "populist" organizations emerged, such as ACORN and Mass Fair Share, which focused on community organizing and emphasized the positive significance of traditional communities. These efforts responded to a critical weakness of the New Left: its distance from ordinary people. The populist movement restricted itself to a narrow politics of self-interest, however, with no vision capable of reaching deeply into people's lives, and no analysis capable of challenging capitalism. The "vision" of these organizations is kept in the back pockets of behind-the-scenes leaders, who typically are socialists of one stripe or another—who want to change all of society, but do not think their constituents or their funding sources would. They therefore keep quiet about their real plans while they lead their members on a "socialist" path.

In the 'eighties, the Rainbow Coalition emerged, centered around the presidential campaigns of Jesse Jackson. Since the early 'seventies, the Democratic Socialists of America had tried to persuade people on the left that the road to change led through the Democratic

Party. Years of organizing within the Democratic Party had hardly resulted in moving the party to the left, however; the party leadership had moved the party farther and farther to the right, always under the pretence that "the American people have moved to the right, and if we want to win elections, we must follow them." The Democratic Socialists' efforts to restore people's faith in the system had come to nought. Not only had the left lost much of its faith in electoral politics and in the Democrats, but millions of working people had opted out of the game. In 1980, nearly fifty percent of eligible voters had chosen not to vote.

How one evaluates Jesse Jackson and the Rainbow Coalition depends on a view of electoral politics in this society as well as on the character and politics of Jackson.

The role of elections in capitalist "democracy" is to legitimize capitalist power by giving people the illusion of democracy and change. They are part of the means by which the ruling class manages the *appearances* of political life. The voting booth is capitalism's isolation cell, by which it breaks up and manages the forces for change.

The role of "anti-establishment" politicians is to keep popular discontent within the system, so that it can be managed and defused. The real force for change in the '60s, for example, was not elections but the mass movement: black people fighting in the streets, antiwar protestors marching and taking over campuses, workers on wildcat strikes. Senator McCarthy was quite open in 1968 about his purpose for running for president; it was "to get the people off the streets."

Now what of Jesse Jackson? Jackson is a powerful and exciting speaker. In a political landscape in which people have long been starved for sustenance, he seems to offer hope. In many rallies and speeches, he has given voice to people's yearning for a united movement of black and white working people. He has even—occasionally—given vent to some of people's anger at the powerful corporations which have devastated so many people's lives with layoffs and cutbacks and runaway shops. He has offered support—carefully qualified—for workers involved in a number of strikes.

But Jackson's role is to take people's aspirations and to bring them back within the system of capitalist relations. This is most obvious in his efforts to bring black and other disgusted working class voters back into the Democratic Party, which, like the Republican Party, is financed and controlled by capital. Jackson announced at the Biennial Convention of the National Rainbow Coalition in October, 1987 that his goal was to "challenge the cynicism and despair which led 83 million Americans to surrender their right to vote in '84."

In 1984 Jackson seemed to offer an alternative to the policy views of the other candidates, though even these alternatives were well within the system. But in the 1988 contest, as Jackson became a more "serious" candidate, he increasingly suited his positions on such key issues as military spending and the Middle East to the needs of American capital.[196]

Though Jackson continued to attack "corporate greed" in the campaign, he was careful to assure the capitalist establishment that his goal was to save the system, not damage it. In a letter to *Business Week*, Jackson wrote:

> I wish to make clear the positive aspects of my position on economic policy: a realistic concern about the practices of American businesses that tend to place short-term profits ahead of the well-being of their employees, their communities, the nation, and their own future financial health.

> To point out these problems and to call for their correction is not "business bashing." A strong, healthy private economy is essential to our national well-being and our hopes for social progress. The future of the business Establishment and of the nation itself are dependent on attention to the long-range effects of current American business practices.

> The long-term interests of American business and the American people are mutual and inseparable.[197]

Jackson's assurances that he saw the health of capitalism and the welfare of the American people as one were not simply for the business audience. In his popular speeches too his theme was that rich and poor, capitalist and worker, are all in one boat, and have the same interests. After the stock market crash of 1987, Jackson said:

> We are all in the economic trenches now, even if, on Wall Street, the trenches are mahogany-lined. Layoffs, farm foreclosures, bank failures, rising debt and falling wealth are our common ground. Wall Street and LaSalle Street [Chicago's financial district] cannot escape Main Street and Rural Route 3. We are one.[198]

Jackson's message was that "we" have to pull together—business, labor, and government—if "we" are going to compete more effectively with Japan and Germany and save American capitalism.

Jackson is inspiring exactly to the extent that he voices some of the feelings and aspirations and struggles that are already present in the working class. He is dangerous to the extent that he tries to lead these aspirations back into loyalty to the system.

The goal of most people active in the Rainbow Coalition, of course, is not to save the system. They are desperate for a way to fight for change and see the Coalition as a possible way to do it. The response of millions of black and white working people to Jesse Jackson when he addressed class issues in the 1988 campaign gave a small indication of the great potential for building a united mass movement against capitalism.

But the Rainbow Coalition has all the problems endemic to the left. The difficulty is not just Jackson's egomania or his political message or the investment of the coalition in advancing the career of this politican. The problem is that the Rainbow Coalition understands people and the world in terms of a capitalist conception of them; its view of political change, not only of how it would happen but of what it would consist, are conceived within a capitalist view of the possible. As the organization gets more deeply into electoral politics, its internal relationships and program and ideas have been increasingly defined by the need to "win," to elect people to office as the basis of change. The members of the Rainbow Coalition, whatever their deep personal goals for social change, are being used to further not just the interests of a handful of politicans, but to further the illusion that meaningful change can occur without challenging capitalism.

The Rainbow Coalition has the same unfortunate effects as the rest of the left: not of building struggle but of containing it; not of developing consciousness, but of keeping it restricted within very narrow bounds; not of mobilizing people for fundamental change, but of demobilizing them, by keeping political activity strictly within the framework of capitalist control; not of giving people an expanding sense of their power to change the world, but giving them an ever diminishing sense of the possible.

Before ending this brief look at the left, I should mention the sectarian left—the assortment of grouplets in the U.S. who cling to a communist view of the world. Still the largest of them, the Communist Party USA (CPUSA) has political views virtually indistinguishable from the liberal wing of the Democratic Party, and vigorously supports the Democrats. The tiny, Trotskyite Socialist Workers Party (SWP), endorses "socialism" abroad and liberalism in the US. Another group, the Revolutionary Communist Party (RCP), is a Maoist organization. It believes that U.S. workers, in particular white workers, benefit from imperialism and are hopelessly reactionary; it supports "national liberation" movements abroad and seeks in the U.S. to organize "the dispossessed," by which it means "unemployed black youths, punks, women, gays and lesbians," and others who it claims "have nothing to lose."

All of these communist organizations exhibit the distortions of Marxism as a failed revolutionary idea. They are about as far from the mainstream of people's lives and thoughts as it is possible to be.

The Left's View of People

As we have seen, the core of capitalist ideology is its view of people. Capitalism views the mass of humanity as passive and brutish. The good in society flows from the cultured elite who have risen by their personal worth and who have the leisure and education to be enlightened. People are only out for themselves; the competitive and hierarchical nature of the society is a function of people's innate need to gain a sense of personal worth by being on top of someone else. The order of society is fixed, because capitalism is human nature.

Since the left does not challenge capitalism, it cannot challenge its view of people—and any movement which does not challenge capital's view of people is condemned to repeat it.

Rather than seeing ordinary people in their everyday lives as the source of a new world, the left tends to see people either as mere victims of oppression, or as deformed by capitalism and carrying its values like so many diseases. The left judges people based on their race and sex, rather than on their values or what role they play in society. The question for the left which determines a person's worth is whether that person belongs to any group it sees as victimized. (The American left has created probably the first social movement in history in which "white male" is accepted as a derogatory term.)

Seeing people merely as victims denies their humanity. What is important about ordinary people is not what is done to them, but what they do: they create the bases of human life. Their struggle is the driving force of history, the source of human value in this society and the basis of a new one. Capitalism does not deny that the people at the bottom of society suffer; it merely denies that they are the source of anything good. Seeing people as victims is a means for elites—whether capitalist or Communist, liberal or leftist—to control them.

The left sees most people—except for those who qualify as sufficiently victimized—as "racist" and "sexist," hooked on consumerism, concerned only with their immediate self-interests, uninterested in and incapable of understanding larger questions concerning the future of the society. For the left, the limits on the possibilities of social change are a function of the people themselves.

Seeing people as imbued with the values of capitalism denies the most fundamental thing about people: that they are daily engaged in a struggle to change society. It is another way of saying that capitalism is human nature and that its rule is eternal. It is also the basis of the left's top-down approach to politics. If you can't trust the people, who can you trust? The enlightened few at the top, that's who.

The left accepts capitalism's idea that society consists of competing interest groups. Since it has no vision of a working class of men and women, black and white and Hispanic and other workers, with common goals, it is left with groups with competing interests which may from time to time coalesce. The left's view of people dooms the movement to perpetual fragmentation.

One positive contribution of the New Left was that it saw that "the personal is political." Feminists and others showed that there is no aspect of life in capitalist society which should not be transformed by conscious action. Without a new vision which went beyond capitalism, however, the powerful cultural insights of the New Left degenerated into special-interest politics and accommodation with the structure of inequality. Instead of a movement for the transformation of capitalist society, groups emerged which compete to secure the interests of women, blacks, Hispanics, welfare recipients, education, labor, the elderly, within an unequal society.

Accepting capitalism as the framework within which it understood and fought for equality changed the left's goals; the struggle became not for the destruction of inequality and the transformation of human society, but for a society which was perfectly unequal—a capitalist society in which blacks and women and all other groups would be proportionately represented at the various rungs of the social hierarchy.

Accepting the permanence of the system also meant that the enemy was no longer identified as the capitalist system, but people's mindsets. Thus "racism" and "sexism" were detached by the left from their moorings in the system of ruling class power and psychologized; they came to be viewed not as weapons of class war wielded by the ruling class, but as free-floating psychological deformations existing in the people at large. People have an attitude problem, which the left sees as its task to solve.

In these ways, the movements for racial and gender equality were transformed into instruments of capitalist rule.

Feminism and Nationalism versus Equality

I have said that equality and solidarity are the chief values which should shape a new society and which should underlie a revolutionary movement. I have also maintained that most people hold these values precious, and in one way or another struggle to bring them into their lives, in the midst of a culture which is profoundly hostile to them.

In this section I want to look more closely at feminism and nationalism in light of revolutionary values. I contend that feminism and nationalism embody the capitalist values of competition and inequality. Rather than being part of the solution, these ideologies are major parts of the problem for anyone wishing to create an equal society.

Let me begin with a couple of definitions. By feminism I do not mean belief in the fundamental equality of women and men, and determination to realize that equality in every area of life—an undertaking essential to a democratic revolutionary movement. By feminism I mean rather that political outlook which believes that men in general, rather than the ruling class as a class, are responsible for inequality, that most men benefit from the inequalities between men and women in society, and that women as a whole have goals and values in opposition to men as a whole.

By nationalism I do not mean a belief in the equality of people of all races and a commitment to realize that equality in every area of life. By nationalism I mean—referring here to black nationalism, but including all nationalism—that political outlook which holds that whites in general rather than the ruling class as a class are responsible for racial inequality, that most whites benefit from the inequalities between blacks and whites in society, and that black people as a whole have goals and values in opposition to whites as a whole.

My objections to feminism and nationalism are essentially that seeing society in terms of race or gender 1) distorts reality and conceals the dynamics of capitalism beneath these categories; 2) inevitably leads to strategies for change which preserve rather than destroy the system of class exploitation; and 3) is based upon and reinforces the capitalist view of human beings.

Since the view of people which a political vision expresses is the most essential thing about it, let me first examine the view of people which feminism and nationalism express.

Feminism and nationalism say that what is most fundamental about human beings is not their values or ideas or their role in creating society or the way in which they relate to other human beings, but is instead their race or sex. Feminism and nationalism reduce humanity to biological traits. They deny that the relationships between men and women or between black people and white people are the products of a class society at war over the future of humanity.

Feminism and nationalism reinforce the idea that human beings are competitive by nature and that society is a war of each against each. They encourage the idea that society cannot change because people do not change. The best that can be hoped for is that individual women or individual racial minorities will make it in the hierarchy, or that women or blacks will set up hierarchies under their own control. Social change is reduced to electing black politicians and promoting female corporate executives.

Feminism and nationalism conceal the substance of oppression beneath its form, hiding the depradations of capitalism on the vast majority of people beneath apparent differences in its effects on different groups of people. To them, "white society"—not capitalist society—is racist; "men"—not the system—are sexist. Feminism and nationalism are in perfect accord with the capitalist view that other people are the enemy, the cause of our unhappiness.

Feminism and nationalism have powerful effects. They attack the fabric of people's lives and militate against revolutionary change. Capitalist culture does not primarily work by saying, "People in general are no good." It is far more specific and sophisticated. The constant refrain of the culture is that whites are racist; blacks are criminals; women are mindless consumers; men are brutal. The general lesson is: trust no one.

Feminism and nationalism in this way intensify the corrosive effects of capitalist culture on people's lives. Relationships among people in this society are under constant attack. People are always being encouraged to be fearful of each other, or to be at each other's throats. The newspapers and TV are filled each day with tales of rape and murder and child abuse and wife-beating and racial attacks. Pay scales and job categories are set up to enforce separations—by race and gender, and in other ways, to keep people from learning from each other and supporting each other. Much about school and college life is set up to encourage people to see each other as the competition at best, or the enemy at worst, and to prevent them from finding what they have in common and acting on it.

In this context, leftist ideology—the idea that men are sexist and whites are racist—plays a powerful role in reinforcing capitalist ideas about people. The power of its role comes precisely to the extent that people look to the left as a way of understanding problems in their lives and as a source of ideas for change. It has the power of being sought as an alternative to the way things are; it has the effect of reinforcing them.

Nationalism in Historical Perspective

Ruling elites have always tried to play different groups against each other, and they have always tried to get the toiling classes to identify with "their" elites against the working people of other nations or groups.

Before Lenin, the international working class movement had always been firmly against nationalism as counterrevolutionary. What is new in the modern era is that nationalism and "national liberation" have been enshrined by Marxism-Leninism as "progressive."

Shortly after the Bolsheviks seized power in Russia, they reversed their historical opposition to nationalism and made "the self-determination of peoples" the keystone of their policies. By splitting them into national groupings, their policy weakened the power of revolutionary workers in the Soviet republics, and prepared the way for the rule of the Bolsheviks as a new elite.

Lenin and Trotsky's policy occasioned a fierce attack from Rosa Luxemburg, a leading German revolutionary of the time, who saw the Bolshevik policies as a betrayal of the revolution:

Instead of warning the proletariat...against all forms of separatism as mere bourgeois traps, they did nothing but confuse the masses...by their slogan and delivered them up to the demagogy of the bourgeoisie....the Bolsheviks...strengthened the position of the bourgeoisie and weakened that of the proletariat.[199]

Luxemburg was right to attack the Bolsheviks for their nationalist policies, but she was wrong to see nationalism as an aberration from Marxism. Lenin's embrace of nationalism was consistent with the Marxist idea that economic forces drive history and that capitalism represents a progressive stage of historical development. This model was the basis of Lenin's view, developed in *Imperialism, The Highest Stage of Capitalism*, that nationalist movements in colonialized countries led by native capitalists are progressive because they supposedly weaken imperialism, even while these national elites oppress and exploit their own workers.

Marxism-Leninism established the theoretical legitimacy of nationalism on the left. It also promoted the growth of nationalism in another way. The failure of Communism as a revolutionary idea undercut the potential for the working class to lead social change, and gave over leadership to the bourgeoisie. Nationalism was thus newly legitimized as the only practical solution to historic problems.

The theoretical and practical impetus which Communism gave to nationalism has had enormous implications for the history of the twentieth century.

The history of Zionism—Jewish nationalism—is a case in point. This history is worth looking at in some detail, for several reasons. History provides no clearer illustration of the failure of Communism leading to the triumph of nationalism. In addition, there are few clearer examples than Zionism of how ferociously reactionary nationalism always is, no matter how progressive a mask it may wear. Finally, there are few instances in which it is more clearly essential to distinguish between ordinary people and the elites who claim to speak in their behalf. Decades of propaganda have identified Israel and Jews; Israeli leaders claim to speak and act on behalf of all Jews. Only by understanding Zionism and its role in the twentieth century can we see that the Jewish nationalist elite do not now and never have truly represented Jewish working men and women; the crimes of the Zionists cannot be laid at the feet of ordinary Jews.

Founded in the 1890s by Theodore Herzl, Zionism held that anti-Semitism was inevitable and could not be fought; the only solution to anti-Semitism was the creation of a Jewish homeland. At a time when the mass working class movement in Europe and Russia was successfully mobilizing against anti-Semitism, the "central stratagems of the

[Zionist] movement" were "accommodation to anti-Semitism—and pragmatic utilisation of it for the purpose of obtaining a Jewish state."[200]

Like other forms of nationalism, Zionism is counterrevolutionary. (Herzl himself was a monarchist. He met with Kaiser Wilhelm in 1898 to solicit support for a Jewish homeland in Palestine; in his diary, Herzl reports, "I explained that we were taking the Jews away from the revolutionary parties."[201]) Zionism calls for Jews to unite as a people, implicitly behind a Jewish elite, rather than to unite with other working people to transform the world. It enshrines the racial purity of Jews as a premier value.

From the time of its founding until the Holocaust, Zionism was embraced by only a minority of Jews, and had "virtually no working class following."[202] Rather than being attracted to racial separatism, the majority of Jews, who were workers, were heavily represented in the unions and the Socialist and Communist revolutionary movements of their time. The appeal of Zionism was to wealthy Jews, precisely because it was counterrevolutionary:

> The only way the Jews could have had any success in fighting for their rights in Eastern Europe was in alliance with the working-class movements which, in all these countries, saw anti-Semitism for what it was: an ideological razor in the hands of their own capitalist enemies. But although social revolution meant equality for Jews as Jews, it also meant the expropriation of the Jewish middle class as capitalists.[203]

Zionism was funded by Jewish capitalists—department store owners and other wealthy Jews—as a means of defeating the unionizing and revolutionary movements among Jewish workers.

Zionism has characteristically made common cause with right-wing and Fascist movements, and shares their ideological and racist underpinnings. Zionists warmly embraced Mussolini and Italian Fascism.[204] They "sought the patronage of Adolph Hitler, not once but repeatedly, after 1933."[205] They sought to collaborate with German Nazism, pointing out to whichever Nazis would listen the essential similarities between Zionism and Nazism as racist philosophies, and their common goal of ridding Europe of Jews:

> Prior to the Nazis, German Zionism was no more than an isolated bourgeois political cult. While the leftists were trying to

fight the brownshirts in the streets, the Zionists were busy collecting money for trees for Palestine. Suddenly in 1933 this small group conceived of itself as properly anointed by history to negotiate secretly with the Nazis, to oppose the vast mass of world Jewry who wanted to resist Hitler, all in the hope of obtaining the support of the enemy of their people for the building of their state in Palestine.[206]

In March, 1933, in protest against Hitler's accession to power, New York's Jewish War Veterans called for a boycott of German goods; trade unions and other organizations from around the world joined the boycott. Several months later the World Zionist Organization (WZO) concluded a pact with the Nazis to break the boycott; according to the agreement, German Jews would put money in a bank set up for this purpose in Germany, and then purchase German goods to be sold outside Germany, in Palestine and elsewhere. Lenni Brenner reports that "Some 60 percent of the capital invested in Palestine between August 1933 and September 1939 was channelled through the agreement with the Nazis." The Zionist boycott-scabbing extended beyond the transfer of Jewish wealth out of Germany: "the WZO started soliciting new customers for Germany in Egypt, Lebanon, Syria, and Iraq. Eventually the Zionists began exporting oranges to Belgium and Holland using Nazi ships. By 1936 the WZO began to sell Hitler's goods in Britain."[207]

In 1941 Jewish nationalists in Palestine attempted to establish a military alliance with Nazi Germany. The Stern Gang, a Zionist terror organization, proposed to the Nazis, in a document discovered after the war in the German Embassy in Turkey, that "The establishment of the historical Jewish state on a national and totalitarian basis, and bound by a treaty with the Third Reich, would be in the interest of a maintained and strengthened German position of power in the Near East." In return for support from Hitler for establishing Zionist power in Palestine, they proposed to train and organize Jewish military units in Europe to "take part in the fight to conquer Palestine," should the Germans decide to open a front against the British there. The Stern proposal emphasized that it was "closely related to the totalitarian movements of Europe in its ideology and structure."[208]

The Stern Gang was not an unrepresentative fringe group. Its operations commander at the time the alliance was proposed to the Nazis was Yitzhak Shamir—presently the Prime Minister of Israel.[209]

It was only after World War II—in the wake of the Holocaust, and the clear failure of Communism as a positive alternative to capitalism--that Zionism became widely accepted among Jews.

With support from the United States and Soviet governments, Zionists established Israel as a Jewish state in 1948. Though it was attended by much talk of "democracy," the Jewish state was established on the basis of racist concepts parallel with German Nazism. Zionism preached in essence that Jews were a "Herrenvolk," a master race chosen by God to rule over Israel. The native people of Palestine were "Untermenschen," subhumans whom Jews have every right to exploit or destroy, as they carry out the task with which God has entrusted them, of expanding the Jewish "Lebensraum," or living-space, of Greater Israel.

Since its founding, Israel has been the most important client state of the United States; it is the focus of U.S. policy and interests in the explosive Middle East. Israel is used by U.S. and Arab elites as a kind of lightning rod, to draw the anger of ordinary Arabs away from Arab rulers and toward the Jewish state. At the same time, Zionist leaders use Arab hostility, which the Zionists themselves have done much to generate, to strengthen their own grip on ordinary Israelis. U.S. and Jewish and Arab elites have thus set up a situation in which their power over their respective peoples is legitimized by the external threats to their people which the rulers themselves encourage.

The disproportionate amount of U.S. aid for Israel and the outspokenness of Zionist advocates in the U.S. for Israel has led some commentators to suggest that the relationship with Israel has become topsy-turvy, and that Israel has too much influence over U.S. policy. This complaint is misleading, however; whatever the Israelis do, they do as an extension of the policy interests of U.S. capital.

The *intifadah*, or uprising of Palestinians against the Israeli state, has brought to light the suffering and the heroism of the common people of Palestine in a way that the terrorism and buffoonery of the PLO nationalist elite never did. The world has watched in horror as Israeli troops murder Palestinian children for throwing stones, or capture them and smash the bones of their hands and arms and legs. The Israelis have taken the idea of collective punishment to new heights. They have deprived entire villages of water to punish them. They have cut down tens of thousands of olive trees, to deprive Arab villages of their livelihood. They have sealed or blown up the houses of those suspected of participating in the uprising. They have put entire populations under house arrest with curfews. They have imprisoned an unprecedented portion of the Palestinian population, under inhuman conditions. And they have killed nearly a thousand Palestinians for resisting Israeli oppression; the incident in the fall of 1990, when 200 heavily-armed Israeli police slaughtered 31 unarmed Palestinians on the Temple Mount, was only the latest in the series of Zionist-sponsored atrocities. The parallels for the actions of the Jewish state are to be found in Nazi Germany and racist South Africa.

The savagery of Zionism is matched only by its hypocrisy. Its claim to represent the welfare and the values of ordinary Jews is an ugly lie. The most grotesque hypocrisy of all is that the Zionists use the genocide practiced against Jews in the Holocaust to justify genocide against the Palestinians now.

We have enough historical experience of nationalism to know where it leads. And yet leftists in the U.S. have joined with capitalist politicians and the PLO to call for a Palestinian state as the solution to the oppression of Palestinians. Surely it is clear that the establishment of a Palestinian state would simply consolidate the power of a Palestinian elite to control more effectively the Palestinian working class, and to make more lasting the divisions between Arabs and Jews. Has statehood made Lebanese or Egyptians or Jordanians or Iraqis free and equal? The idea is absurd, yet it is all that the left has to offer.

There is only one solution in the Middle East, and it is the same solution as everywhere else. The solution is democratic revolution throughout the Middle East, and the creation by working people themselves—ordinary Jews and Palestinians and other Arabs—of a new and classless society, in which inequality and national conflict and the exploitation of one human being by another is finally put to an end.

Ruling elites will be able to play off people against each other until we build a new revolutionary movement, constructed on the social relations and values of working people. Only then will it be possible to fulfill Marx's rallying cry, "Workers of all countries, unite!"

The Basis Of A New Movement

Many people on the left see the failings of the left and yearn for a different way, a "new New Left"—without seeing a way to create one.

I hope to have shown in this brief review that the necessary basis of a new movement is a new way of seeing the world. In a later chapter, I will outline what I believe a real movement for change should look like. From all that has been said, however, it should be clear that a real movement should enable people to feel new confidence in themselves and in other people, and new faith in the power of people to make a new world. It should help people to see the world in a new light—to understand in a new way, with more sense of depth and connection, what is wrong with the world as it now exists, and at the same time to see the good in it which people already accomplish. It should help people—black and white, men and women, Arab and Jew—see what they have in common with each other, and build a new vision out of their shared strengths.

In a real movement for change, every issue should be a prism through which the entirety of capitalism becomes more visible. Every analysis should be a way of seeing something new and profound about people which capitalist culture strives to conceal. The practice of a movement should build on people's real strengths, and show where real power and good come from; political practice should build people's sense of *themselves* acting together as the creators of change and the source of value. The relationships encouraged by a movement should allow people to grow and develop, by contributing what they know and by permitting them to learn from other people. The relationships should reflect the society which they want to build: equal, collective, and based on struggle and criticism: not on sucking up to the powerful, but on concentrating power within the class of people whose labor creates human society.

Above all, a real movement should fill people with hope. It should give people an entirely new sense of what it is possible for human beings to achieve together. A real movement would never accept capitalism and Communism—would never accept the way things are—as the measure of human possibility.

10

THE ROLE OF THE UNIONS

After the mid-1970s, the retreat of the U.S. labor movement in the face of corporate attacks turned into an unparalleled rout. Union membership declined from over 22 million in 1975 to fewer than 17 million in 1985. The percentage of non-farm workers organized into unions dropped from a 1953 high of more than 32% to about 17%. Average wage increases won in contract settlements of unionized workers dropped from nearly 10% in 1981 to about 1% in 1986.[210]

The picture suggested by these figures, however, is misleading. They present "the labor movement" as a unified whole, and paper over conflicting roles played by union leaders and members. They thus obscure certain fundamental questions: Who has suffered from the corporate attacks? What role do the unions play now in the working class movement? Where does the future of the union movement lie?

The Evolution Of Labor's Role

The modern labor movement in the U.S. was founded in the 'thirties on the basis of struggles which challenged capitalism, sometimes implicitly, sometimes openly. From the time of the massive hunger marches of 1930, class warfare raged around the country: in New York slums and Pennsylvania steel plants, in Michigan auto and Ohio tire factories, in the coal fields of West Virginia and the cotton fields of Alabama. General strikes broke out in San Francisco and Minneapolis. The system was in crisis, and millions of people sought an alternative to capitalism. In this context, "Labor...was not just an economic program. It was a way of life, a holy creed, a passionate belief, a blazing crusade for which thousands were ready to give their lives."[211] Wall Street financiers and Detroit auto lords and Pittsburg steel kings feared revolution.

The great Flint sit-down strike in auto which first established the CIO was followed by a wave of sit-downs and other strikes across the country—more than 10,000 in 1937:

> What had been a labor tactic seemed to become a universal mania....Woolworth girls jitterbugged in the aisles of stores closed tight as the result of sit-downs. Waiters in exclusive clubs, sitting down in the seats of the mighty, stared coldly and impassively at bankers demanding service and their chairs....One might walk into a barbershop and find the barbers sitting down, go to lunch and find the restaurant occupied by sit-down cooks and waitresses. Teachers, WPA workers, artists, bus boys, bellboys, municipal employees, clerks, stenographers, cooks, steel workers, longshoremen, garment workers, fur workers, waiters, bartenders, miners, sailors, firemen, power house workers, lumberjacks, sharecroppers, salesmen, thousands who had scarcely heard of unions before, were talking solidarity as they organized, sat down, got contracts, raised wages."[212]

The more far-seeing members of the corporate class correctly saw that their best response to trade unionism would be to sanction and legalize it. They could then strive to keep trade union struggles within the economic dimensions of capitalism. With their struggles regulated within an institutional framework, union members could be demobilized by union officials, who would have the legal obligation to uphold labor contracts negotiated with management. In 1935, Congress passed the Wagner Act, which granted collective bargaining rights to labor; in 1937, in the face of spreading class war, the Supreme Court acknowledged the law's constitutionality.

With the signing of contracts, the role of union leaders changed: from being militant organizers, they became contract administrators, who cooperated with management to insure production according to the terms of the contract. Local leaders who had difficulty making the change were fired by the international unions.[213] The union leadership began to suppress as well as it could the collective relations formed by workers, and to substitute for them the top-down institutional relations characteristic of corporate capitalism. Unions became responsible for imposing the work discipline which capitalists previously had to impose themselves—expelling rank-and-file militants, shelving grievances, breaking-up slow-downs and wildcats. The discipline was the more effective for coming from within the ranks of labor.

The establishment of unions was thus a two-edged sword for workers: it promised them a certain amount of protection from the company—protection which they would otherwise have had to win by their own collective action—but at a great price. As John Sargent, a worker at Inland Steel since 1936, observed, "The union has become a watchdog for the company. The local union has become the police force for the contracts made by the international union."[214]

The trend towards top-down control of unions accelerated during World War II. A number of factors contributed to bureaucratization. Capital itself became greatly concentrated during the war, as the War Production Board awarded enormous defense contracts to a relative handful of large firms. As the largest corporations grew larger, unions in key industries developed parallel bureaucratic structures. The alliance of top labor leaders with Roosevelt cemented at the level of the capitalist state the relationships which many of the leaders already had with the corporations. Top leaders of the AFL and of the CIO took a "no-strike pledge" for the duration of the war, and used the union apparatus to enforce it.

There was another factor which undermined the power of the rank-and-file, however, which is critical to understanding the history of the unions. The Communist Party fervently championed the war effort and enforced the "no strike" pledge. Communist militants had played an important part in building industrial unions; with 60,000 to 80,000 members in the workforce, and fellow-travelers and ex-members many times these numbers, Communists were the most disciplined and influential political force in the core industrial unions.[215] While Communists still had the reputation of being firmly revolutionary, the party leadership had become enthusiastic supporters of capitalism. (See Chapter Seven.)

Communists formed a bloc with conservative union leaders to build the war effort. Together they played a key role in disciplining workers, attacking shop floor struggle and helping to fire rank-and-file militants who organized walkouts. They championed incentive pay and speed-up. Nelson Lichtenstein describes this development:

> Communist spokesmen urged the labor movement to agree to all concessions demanded by the government, not so much as a necessary tactical retreat...but as a progressive step in itself, one that mirrored on the home-front the Big Three unity that Churchill, Roosevelt, and Stalin would forge at the Teheran Conference in mid-1943. "'In the United States we have to win this war

under the capitalist system,' declared Communist leader Earl
Browder in his *Victory and After.* 'Therefore we have to make
the capitalist system work...we have to help the capitalists learn
how to run their own system under war conditions.'"[216]

In 1944 Browder declared that "Capitalism and Communism have
begun to march together towards the peaceful society of tomorrow."[217]
Harry Bridges, Communist leader of the powerful International Long-
shoremen's and Warehousemen's Union, called on the CIO leadership
to organize speed-up, and his union sponsored a well-advertised campaign to continue the "no-strike pledge" after the war, as the domestic
version of the Teheran agreements in a post-war world dominated by
Soviet-American detente.[218] Bridges was true to his word. When
Montgomery Ward workers in Chicago walked out, Bridges ordered
the ILWU-organized Ward local in St. Paul to work overtime to
break the strike.[219]

Workers now fought for change in a world in which the most prominent adherents of revolution had become the most fervent supporters of capitalism. The working class was hemmed in on all sides:
caught between capitalism and Communism and between the company
and the union.

In spite of the efforts of the government, the corporations, union
officialdom, and the Communist Party to control them, authorized
strikes and unoffical rank-and-file action continued to challenge corporate power and official control of the unions. In 1943, fifty percent
of the workforce in auto participated in wildcat strikes.[220] Shipyard
workers engaged in sit-ins and slow-downs. United Mine Workers
went out on authorized strikes. A huge strike wave commenced in
1945 and reached a peak in 1946, when 4.5 million workers hit the
bricks and the number of days lost to strike activity hit its historic
high.[221]

But by the war's end, the labor leadership had consolidated around
hopes for a labor-corporate-government alliance to direct American
society after the war. In 1945, the CIO, along with William Green of
the AFL, and Eric Johnston, president of the U.S. Chamber of Com-
merce, sponsored a "Labor-Management Charter," in which, in return
for management support for the Wagner Act, the unions pledged to
defend "a system of private competitive capitalism" including "the inherent right and responsibility of management to direct the operations
of an enterprise." The Charter was drafted by CIO staffers close to
the Communist Party.[222]

The 1947 Taft-Hartley bill made mass picketing, secondary boy-cotts, and other important weapons of labor struggle illegal. The lead-ers of the AFL and CIO, using Taft-Hartley's requirement for loyalty oaths, ejected Communists—whose position had been weakened by their attacks on the rank-and-file during the war, as well as by the Cold War—and Communist-led unions from the federations. The "purge of the Communists" had a chilling effect; it "undermined the legitimacy of all opposition groups, Communist and anti-Stalinist alike."[223] The unions were now thoroughly in the hands of officials dedicated to upholding the corporate order.

During the war, labor had disciplined its ranks with the rationale that cooperation with the bosses was necessary to defeat Fascism. After the war, labor leaders disciplined the members with the ration-ale that capitalism was the source of progress in American society, and was the best available form of society. George Meany, then pres-ident of the AFL-CIO, made a speech in 1965 which accurately char-acterized the AFL-CIO leadership's long-held attitude toward the system:

> We believe in the capitalist system, and we are members of the capitalist society. We are dedicated to the preservation of this system, which rewards the workers, which is one in which man-agement also has such a great stake. The investors of risk capital also must be rewarded. It is, perhaps, not a perfect device, but it is the best that the world has ever produced, and it operates ef-fectively in a free society. We are not satisfied, no, but we are not about to trade in our system for any other.[224]

The role of the AFL-CIO became to enforce the regime of capital at the workplace and within the wider society.

The Best That The World Has Ever Produced

The goals of workers and the goals of capitalists are in fundamen-tal conflict. This conflict is always present—in open class struggle, such as the Hormel and British miners strikes which we examined earlier, and in the less obvious everyday struggle of working people to shape their lives with their values. Behind the traditional union values of solidarity and equality lies a vision of a different society, incompatible with capitalist society and its values of competition and inequality.

Having made their deal with capital, the union leaders could not admit that the goals of working class and capitalist class are in conflict. Instead, they had to try to suppress the struggles of workers to achieve their goals, and to substitute for them goals and values compatible with the corporate agenda.

Union officials tried to get workers to accept a revised vision of unionism compatible with the capitalist definition of the American dream. This revised vision consisted of participation in the general consumerization of American life. Labor leaders accepted with a vengeance Charles Wilson's phrase, "What's good for General Motors is good for the country." The welfare of workers was defined, by labor and corporate leaders alike, in terms of the profitability of the corporations, while the welfare of American society was defined in terms of the growth of the economy. The term "capitalism" largely disappeared from their vocabulary; it was replaced by "democracy" and "freedom," with which capitalism was taken to be synonymous. Human and social development were defined in terms of economic development, and "democracy" and "freedom" advanced around the globe as U.S. capital penetrated new lands and subdued new peoples.

Consistent with their belief in the right of capital to run its corporations as it saw fit, union leaders began to cede greater control to management over work rules and conditions—control which workers had won through militant shop-floor organizing in the mid-'40s. The 5-year contract concluded between GM and the UAW in 1950, for example, granted work rule and line speed concessions and a guarantee of labor peace to the company in exchange for higher wages. Autoworkers wildcatted against the contract around the country in 1955 with the demand, "Humanize working conditions."[225]

Union leaders and management had a joint interest in whittling away at work rules. Rank-and-file power is centered on the shop floor; here, at the point of production, is where ordinary workers have real leverage against the company—and against union officials. The more this power could be wrested away from workers, through work rules changes, elaborate grievance procedures, Taylorism and technology, the more the rank-and-file would be vulnerable to control by company and union officials. As the '50s advanced, so did the efforts of the labor establishment to grab power away from the rank-and-file.

In the '60s and '70s, workers waged an unprecedented number of wildcat strikes against labor officials as well against the corporations. (See Chapter Five.) These strikes found their source in the values of worker solidarity and equality, in movement from below and confrontation with authority—values long under attack by the labor establishment. They began to shift some power back to the workers themselves.

Sometimes management was able to defeat these strikes with only the back-room cooperation of union officials. At other times, union officials had to play their role as corporate police and strikebreakers more openly. In the summer of 1973, for example,

> a wave of sit-down strikes swept through the Chrysler Corporation plants in Detroit....The movement was broken decisively only on the morning of August 16, when high officials of the UAW, many veterans of the union's early battles, assembled a "flying squadron" of 1,000 local officials and staff representatives that dispersed the picket lines, manhandled the militants, and persuaded hesitant employees to return to their jobs.[226]

The struggle of the rank-and-file had forced the labor leadership to show its true colors. That leadership, having accepted the goals and value structure of capitalism, had become the most ferocious enforcers of capitalist relations on the front lines of the class war.

Policing The Empire

The AFL-CIO leadership accepted the legitimacy and permanence of corporate domination of American society and, what necessarily followed, American capital's dominance of the globe. They became capital's representatives within the ranks of labor at home and abroad, attacking working class struggle wherever it arose to challenge corporate power, whether on the shop floor in the U.S., or in factories and slums and jungles overseas.

The AFL had begun cooperating with the government overseas during World War II. After the war, it cooperated with the CIA in the overthrow of the reformist Arbenz regime in Guatemala in 1954 and the establishment of a reign of terror in that country which has still not subsided.

In 1962, working with the Kennedy Administration, the AFL-CIO established the American Institute for Free Labor Development. AIFLD worked with the CIA to overthrow the liberal Cheddi Jagan government in British Guyana in 1963. In Brazil, it established the *Movimento Democratico Sindical*, under the motto, "God, private property, and free enterprise," and assisted in the 1964 coup against Goulart. It helped organize the U.S. invasion of the Dominican Republic and overthrow of the Bosch regime in 1965. Working jointly with the CIA and ITT, it was instrumental in the bloody overthrow of the Allende government in Chile and the establishment of the Pinochet dictatorship.[27] AFL-CIO leaders were outspoken supporters of American capital's murderous war on the Vietnamese people. Even now, AIFLD personnel play a key role in the rural "pacification" campaign in El Salvador.

The AIFLD has long been exposed, and labor and left activists have made numerous attempts to break AFL-CIO links with the CIA. But their efforts miss the point. The AIFLD is no aberration. The international role played by the AFL-CIO is the mirror image of its domestic role, and springs from it. Chairman J. Peter Grace described the purpose of AIFLD to be to bring "an end to class struggle" and to promote harmony between business and labor in Latin America. But this, of course, has been the direction in which the unions have headed in the U.S. as well as overseas ever since their establishment on a friendly basis with capital.

Having concluded a pact with management to control the workers, the relationship of union officials both to the working class and to the forces of capital profoundly changed. Policing the contract for business led to policing the empire.

The Attack On Labor

When the corporations went on the counteroffensive in the 1970s, the unions were in a very weak position to resist. They had long since abandoned moral and political leadership of the society to the capitalists, and had identified the welfare of workers and American society with corporate profitability. When the corporations claimed that foreign competition was ruining them and workers would have to take cuts to protect profits, "progressive" unions like the UAW called on their members to unite with their American bosses against the Japanese "invaders."

But there was a more direct reason for the rout of the unions. The union leadership and the corporations had a common interest in destroying the power of organized workers. The upsurge of labor militancy of the '60s threatened the labor leadership as much as it challenged the corporations. The corporate counteroffensive was an opportunity to consolidate the power of labor bureaucrats, while it undermined the power of the rank-and-file.

The attack on the ranks of labor of the past two decades has been a joint attack, co-managed by corporate leaders and the officials of the AFL-CIO. This is why it has enjoyed such success. In union after union, international leaders have joined with corporate officals to force locals to make concessions. These concessions are not only in terms of wages and benefits. They also include structural changes which institute two-tier wage structures, undermine work rules, establish "quality of working life circles" (QWL) for "labor-management cooperation," and put locals into competition with each other.[228] The company and the union leadership want these changes for the same reason: they weaken the power of workers and make them more easily controllable.

The interest of labor officialdom in undermining the power of the rank-and-file explains why, when workers have mounted anti-concession struggles on their own, the AFL-CIO leadership has moved against them. It explains why the international leadership of the United Food and Commercial Workers and the AFL-CIO were determined to destroy the militant meatcutters' Local P-9 at Hormel. Mobilization of the membership against Hormel would have threatened the relationship between the company and the International. An active membership would also have threatened the International's control of the union, a control which depends on the members' passively accepting the dictates of the union bosses. An activist P-9 membership would have offered a dangerous example to other union locals.

Nearly the entire labor establishment, not merely the right-wingers, joined ranks to destroy P-9. William Winpisinger, for example, "Democratic Socialist" president of the International Association of Machinists—who had left the air traffic controllers twisting in the wind in 1981—on March 7, 1986, after the meatcutters had been on strike for nine months, sent a letter to thousands of union locals, urging them not to offer any money or moral support to the Hormel strikers.

At about the same time, Winpisinger directed his machinists to cross the picket lines of striking TWA flight attendants. The flight attendants subsequently lost their strike and their jobs. In a 1989 ruling, the Supreme Court upheld the right of TWA to keep the scabs hired during the strike and not to rehire strikers—a stunning defeat for workers, which passed without notice from the labor establishment.

Unions and the Goals of Class Struggle

At the heart of the unions there is a conflict over the forces that will control them, the goals they should pursue, the values that should shape them, and the role of the members within them. This struggle is sometimes open, sometimes hidden from view.

Capitalists and their allies among union officialdom work to control the unions from the top, to reduce their goals to disagreements within the corporate agenda, to shape ther values with competition and inequality, and to reduce the role of members to passive acceptance of the decisions of the leadership. Their objective is to prevent the articulation of the goals and values of workers as an alternative vision, and the emergence of a democratic movement which fights for a new world based on these values.

The problem with the unions is not that they are weak, but that they are dominated by the forces of capital, and have come to play a role of containing, misdirecting, and suppressing class struggle—a role of managing workers on behalf of capital. It is working men and women, not union bureaucrats, who have borne the brunt of the corporate assault of the last two decades. The international leaders of the AFL-CIO unions have cooperated in these attacks, and their control of the rank-and-file has been strengthened by them.

As their history makes clear, the role played by the unions is not a function simply of bad leaders. It stems from the collaboration between the union leadership and capitalism. This collaboration in turn is a function of the absence from society of a viable revolutionary vision on which to build a practical challenge to the capitalist system. The labor movements of the United States and other countries have been profoundly shaped by the failure of Communism as a revolutionary alternative to capitalism.

As they came to believe in the permanence of capitalism, union leaders came to accept the corporate structure as the framework which would define union goals and internal relations. Union officials took on the role of managing workers on behalf of capital and systematically undermined the power of the rank-and-file, so that they would be more easily managed.

What then can be done to reverse the role played by the unions? How can they be made into organs of class war on the side of working people?

Workers can only become the leading force within the unions by becoming clear about the values and goals they want to shape all of society, and fighting for them in the unions and beyond. The only movement capable of transforming the unions is a revolutionary movement, rooted in the values and social relations of the working class.

Workers must build a movement which rejects the claims of capitalism to legitimacy and to permanence. The movement must challenge the vision, goals, values, social and economic relations, and political power of capitalism with the goals and values of working people. It must articulate as a social vision the values of solidarity and equality which are at the heart of unionism, and fight to extend that vision to all of society. The goal of this movement must not be to negotiate better conditions of exploitation, but to end it.

11

THE COLLAPSE
OF COMMUNISM

The end of the 1980s witnessed extraordinary developments in the Communist world: an historic uprising in China; the collapse of Communist rule in Eastern Europe; the reunion of Germany. As startling as these events have been, there is surely more to come, as the Soviet Union and China themselves become swept up in change. We have seen only the opening acts of the drama.

What are we to make of all this? Various analysts have proclaimed the triumph of capitalism on a world scale: "The Cold War is over, and we won."[229] The Western media have by and large presented the collapse of Communism as a revolt *for* capitalism. The media translate mass demands for democracy in socialist bloc countries as demands for what Americans have: consumer goods, freedom of the press and travel, "free enterprise" and a market economy.

These are surely very profound developments—perhaps the most important events since the Russian Revolution of October, 1917. But their meaning, I believe, is quite different from what the capitalist media and political analysts say it is.

Revolt In The Soviet Bloc

Trying to understand the developments in the Soviet bloc, one is immediately struck by a paradox: the changes in Eastern Europe have swept the Communists out of power in country after country—and yet these changes were initiated and still are largely led by Mikhail Gorbachev, the leader of the most powerful Communist Party in the world. Why would Communists initiate their own destruction?

This is not the only paradox. Why are Western capitalists so vocal in their support for "democracy" in Eastern Europe? The savagery of the capitalists in the countries under their control knows no bounds; even as they call for democracy in Eastern Europe, they drown El Salvador in blood, to prevent the people of that tortured land from enjoying what Western politicians claim to support in the Soviet bloc. Clearly something must be happening in the East quite different from what the representatives of capital are saying.

The dynamics of the struggle in the Communist world become more clear if we consider several things: one, the nature of the changes which Gorbachev is proposing; two, the dynamics of the economic situation in the Soviet bloc which is a key focus of the reforms; and three, the history of working class revolt against Communism which is the context of the reforms.

Gorbachev launched his campaign for reform in 1985. His reforms are usually summed up by two terms, "*glasnost*" and "*perestroika*." Glasnost, translated as "openness," refers to the new policy in the Soviet bloc of relaxing media censorship and allowing some freedom of discussion. Perestroika, or "restructuring," refers to the economic and political restructuring encouraged by Gorbachev and other Communist reformers.

The West paints the crisis in the Soviet bloc largely as an economic crisis—with primarily an economic solution. Communism, the story goes, with its central planning rather than marketplace regulation of the price and supply of goods, and its lack of the profit incentive for individual entrepreneurs, is economically inefficient. The people of the Communist world are unhappy because of the constant shortages of consumer goods, and the lack of individual freedoms enjoyed in the capitalist world. The solution of these problems is to replace the centralized economy with market forces as the regulating mechanism, to encourage private enterprise, and to grant people a measure of "democratic" freedoms.

But this description of the crisis in the Communist world is misleading, because the apparently economic crisis there is actually political. The problem is that the Communist system has a "command economy" in which nobody follows the commands anymore. It is true that the economy of the Communist world is in shambles. But the reason for that is not a technical reason having to do with the formal design of economic systems. It is because the working people of the Soviet bloc have been on a decades-long slow-down strike. (In March, 1990 I asked Miklos Patrubany, the Senator representing the

Hungarian ethnic minority of Cluj-Napoca, Romania, the cause of the economic crisis under Ceausescu. He said, "Workers in Romania have been on strike for five years. They show up for work, yes, but nobody works for more than two hours a day. They smoke, drink, play cards, talk. Nobody works." I asked my guide and translator in Torun, Poland, the cause of the economic breakdown there. We were sitting in a hotel bar at the time, around ten o'clock on a Thursday morning. He said, "You want to know the reason? Look around you!" The bar was full of people talking and drinking. "All these people are at work. They check in, then say, 'I have to run an errand.' Then they go out to drink.")

Communism clearly does not work over the long haul as a strategy for economic development. But why is this? It is not because Communism is top-down and undemocratic; so is capitalism, which in its perverse way certainly works. So what is the reason for the difference in performance between the two systems?

The chief difference is that Communism, based on an ideology of collectivism, does not have the same means to enforce its everyday rule as capitalism. In Commmunist countries, workers cannot be fired. They cannot be laid off. There is no unemployment. Social services like education and medical care are free and available to everyone. Secret police and gulags may be useful to prevent uprisings, but, as a Hungarian official commented, "Dictatorship can control people, but it cannot make them work."

Capitalism is more efficient than Communism not primarily as an economic system but as a system of social control. Capitalism is based on an ideology of individual competition and on social structures, such as the labor market, which force the individual to compete to sell his labor power. Through the market and the ideology of competition, capitalism is able to fracture ties among people and force them to face their fate alone. Capitalism thus strips the individual of his security and forces each person constantly to face the possibility of failure. In this way capitalism makes people far more vulnerable to control.

The Soviet elite need capitalist restructuring because they need a source of day-to-day discipline to enforce their control and to make workers produce. The purpose of economic reforms is not more "democracy" or freedom, but more effective labor discipline to strengthen the hand of the Eastern bloc elite.

Economic restructuring consists of introducing capitalist economic forms, dismantling the system of social services and planning in the

Soviet countries on behalf of market capitalism, and replacing official equality backed up by state repression with inequality driven by the "invisible hand" of the market.

By introducing the market into Communist societies, perestroika will make workers less secure and more vulnerable to management control. Perestroika will enable the ruling elite to pit workers against each other for jobs, and factories against each other for markets. It will produce massive unemployment in these societies, and the massive insecurity which goes with it. It will wipe out the system of social services. Finally the Eastern bloc elite will have at their disposal the same means of enforcing labor discipline which have served capitalists so well.

Economic restructuring of this sort would never work, of course, if everyone obviously lost by it. As the factories and other public wealth of Communist societies are sold off to private interests—often the former Communist factory managers themselves—and private enterprise is encouraged, perestroika will lead to the creation of a large class of private entrepreneurs, free to exploit the labor of others and free to get rich. The Eastern bloc elite hope by this strategy to win the allegiance of a portion of the population, who will support the government in the continued exploitation and suppression of the working population.

The purpose of political restructuring, such as free elections and easing the Communist monopoly on power, is to prepare the way for economic restructuring. Political reforms are intended to give people an illusion of popular power, in the same way as "democratic" elections are intended in the West. In no instance has political restructuring meant profound change in the distribution of power. In no case has it meant the real enfranchisement of working people and the destruction of elite control—nor was it intended to.

The "velvet revolutions" already concluded in Eastern Europe and now unfolding in the Soviet Union represent a new strategy of domination designed to maintain elite control. While the pressure for change in the East has come from below, the direction of that change—in which the "free market" and parliamentary politics substitute for real democracy—has been dictated from above.

Communist elites have found that they cannot continue to rule on the old basis, using state socialist forms and language within a repressive social structure. They are trying to create, through economic and political reform, more stable means of social control which emphasize competition, individualism, and inequality within less obviously repressive structures. The reforms are new mechanisms for managing the population, while preserving intact if not all the personalities and party titles, at least the power and authority of the ruling class.

China and the Soviet Union have pursued different strategies in making these changes. The Chinese Communist Party imposed wide-ranging capitalist economic reforms in 1982, but has not opened up the political life of China; the Soviet Union and the Eastern bloc have begun by making some political concessions, in preparation for imposing capitalist economic forms. Both these strategies are directed toward the same end, of preserving intact the hierarchy of power and control in their societies.

The Historical Context of Perestroika

Gorbachev's calls for reform from the top must be understood against a backdrop of decades of working class struggle against the whole hierarchy of power in the Communist world. He has been taking an enormous risk—encouraging movement from below to serve as a battering ram against the structures he wishes to change at the top. It is the kind of risk ruling elites take only when they have concluded that they cannot continue to rule in the old way.

Pressures for change have been building throughout the Soviet bloc for years. Workers' uprisings in East Germany in 1953 and in Hungary in 1956 were put down only with Soviet tanks and much bloodshed. The 1968 uprising in Czechoslovakia required armed Soviet intervention for its suppression. Each of these uprisings chipped away at the Communist myth of workers' power which served to legitimize the ruling class throughout the "socialist bloc."

The Communist system in Poland had been unravelling for two decades. Worker uprisings there in the 'sixties and early 'seventies preceded and built the foundations of the Solidarity movement in 1980-81. The Solidarity movement, an illegal union of more than 10 million members—virtually the entire working population of Poland—was only forced underground by martial law and the arrest of hundreds of activists in December of 1981.

No doubt the Kremlin understood that events in the satellite countries could only foretell events to come in the USSR.

It has long been difficult to get information about developments within the Soviet Union. With the new openness, however, some information about the past is coming to light. In June, 1989, for example, the Soviet newspaper *Komsomolskaya Pravda* confirmed rumors that in 1962, in the southern city of Novocherkassk, soldiers killed as many as seventy strikers in a blaze of machine-gun fire. Reportedly, "strike organizers were arrested the next morning, but other factories went on strike, and the military was deployed with tanks and armored personnel carriers." Soviet officials had long denied reports of the massacre. One teacher told the newspaper that, after the massacre, "they tried to wash the blood from the square for a long time, first with fire engines, then other ways, then brushes, and at last called in a steam roller and laid a thick layer of pavement."[230]

Presumably there have been other strikes, and perhaps other massacres, which Soviet officials have succeeded in covering up. But we hardly need other examples of working class struggle against the Communist regime to realize that not for nothing has the party maintained its police state—the gulags and secret police and torture cells and "psychiatric" institutions. These are not the institutions of a people who are governed by consent.

It would be a mistake, however, to assume that the Communist elite have had only these crude means at their disposal to enforce their rule. If that was all it took to govern a country, there would still be little threat to party dictatorship now.

The Soviet Union was governable in the past to the extent that the majority of people continued to believe that the society was moving toward fulfillment of the Communist vision of a classless, cooperative, and democratic society. Communism cannot work without moral credibility; it has to *appear* to be revolutionary to gain people's allegiance. In the Soviet bloc it has long since lost that credibility, resulting in a disillusioned and restive populace and an economy in disarray. The Russian newspaper which reported the massacre at Novocherkassk said that the strike broke out when people ceased to believe in "promises of success and the rapid approach of Communism." Popular disaffection runs very deep in the Soviet Union; its source is that the Communist Party seems unwilling and unable to fulfill the revolutionary ideals by which the party had historically won people's allegiance.

The Dynamics Of Change

The struggle over change in the Soviet Union shows the opposing class forces involved in the struggle. It also shows that workers will not be satisfied with what perestroika has to offer.

In the summer of 1989, more than 500,000 coal miners and other workers in the Soviet Union went out on the largest strike in the Soviet Union in seventy years. The strike displayed something of the workers' attitude toward perestroika. One miner said:

> "We were told for years: 'Put out more coal and don't worry about anything. We'll feed you and dress you, give you housing and child-care centers, houses of culture and sport,' miner Nikolai Yatsenko said. "And we worked our heads off, put out coal, and now we hear, 'Not only do you have to put out coal, you have to take care of yourself and everything else too.'"[231]

The workers did not appear to feel that being exploited without the benefits of the old social welfare system is much preferable to being exploited with them.

Gorbachev complained to the Supreme Soviet that the strikers had perestroika "by the throat."[232] The Soviet government ended the strike only with huge concessions to the strikers. One Moscow writer remarked that "Gorbachev had little choice but to satisfy the miners' demands. He could hardly say, 'Sorry, perestroika is just for the intellectuals.'"[233]

Included in the strikers' manifesto of demands was one that received little notice in the United States. The miners "called for abolishing or sharply curtailing the freewheeling private entrepreneurs who have amassed wealth and huge resentment under the new economic order that Mr. Gorbachev is trying to build." The flourishing private sector is reportedly the focus of "bitter envy" in the Soviet Union. According to public opinion polls in the USSR, "most workers believe that the state has an obligation to prevent some citizens from prospering while others fall behind."[234] Some of the profit-making companies, called "cooperatives," have been burned to the ground by citizens who disapprove of the profit motive.

In the wake of the miners strike, Russian workers formed a nationwide organization to oppose capitalist-style economic changes and the growing nationalism and ethnic strife in the Soviet Union. According to the daily *Sovietskaya Rossiya*, the United Front of Workers of

Russia held its founding conference in the Siberian city of Sverdlosk in early September, 1989, with 110 delegates from 29 industrial centers taking part. Stressing the delegates' alarm at Gorbachev's plans to increase private enterprise in the country, the newspaper quoted one delegate, V. Yakushev, as saying, "If we stake our future on developing completely unjustifiable market relations in the economy, the situation in the country will deteriorate even further."[235]

Two months after the conclusion of the national walkout, at least 20,000 miners in the Soviet Arctic city of Vorkuta resumed their strike—in defiance of a new "reform" law outlawing strikes in mining and other key industries—to demand full implementation of the government's concessions. The strike soon spread to other regions.[236]

Worker opposition to perestroika is intensifying. There were more strikes in the Soviet Union in the first quarter of 1990 than in all of 1989, which itself represented an historic high.[237] In the face of popular protests, the Soviet government postponed price increases scheduled to go into effect on July 1, 1990. On July 11 hundreds of thousands of miners, supported by farmers and other workers, went on a one-day national strike. They called on the Communist government to step down, and promised that this strike was only the beginning of their campaign.[238]

Nationalism and Perestroika

In addition to working class struggle, there is another kind of conflict sweeping the Soviet Union: conflict between national and ethnic groups. Nationalist fighting has become widespread in several Soviet republics. By early July, 1989 more than 100 people had been killed in ethnic fighting in Armenia, Georgia, and Azerbaijan.[239] In late July, fighting intensified in Azerbaijan, with a reported 5,000 heavily armed Azerbaijanis attacking Armenian settlements and slaughtering over 200 people. In January, 1990, 60 more Armenians were killed, leading the Kremlin to send in troops and impose emergency rule in Baku.[240] The Soviet republics of Lithuania, Latvia, Georgia, the Ukraine, Uzbekistan, Moldavia, and Russia itself have declared varying degrees of independence from the Soviet Union.

Here is yet another paradox. Growing nationalism has led to the very real possibility that the Soviet Union will break up into a loose federation of sovereign republics. And yet Gorbachev has repeatedly encouraged the nationalist movements, while party reformers under

Gorbachev's leadership have encouraged nationalism through the formal programs of perestroika. The 19th Party Conference of June, 1988, which developed the principal strategic elements of perestroika, called for "free development of each nation and ethnic group" in the Soviet Union,[241] with "an economic self-management system by the different republics."[242]

Why would the Soviet elite endorse an ideology which threatens the very existence of the Soviet Union?

As we have seen, nationalism is a capitalist ideology. By denying the significance of class exploitation and conflicting class roles in society, it legitimizes the power of national elites. Nationalism reinforces the capitalist idea of competing interest groups in a hierarchical society, and thereby provides the ideological cover for elites to manipulate people against each other.

Nationalism is the means by which Gorbachev hopes to break apart a potentially revolutionary working class movement and make it more susceptible to elite control; the Soviet ruling class would much prefer to have various ethnic groups killing each other than to have a united working class directing its anger at the elite. By encouraging nationalism, the Soviet ruling class hopes to strengthen national elites in the various Soviet republics and encourage the competitive and hierarchical approach which the party is trying to put in place. Gorbachev is using nationalism for purposes not very different from those for which Lenin used it in the years following the October Revolution. (See Chapter Nine.)

Gorbachev's promotion of nationalism suggests how dire the situation in the Soviet Union has become. Gorbachev would rather bring about the dissolution of the country than risk the revolutionary overthrow of the Soviet elite.

The Communist leadership has not merely paid lip-service to nationalism. Evidence has come to light that Moscow itself organized and stage-managed the ethnic conflict in Azerbaijan "to create political chaos in the region that would justify strong central controls." According to reports, "Communist Party officials actively encouraged the growth of a nationalist political movement in Azerbaijan, the Popular Front, and tried for almost a year to turn it toward more chauvinist and militant activities." In addition, "The police and the KGB appear to have had advance knowledge of the anti-Armenian attacks that broke out in Baku on Jan. 13, but did not move to prevent them." Communist Party officials created "an unofficial Azerbaijani paramilitary organization, the so-called National Defense Commit-

tee...in an attempt to discredit the [more moderate] Popular Front."
As one local non-Communist leader put it, "I think now that all these
events were planned by the KGB, and the main director was [the
second secretary of the Azerbaijani Communist Party]."[243]

By both endorsing nationalism and attacking nationalist demonstrations, the Soviet elite is choosing the enemy and the ground on which
it wants to fight for continued control of the country. With this approach, the Soviet rulers can seem to be the arbiter between conflicting interests, and the only source of order in the society.[244]

The Future of Perestroika

Where will developments in the Eastern bloc lead? That is impossible to predict, of course; but developments in Poland, the Eastern
bloc country where events have unfolded most fully, point to the
uncertain future of the reforms. They also illustrate the counterrevolutionary role of the reformers.

The Solidarity movement in 1980-81 was at a crossroads; as an illegal organization of ten million workers, it had either to mount a
revolutionary challenge to Communist power, or to accept the continued existence of an hierarchical system in exchange for some reforms within it. By a series of maneuvers, Lech Walesa and a group
of Solidarity intellectuals clustered around him—Jacek Kuron and
others—wrested control from more radical leaders in August, 1981,
and suppressed the democratic tendencies of the mass movement.

When Solidarity failed to press forward to challenge the regime,
the Communists seized the moment to impose martial law in December of 1981. The Walesa leadership, with its allies in the Catholic
Church hierarchy and the Western ruling class, called on workers not
to resist. Silesian coal miners and others heroically fought against
martial law; at least nine miners were killed.[245] But Walesa succeeded
in isolating them, and the resistance was crushed. Walesa used the
period of martial law to dismiss the popularly elected members of the
National Council of Solidarity and replace them with his own appoin-
tees. By the end of the martial law period, Walesa's grip on the organization was complete.[246]

In the summer of 1988, strikes began again, over the objections of
Walesa, at the shipyard in Gdansk, the Lenin steel mill, the mines of
Silesia, and elsewhere. The reformist Solidarity leadership was able
to persuade the strikers to give up their strikes only by reaching

agreement with the Communist government of General Jaruzelski; the strikers would return to work if Solidarity was officially recognized. With Solidarity recognized, Walesa set energetically about the task of trying to prevent further strike activity.

The Communist government had repeatedly been frustrated in its attempts to impose an austerity program on Polish workers; every attempted price rise brought strikes and protests. Mass strikes broke out again in January and February, 1989. Communist leaders for some months had called on Solidarity to join the government, wanting Solidarity to take responsibility for enforcing austerity; Solidarity leaders had repeatedly refused.

Finally in the spring of 1989 the Communist government and the Walesa leadership together called for elections, in which Poles for the first time in 40 years would have the opportunity to vote for non-Communists as well as Communists. More than 85% of the popular vote went to Solidarity candidates. The astonishing thing about the elections was not the unpopularity of the Communists, which was to be expected, but that, in this first chance to participate in "democratic" elections, only 62% of those eligible to vote did so.[247] Nothing could say more about popular disgust with the Solidarity approach of negotiations and reforms.

In the new government, the Communists continued in control of the police and armed forces, while Solidarity officials took public responsibility for capitalist reforms—an arrangement which displays the level of Communist-capitalist cooperation in perestroika. Walesa, in a "tactic designed to leave more room for maneuver, [so that he would not be] directly involved in making unpopular decisions," installed his friend, Solidarity leader Tadeus Mazowiecki, as prime minister.[248] General Jaruzelski, the Communist leader responsible for martial law, was made president.

Once in power, Solidarity imposed a painful new capitalism by shock treatment. The government brought about a 30 percent cut in economic activity. It devalued the currency, drastically raised prices, and closed down many factories and mines which were strongholds of union power. Unemployment, non-existent in Poland for forty years, in June, 1990 stood at 4.2%, with 570,000 out of work; it was expected to reach 10% by the fall.[249]

The Solidarity government embarked on a program of privatization. Initially it gave self-managing groups of workers the power to sell off assets, in hopes that workers themselves would break up large combines and shut down less productive enterprises. But the workers refused to put each other out of jobs. "'Those bloody self-management councils,' complained Jacek Bukowski, an adviser to the finance minister and strategist in privatization planning. 'They are very afraid of firing people and are trying to protect everyone.'"[250] The government found itself forced to change its approach. In July, 1990 it passed legislation which broke the power of the workers self-management councils and provided for the sale of 7,600 state enterprises, comprising 80 percent of the national economy, to private investors.[251]

Solidarity's policies have created a nation of paupers, who now can be forced to work for nearly nothing. The shutdown of Polish industry will further drive down wages. Walesa has warned that the changes could explode into "civil war," and complained that, "My house will be the first to be burned down."[252]

The Polish people have tolerated policies under the Solidarity regime which they would never have tolerated under the Communists, for two reasons—there seems to be no alternative, and they have been told that these hard times are merely a necessary transition period to a newfound prosperity.

It is not clear, however, that prosperity will come any time soon to most Poles. Indeed Western capitalists may be planning a quite different future for them. When questioned about the value of the changes in Poland to the West, one Western economist exulted, "The attraction of Poland for the West is that it has 38 million people and a very cheap labor force who will work for Filipino wages."[253] The most likely fate of Polish workers under capitalism is to be a continuing source of cheap labor. Even if development does come to Poland, it will be capitalist development—that is, development of a type which will attack the social relations and values which Polish working people hold dear.

But there are indications that time may be running out for the capitalist reformers and their Communist allies. Once an organization of over ten million, Solidarity now includes fewer than two million members. When miners in Polish Silesia went on strike in January, 1990 they refused to have any contact with representatives of Solidarity—suggesting that these workers, at least, have become aware that the Solidarity leaders are traitors.[254] Railwaymen went out on wildcat strike in May, 1990 refusing the leadership of Solidarity or the unions; a national crisis was averted only by the personal intervention of Walesa. At the same time, the first elections in Poland in forty years in which no Communists were guaranteed seats were conducted; only 42% of the eligible voters participated.[255] A sit-in by Polish

ed a leading role in Solidarity since the imposition of martial law
981.

a February, 1990, in Gdansk, I spent many hours talking with
llectuals active in Solidarity. Woitek Kubinski had been a trans-
r for Lech Walesa in 1980-81. During martial law he was impris-
d for a year for producing an underground newspaper; after his
ase, he was elected to a leadership position in Solidarity. At the
e of our meeting, he was a rank-and-file member of the organiza-
, Richard Wenzel was Chairman of the Solidarity Humanities
lty and on the Executive Council of Solidarity for the Gdansk
on. Both were assistant professors of linguistics at the University
dansk.

oth were ferociously right-wing. They saw Margaret Thatcher and
ald Reagan as "the greatest political leaders of the twentieth cen-
." Their goal for Poland is capitalist economic development, gui-
by the International Monetary Fund, so that, "in 15 years or so,
nd might be on a level with Spain or Greece." They fear only
Polish workers might not share their vision.

hey lamented that "Many Poles still see capitalists as bloodsuck-
They still identify capitalism with the exploitation of labor." This
cause "These people [Polish workers] have been misled by Com-
ist propaganda." What workers need to learn, they claimed, is
"Capitalism is the only natural form of human society....capital is
ifeblood of society." It is true that "Many people think that capit-
n is undemocratic. But," they explained, "that is because these
le do not understand the difference between politics and econo-
."

admit that I was taken aback by the discussion. I had hoped to
activists who were critical of both Communism and capitalism.
ad these Solidarity leaders refused to admit that capitalism is a
al system, or in fact that it has any serious problems. Their re-
se to me was, "Yes, capitalism may have some problems. But
talism is like a cold; Communism is like cancer." Communism,
said, is a "Mafia system; Communists are like gangsters who
t and steal from everyone and produce nothing. Capitalists are
ucers. Capitalists would not cheat or steal from their workers.
y bring wealth to the society...."

felt like I had been transported to Never-Never Land. These in-
ctuals—Solidarity officials, to be sure, so they had a stake in de-
ing the policies of the organization—were living a fantasy. In op-

farmers at the Ministry of Agriculture in June, 199
by the first use of police violence by the Solidarit

Developments in Poland make clear that the ch
italist reforms is to destroy the growing power of
the Soviet bloc. They also illustrate the need fo
overthrow of the capitalist reformers as well as tl
lies.

The great fear of the Soviet and the world elite
Communist bloc countries, in particular the Soviet
in authentic democratic revolution that could swee
over the Communist world and into the capitalist \

They take the possibility very seriously. Boris '
head of the Communist Party in Moscow and no
republic of Russia, said on "Good Morning, Ame
of 1989 that Gorbachev has "not more than one
about six months....before he could face revolution
has already started in the form of strikes, but to
strikes, hot spots here and there in the country. /
occur when these hot spots spread and the whol
ted."[257] In an appearance before the Council on F
New York, Yeltsin warned that the Soviet Union I
or less to succeed in reform from above. "We are
abyss, and if we go over the edge, it will lead t
only for the Soviet Union but for the whole wor
December, 1989, Gorbachev urged caution movin
economy, arguing that "a rapid transition would i
revolution that would sweep away the most well-i
ment."[259]

The Role of Intellectuals in Perestro

With the exception of Poland, there has been a s
workers playing an organized role in these Eastern
utions." The leading forces have been intellectuals
professionals. Demonstrations which led to the resi;
German government were organized by church activ
unions. Communist governments in Czechoslovakia
rendered power after a few demonstrations by s
citizens and brief token strikes. Even in Poland,

posing Communism, they had closed their eyes to the horrors of capitalism.

The role of intellectuals in the Solidarity movement was evident in
this and other discussions in Poland. The intellectuals function as the
ideological henchmen of the new capitalist order—precisely in the
way they functioned decades ago on the opposite side, as the ideological champions of Communism. Their role is to wrap a vicious system in a dressing of philosophy and history, and to beat down with
their intellectual "superiority" the misgivings of workers who persist
in the delusion that capitalism means exploitation.

The role of intellectuals in other countries of the Eastern bloc and
in China has been similar: to equate democracy and capitalism, and
to champion privatization and the "free market" as the answer to
Communism.[260]

Why are the intellectuals of the Communist countries fighting for
capitalism? There are two reasons. One is the lack of an alternative
social paradigm to capitalism and Communism. The second is the
nature of the relationships which characterize the lives of people in
the professional and intellectual classes.

The reason that Polish intellectuals have championed the new capitalist order is essentially the same reason that Polish workers have
tolerated the suffering brought about by it—because capitalism seems
like the only possible alternative to the hated Communist system.
Professionals in the Eastern bloc are caught in the same bind as the
working class; most of them aspire to a society based on equality and
cooperation, but there has been no revolutionary alternative to Marxism and capitalism put forward for them to fight for. (The Solidarity
intellectuals with whom I talked all agreed that there was a time—in
1980-81, when Solidarity included 10 million workers, and was led
by the working class—that they thought they could create a truly new
society, a "Solidarity Society," not capitalist and not Communist. But
that no longer seemed to be a real possibility.)

There is, however, an important difference in the reactions of intellectuals and workers to the imposition of capitalism. Individuals of
the middle class, by training and life experience, have fewer collective social relations than workers; their social relations have been
more fractured by the hierarchical culture in which they have risen to
or have been trained in their middle-class status. Unlike workers,
intellectuals do not have in their own social relationships a source for
an alternative view of life as a vantage point from which to criticize
capitalism or to imagine an alternative society. Intellectuals do not

shut down shipyards; they have little experience of collective struggle against authorities. They turn more naturally to a competitive view of life than to an egalitarian and collectivist one. The different reactions of intellectuals and workers in the Eastern bloc to capitalism is not based on mere self-interest; that would be an economistic explanation, consistent with capitalist or Marxist views of human motivation. The differences are moral and cultural, based on class understanding rooted in their everyday social relations.

In an important sense, the Eastern bloc intellectuals' embrace of capitalism is based on intellectual and moral despair. I asked a leading intellectual of the Hungarian community in Romania, Salat Levente, whether he or his colleagues believed in the possibility of creating a democratic "third way," not Communist and not capitalist. He said to me:

> "In the '70s we believed for awhile that the West is in a crisis of moral values. We thought we had something to say to the West about values. Then in the '80s we learned how lying and false was Communist society. Now we see that our only possibility is to create civil society."

It seems that the discovery by East bloc intellectuals of the falseness of Communism has led them to abandon all that they understood about the falseness of capitalism. "We are all convinced now," said Salat Levente, "there is no third way."

The large class of professionals and disaffected intellectuals in the Communist bloc is capable of taking either a revolutionary or a counterrevolutionary path. They will take a revolutionary path, however, only when a new model of social change, rooted in the values and social relations of the working class, which makes an alternative to capitalism and Communism seem possible, is held out to them.

The Uprising In China

In contrast to events in the Soviet bloc, the 1989 spring uprising in China represented a revolt against nearly a decade of capitalist restructuring. The China spring can only be understood against the background of the economic reforms put in place by the Chinese Communist Party as part of its response to the Cultural Revolution of the 1960s.

Background To Revolt:
The Economic Reforms In China

The genuine revolutionary movement of the 1960s ignited by Mao's "pseudo-revolution" came perilously close to overthrowing the Chinese Communist Party. With the defeat of the ultra-left revolution, the party began a long struggle to consolidate its hold on the political and economic life of China. Its efforts to reassert control coincided with the counteroffensive of capital on a world scale against the revolutionary upsurge of the 1960s, and were at least to some extent coordinated with it. Mao met with Nixon in 1972, in an historic opening to the West which signalled the Chinese elite's desire to become one with the world elite. The Chinese Communist Party increasingly integrated the Chinese economy into world economic structures, even as it increasingly adopted the political and managerial techniques of Western capitalism to control its restless population.

It had become clear to the Chinese elite during the Cultural Revolution that they could not continue to rule China with a collectivized population mobilized to achieve avowedly revolutionary goals. To reassert control, the Chinese elite embarked on a program of capitalist reforms. These reforms accelerated after Mao's death in 1976, and have been in full force since 1982.

The reforms broke up peasant communes, privatized agriculture and much industrial production, introduced piece rates and large wage differentials among workers, encouraged private enterprise and entrepreneurs, created widespread unemployment among peasants and workers while they destroyed social welfare programs, and opened up large sections of China to foreign investors.

Though these reforms were promoted in the name of modernization and economic development, their real purpose was to consolidate the political power of the Chinese elite.

In spite of the turmoil in China during the 1960s, the Cultural Revolution spurred real advances in the economy. Mao's policies encouraged collective development of Chinese land and industry, with mass participation in deciding the goals and methods of production. Maoism emphasized the human factor in production, and stressed moral incentives—rather than material gain—and political consciousness as the basis of economic effort. Millions of peasants planted forests and built dams, irrigation systems and roads, terraced hillsides and reclaimed waste areas for agriculture. Workers collectively designed new machines and production techniques. Small- and medium-scale industries sprang up around the country, based on economic decentralization, local initiative, and the Maoist idea of Chinese self-reliance and cooperation.[261]

The problem with these policies for the ruling elite, as the Cultural Revolution developed, was not economic but political: they encouraged a level of popular mobilization which had turned revolutionary and threatened to break the grip of the Communist Party on Chinese society. Egalitarian and collective social relations were part of traditional Chinese peasant culture and were nurtured by Maoism. In the ultra-left current in the Cultural Revolution, these egalitarian and collectivist relations became an openly revolutionary culture. Capitalist economic reforms were intended to demobilize the people by fracturing their communal relationships, promoting competition and inequality in their stead.

These reforms brought huge dislocations to the lives of ordinary people:

> Fifty million peasants have left their homes in search of work in the towns and cities. They overload trains; turn railroad stations into flop houses; strain the supplies of food and water in urban areas; and provide an industrial labor force for industry and municipal services as they seek wages that are superior to those available in the countryside. Free-market experiments [have] opened the floodgates to a revival of regional and class distinctions. A flourishing private sector has engendered wealthy entrepreneurs, private financiers, merchants large and small, and a class of managers and executives who work for foreign companies....Prostitution, one of the first diseases of the old regime to be suppressed by the Revolution, has also returned, as has the use of opium.[262]

China's constitution was amended in 1982 to outlaw strikes, and special economic zones were established to which foreign capital was invited to exploit cheap Chinese labor. A 1988 *Business Week* article reported that, in these zones and spreading farther into the mainland, "Chinese investigators recently discovered children as young as 10 making toys, electronic gear, and artificial flowers. They work up to 14 and 15 hours a day at salaries ranging from $10 to $31 a month. Often workers sleep two or three to a bed in dormitories." To meet toy orders for the Christmas rush, workers were required to put in one or two twenty-four hour days, with only two meal breaks. The

Chinese government, *Business Week* reported, was concerned at rising levels of worker unrest. One factory alone experienced 21 work stoppages and strikes in 1986 and 1987.[263]

The privatization of land, with the consequent beaking up of large fields into tiny family plots, has rendered most of China's farm machinery useless; thousands of tractors and other items of mechanized equipment sit idly rusting in fields and warehouses. Government investment in agriculture, "measured as a proportion of its total budgetary expenditures, has plummeted to a third of 1978." Along with privatization, the government has shut down fully half of China's schools, reducing their number from 1,620,000 to 744,000 while the school-age population rose.[264] The government has thereby accomplished two important goals; it has freed up children to be laborers on de-mechanized family plots, and it has acted to lower the expectations which education might have brought the children of peasants and workers.

In an article based on repeated visits to the mountain village of Dazhai over a period of fifteen years, William Hinton reported on the effects of economic reform there. Dazhai had been held up by Mao as "a model of rural development, primarily because it practiced co-operation and self-reliance." Now the reformers hold it up as an example of the superiority of the "responsibility system"—the privatized system in which each family is responsible for its own profits and losses—over the cooperative egalitarianism practiced under Mao.

It is true, said Hinton, that under the system of private incentives, certain profit-making sidelines have flourished. But they have flourished at the expense of the agricultural infra-structure—terraced fields, irrigation systems, and the like—and other undertakings which depended on collective labor and a sense of responsibility to the whole community.

As a result, while some in the community have indeed been getting rich—by hiring out contract labor, and other forms of entrepreneurialism—agriculture is deteriorating, and "Dazhai, the village that once sold a higher proportion of its crop to the state than the big mechanized state farms on the virgin lands of the northeast, this year...raised too little grain to feed its own population." This is not just a problem in Dazhai but all over China. Following a peak year in 1984, grain output dropped substantially in 1985 and "has virtually stagnated since."

Describing the effects of reforms on Dazhai, Hinton says:

So what used to be a community of relatively equal laboring people who shared their collective income on the basis of work performed, is rapidly turning into a stratified community consisting of a well-to-do minority moving into position to realize unearned incomes, a middle income majority (many of them primarily wage workers), and a substrata of the poor, handicapped primarily by the lack of labor power. Capital assets including means of production held or controlled now have more to do with income levels than work done.[265]

It is true that there has been massive development in China in the past decade, but it has been development of a particular kind in a particular direction. The opening up of great areas of Southeast China as "special economic zones," the building of world-class hotels and office towers in Beijing to accomodate foreign businessmen and tourists, the privatization of communal property: all these both reflect and reinforce the consolidation of hierarchical power in a class society.

The creation of a new social hierarchy in Chinese society was no accident of the reforms; it was central to their purpose of forming a stable social basis for continuing rule by the party hierarchy. The Communist elite was attempting to create a large class of bureaucrats and businessmen and entrepreneurs sufficiently tied to the regime to support it against the impoverished masses.

The Communist Party hoped to achieve the same fragmentation within Chinese society that has served other ruling classes so well in theirs. The encouragement of individualism and competition, of enriching oneself at others' expense; the creation of a mass of unemployed and the withdrawal of means of social security; the conscious exacerbation of hierarchical divisions among workers and among peasants; the privatization of production and of social life: these were no more mere economic strategies in China than they are in contemporary England or America. Rather, they were strategies for social control, undertaken by a ruling class which, in the 1960s, had seen its power deeply threatened by an aroused people, and was determined that it not happen again.

China: The Media Picture
of the Spring Uprising

The revolt in China caught the official China-watchers by surprise. Before the uprising, China was the showcase among Communist nations turning to capitalist means of social control:

> Before the turbulence, experts looked at China and saw an economic miracle—a society that in little more than a decade has managed to propel itself from the bland egalitarian poverty of Maoism to the new-found consumerism of color television sets, earrings and disco dancing. During the last ten years, the average income in China has more than doubled.[266]

The picture of the spring uprising presented most consistently by the media is that: 1) the demonstrations were a student affair, though with much support from the people of Beijing; 2) the uprising was essentially a Beijing phenomenon, with little support in the provincial cities or from the peasants of the countryside; and 3) the goals of the uprising were for capitalist economic reforms, and for such freedoms as freedom of the press.

By treating the Chinese uprising as a fight for more capitalism, the media and politicians hoped to distort people's understanding of its significance and to limit its effects—to sympathy rather than imitation. It was presented as the triumph of capitalism rather than as a potential harbinger of world revolution.

The Goals of the Uprising

There were divergent class forces in the China uprising with divergent goals. Reform intellectuals and student leaders with ties to the party elite sought freedom of speech and the press and an end to the favoritism and corruption which characterize the Communist bureaucracy. As the Western media reported, they desired a continuation into the political sphere of the capitalist economic reforms which the Communist Party had imposed eight years earlier. Their goal was not revolution but reform under the continued guidance of the Communist Party.

The goals of workers and peasants in the struggle, and of students from less elite backgrounds, were not so clearly articulated, at least not in the Western media. Workers and peasants called for an end to inflation and unemployment, and they too were against corruption. But it hardly seems likely that the Chinese masses were in favor of more of the reforms that have ravaged their lives in the past eight years. More likely is that the uprising expressed deep popular revulsion against the changes in Chinese society brought about by the reforms.

As we have seen, the capitalist reforms attacked the egalitarian and collective relationships which reflect traditional peasant values and which have been central to Chinese life since the revolution of 1949. Communist Party literature reflects the struggle in China over social relations. For example, a 1987 article, "Socialism Is Not Egalitarianism," in *Beijing Review*, an official organ of the Chinese Communist Party, lamented that "many people [from 1958 to 1978] confused socialism with egalitarianism." It ascribed this confusion to "the traditional ideology of the peasantry and petty bourgeoisie." Peasant traditions of egalitarianism, it asserted, are the main obstacle to economic progress in China. The article called for overcoming egalitarianism through piece rates and market relations, "so that some people may become affluent first," and the economy may thereby be developed. Thus the "Marxist truth" would be fulfilled, that "Socialism promotes the development of economic forces, whereas egalitarianism hinders them."[267]

The values of Chinese workers and peasants and their goals for the society are embodied in their social relations. These communal relations have always been the engine of class struggle in China, and, as we have seen, have fueled frequent strikes in the past few years against the growing inequality in Chinese life. How fully these values were articulated by workers and peasants as goals for the spring uprising is not clear. To fulfill the vision of society implicit in these values, however, will require the overthrow of the Communist Party and the transformation of Chinese life by the people themselves.

The diverging goals of workers and peasants on the one hand and of the intellectual elite on the other led them to play diverging roles in the uprising.

The Role Of The Students

A Chinese writer, Liu Binyan, wrote in early May, 1989:

In China, student protest movements have always been the earliest reflections of the political mood of the people. Yet the scale
and momentum of this latest one reflects that the Chinese people's dissatisfaction with and anger at the Chinese Communist
Party have reached the highest level in 40 years. This mood reflects the seriousness of the Chinese political, economic, and
social crises.[268]

The student demonstrations gained their significance and momentum
from feelings shared by the people of China.

The role of the students in the mass uprising was complicated, but
quite different from the picture presented by the media. While they
may have sparked the revolt, the leading group of the students, as the
young elite of the country and in many cases the sons and daughters
of the present rulers, also attempted to hold the struggle back, to limit
its scope to capitalist reforms and prevent it from challenging the
Communist Party's grip on power. The original student protesters
were much like the original Red Guards in the Cultural Revolution,
who had close ties with the party elite, and whose goal was to reform
the party in order to strengthen it. (See Chapter Five.)

According to a prominent China scholar who witnessed the events,
the students who led the first pro-democracy protests were from the
Party History Department of the prestigious People's University:

"These kids have all been carefully screened before they are admitted to the Party History Department....Everybody knows they
are well-connected and are being groomed to be the future Communist leaders of China." The pro-democracy protests "were
originally not a movement against the party but a movement to
reform the party....Their goal was to restore the prestige of being
a party member, not to destroy the party."[269]

The prestige of the Communist Party in China had been in drastic
decline ever since the Cultural Revolution failed to result in revolutionary change. Writing before the June 4 massacre, Nicholas D.
Kristof, the *New York Times* bureau chief in Beijing, reported that:

long before the demonstrations....the party...suffered a prolonged
erosion of its moral authority—and its ability to intimidate.
Throughout the country, the love, fear and awe that the Com-

munist Party once aroused have collapsed into something closer to disdain or even contempt.[270]

One measure of that decline, said Kristof, is that, according to the *People's Daily*, since 1985 "13 tax collectors have been murdered, 27 crippled and 6,400 beaten up." Another is that "Waves of illegal migrant workers are sweeping across China, workers who search for new jobs without waiting to get permission." Fully 2.5 million of Shanghai's 14.5 million residents are there illegally. "In February and early March, more than 2.5 million laborers flooded into Canton, ignoring sharp warnings from the government."

The student leadership acted to suppress the potentially revolutionary character of the uprising, by keeping the demands of the movement within narrow bounds which did not threaten party domination and by physically protecting soldiers and government buildings from angry workers. The elite students played the role that they had been trained to play. Eventually, however, like the original Red Guards, the students helped ignite a revolutionary process which neither they nor the party could control.

The Breadth Of The Uprising

The uprising began with student protests after the death of Hu Yaobang, a Chinese official, on April 15, but quickly turned into riots "primarily by nonstudents" in two provincial capitals, the central China city of Xian and Changsa in southern Hunan Province. Authorities imposed martial law in Xian *a month before declaring martial law in Beijing*, after 50,000 demonstrators marched into the city center and destroyed government administration buildings.[271] The profile of those arrested in Changsa as "looters," charged with attacking 22 shops and a shopping arcade, gives some indication of the makeup of the demonstration: those arrested included "six students, 32 urban workers, 26 peasants who had come to work in the city, and six self-employed people."[272]

Western intelligence sources report that "protests flared across the length and breadth of China during the tumultuous months of April, May, and June." "'Serious unrest,'" involving hundreds of thousands of workers, students, and the unemployed, "broke out in more than 100 cities and major towns," according to an Asian diplomat interviewed by the *Boston Globe*.[273] On May 20, 300,000 protesters, marching in defiance of martial law there, "brought Xian to a standstill," while 500,000 demonstrated in Shanghai. Rallies "were reported in at least half a dozen other cities and even small villages."[274] In Shanghai, workers totally destroyed a troop train bound for Beijing when it ran over six workers blocking the tracks. (Two of the workers who burned the train were the first to be executed by the government after the uprising.) In Chengdu, at the time of the Beijing massacre, as many as 30 workers and peasants were killed and up to 300 injured when they went to the defense of students camping at the base of a statue of Mao Tse-tung. In the ensuing battle, the people "set fire to a sprawling market and a movie theater, ransacked vendors' stalls and trashed two tourist hotels." (The focus of these attacks—private markets and tourist hotels—may reflect a lack of popular enthusiasm for the capitalist reforms.) Similar events occurred in Shanghai, Xian, Lanzhou, Harbin, and Nanjing.[275] In Beijing itself, according to the *New York Times*, on May 4 and thereafter workers far outnumbered students in the continuing demonstrations.[276]

The Focus On Beijing

To some extent the media focus on Beijing and the lack of information about provincial China can be explained simply by the fact that Beijing is where the networks and the reporters were. But other areas of China were not inaccessible to Western reporters and observers until the government began to black out the news from all over China, Beijing included.

There was an important political reason for the near-total focus on Beijing. The concentration of attention by both the Chinese government and the Western media on the student hunger strikers and demonstrations in Tienanmen Square helped to maintain the leadership role of the students and to keep the movement within the reformist confines of the students' demands. It also helped to distort the Western public's understanding of the Chinese events.[277]

The student leaders made the hunger strike by two to three thousand students the focus of the protest movement. The hunger strike did not begin until more than two weeks after martial law had been declared in Xian, and workers and peasants had taken action in Changsa and some other cities. The hunger strike was thus a way of dampening the already explosive movement of workers and peasants. While the hunger strike was an effective tactic for rousing the interest

of the country in the student movement, it also kept the growing mass
movement within the bounds of the passivity of the hunger strikers,
as they awaited an offer of dialogue from the government—the future
leaders of the country offering to talk with its present leaders.

The hunger strike thus had the effect of demobilizing the population, by encouraging people to allow the student hunger strikers to act
on their behalf. The student elite in this way hoped to reduce the
population to the role of spectators in social change which would be
managed by the students.

Government power began to unravel soon after the demonstrations
began—an indication of the depth of popular feeling against the Communist Party. Government workers and even the staffs of the Communist Party newspapers declared their solidarity with the uprising.
The Communist leadership declared martial law in Beijing on May
20, but could not get its troops to enforce the order. Tens of thousands of citizens blocked the entrance of the troops into the city, and
the troops themselves clearly had no interest in carrying out their
orders.

For a substantial period—from some time after May 4, until shortly
before the successful crackdown of June 3-4—China was essentially
without a government; the leadership of China was up for grabs. CBS
News later reported that Deng Xiaoping and the other top party leadership had thought their time was up after the May 4 demonstration
brought over a million people into the streets, and spent from May 5
until May 20 converting their wealth into $27 million in cash with
which to flee to the West.

The situation cried out for the aspirations of the great majority of
Chinese to be articulated as a revolutionary vision of a new China,
and it cried out for revolutionary initiative—for the mass movement
to take over the government buildings and the factories, set up
workers' and peasants' and soldiers' councils, and declare itself for
the destruction of the Communist Party and the building of a new
society.

The elite students not only were not prepared to offer revolutionary
leadership—they actively tried to prevent it from emerging. The elite
students struggled to maintain leadership of the movement, even while
they kept their demands within the bounds of reform, and declared
themselves on the side of "non-violence." Student leaders actively
prevented the participation of workers in the discussions in Tienanmen Square, fearing that the demands of the workers were too radical. When workers organized a Workers' Autonomous Federation—an

independent workers' organization parallel with the Students Autonomous Federation—in Beijing, student leaders kept it at arm's length and refused to allow it to establish a headquarters in Tienanmen Square.[278] The students frequently acted to prevent workers from attacking soldiers and government buildings. Student leaders set up an around-the-clock guard to protect the Communist Party headquarters from the wrath of workers.

The passive approach encouraged by the students allowed the initiative to pass over to the hands of the government at precisely the time when a revolutionary situation had developed in the country. It is true that, had the mass of workers clearly understood that revolutionary change was possible and necessary, nothing the students could have done would have stopped them. But in the absence of organized revolutionary leadership among the workers, and given the students' enormous prestige and connections, the student elite was able to prevent the initiative in the crisis from passing from the government to the people.

The students themselves were divided. Students at Beijing University rejected pleas to return to their classes by the leaders of the United Association of Beijing Universities, the new organization begun with the student protests, and voted on May 7 to continue their boycott of classes.[279] According to reports, students coming from the provinces to join the demonstrations in Beijing were more radical than the Beijing students; not being from elite backgrounds themselves, the provincial students wanted to push for far more drastic change—again, in much the same way as the rebel Red Guards, without ties to the party leadership, were prepared to attack the party. While many of the original students reportedly had departed by the time the crackdown came, the more radical students stayed in the square and fought the troops alongside workers.

The breathing space handed by the elite student leadership to the Communist Party allowed the government to regain its composure and organize its forces for the violent suppression of the movement. Probably no one will ever know how many thousands of brave workers and students and other people died at the hands of the government troops on June 4 and in the following weeks. The U.S. government estimated 3,000 on June 4 alone. Other estimates were as high as 20,000.[280]

The Future of China

The Western media presented the most important struggle in China as one between leaders at the top, the "hard-liners" against the "reformers." According to the media, Deng Xiaoping and Li Peng, who headed the government, were "hardliners"; Zhao Ziyang, who fell from government favor after supposedly disagreeing with the crackdown on the students, was the leading reformer. The media and Western political figures consistently promote the idea that the real change needed in China is not the overthrow of the Communist Party, but some new faces at the top—chiefly, that of Zhao.

This is a farcical distortion of the situation by the capitalist media. It was Deng the "hard-liner" who championed and imposed the capitalist reforms against which people are rebelling. Beneath the distortion one can perceive the deep fear of the Western elite that the Chinese Communist Party might lose control, and that China will undergo real revolution from the bottom-up. In addition to confusing people here, the Western elite hope (through Voice of America broadcasts, and by influencing the tens of thousands of Chinese students in the West) to deflect the Chinese people's anger from the Communist ruling class as a whole, and to persuade them to be satisfied with a shuffling of personalities at the top, in much the same way that "democracy" works in the West.

The prestige which the Chinese Communist Party enjoyed historically among the Chinese people came from its leading role in a revolution which people thought would lead to an equal and communal society. In the wake of the government crackdown, the Communist Party clearly feels that, to regain popular support, it must try to re-establish its image as the champion of the values and hopes of ordinary Chinese. The government has backed away from its slogans of the era of capitalist reforms, such as "To get rich is glorious," and dusted off some of the more egalitarian-sounding slogans of the previous era. In an attempt to stifle popular discontent with the growing gap between the rich and poor, the Chinese government has clamped down on the private sector by withdrawing government loans and restricting the supplies of scarce raw materials available to private businesses. According to reports, "more than 15% of small private businesses have been forced to shut down this year for lack of loans or raw materials."[281]

As we have seen, elite forces—students from ruling class backgrounds and intellectuals—played a critical role in preventing the spring uprising from taking on a revolutionary character. In the wake of the Communist Party's violent suppression of the democracy movement, capitalist institutions in the West are doing what they can to promote the dissident forces inside and outside China who oppose overthrowing the party and seek only a measure of political reform within a hierarchically-controlled society. The U.S. media have lionized students like Wu'er Kaixi, "the Chinese Lech Walesa," and dissident physicist Fang Lizhi, whom they hope will prevent any movement from becoming explicitly revolutionary. Wu'er, who has fallen into some disrepute for high living and accepting large cash gifts from wealthy Americans, has called for "a campaign of non-violence" to reform China. From his refuge in the U.S. embassy in Beijing, Fang has repeatedly expressed his devout wish that Chinese will "refrain from violence" in making change.[282] Yan Jianqi, chairman of the Front for a Democratic China, affirmed in the fall of 1989 that its goal is not transformation of Chinese society, but power-sharing with the Communists: "Our goal is to overturn one-party rule by the Communist Party, not to overthrow the Communist Party. We want to use peaceful, non-violent means."[283] Of course, the key to change in China is not that it be violent, but that it be democratic and thoroughgoing; by their emphasis on non-violence, these leaders are making plain that they only want such change as can be made without seriously jeopardizing the existing power structure.

The key questions are what kind of change is necessary in China to achieve democracy, and what kind of movement will it take to achieve it. Real democracy cannot consist of capitalist economic reforms plus political "pluralism." Multiplying the number of parties at the top of Chinese society would simply be a way for new elites to share the power and privileges of the Communists, while they exploit the working people of China. Truly democratic change must reflect the values and express the aspirations of the great mass of people—the peasants and workers and students—and must be created by them. The capitalist economic reforms of the last decade and the Chinese Communist Party must both be swept away as part of the process of creating an egalitarian and communal society.

The first task of a movement is to make explicit the revolutionary values of equality and solidarity which should shape Chinese society, and to show that these values already exist in the lives and aspirations of ordinary Chinese.

A movement for democracy in China cannot have its source in the elite classes. While it should encourage the participation of students, a new movement must express the aspirations of working people and peasants. The movement must push from its path those intellectuals and students who block the road to revolution. It can only do this by breaking with the Marxist model of revolution which legitimizes the dominant role of intellectual elites, and the capitalist model which legitimizes the rule of the wealthy. A new revolutionary movement in China must establish itself on a view of people which sees in ordinary Chinese the source of a new society.

The events of the spring of 1989 have exposed the destructive role of the Communist Party in Chinese society in a way without parallel. However ferocious and effective the government crackdown may be in suppressing revolutionary struggle in the short run, in the long run it cannot succeed. The heroism of the uprising has brought authentic democratic revolution in China immeasurably closer.

In the wake of the rebellion a Chinese economist predicted, "The economy will face a crisis situation within two years, and next time people rise up they won't be led by students and it won't be so peaceful."[284]

What Do People Want?

It is hard for us in the West to get a very clear sense of what people in the East are after. Western politicians and the media have gone to great lengths to make us believe that the people of the East want capitalism. Capitalist commentators use "democracy" and "capitalism" interchangeably; a demand for democracy is a demand for capitalism. Indeed, don't the hundreds of thousands of East Germans who fled to the West seem to support these claims?

In February and March, 1990 I traveled in the German Democratic Republic (East Germany), Poland, Romania, and Hungary, interviewing intellectuals and activists, political leaders and ordinary working people, to discover the real situation and what people thought about it.

At a small restaurant in East Berlin, I asked the East German workers seated with me their opinions of "the changes" and their hopes for the future. Like most other East Germans I spoke with, they did not want reunion, though they felt it was inevitable. They wanted, they said, "a Europe without weapons, without NATO and without Warsaw Pact, without nuclear power plants and without dirty air. We want that all people should be one big, happy family." We discussed the situation in Poland. They said that "If the bosses here cut our wages or try to close our factories...we sit down in the factories, we sit down in the streets, we sit down everywhere." (Later that afternoon, walking in Berlin, I spoke with an American investor on his way to Leipzig, in what was then the German Democratic Republic. He was going there, he said, to meet with the leaders of the opposition, to find out if they thought they could control the workers; he had a great deal of pension fund money to invest if they could promise a smooth transition to capitalism. I told the investor what the German workers had just told me about striking. He said, "Oh Christ, that's just what we're afraid of.")[285]

I had expected to find optimism and a sense of possibility in the countries I visited. Instead I found fear and bleak resignation. When I asked a young woman in Poland, "What are your hopes for the future," she replied, "I have no hope for the future." Her husband was somewhat embarrassed by her reply, and said, "My wife is younger than me. This is the way young people think." (She was 28, her husband 34.) "Is this true?" I asked. "Do other young people think this way?" "Yes," she said, "all of my friends feel this is true. There is no hope."

People in other countries expressed similar feelings. A retired skilled worker in Romania told me he had "only terrible fears" for the future; a Romanian locomotive engineer said that "my hopes in the [December] revolution have diminished by 50% since December." A newspaper editorial in Budapest pondered whether Hungary was a nation bent on suicide, the feeling of depression among the people was so palpable.

The widespread hopelessness in Eastern Europe seemed to reflect something more fundamental than the economic dislocations of the transition from Communism to capitalism. What seemed to underlay people's pessimism was a feeling that their future was not in their hands. These were not people who were confidently creating a society which expressed their hopes and their values. They were people who had thrown off Communist dictatorships, only to have them replaced by regimes from which they already felt distant, and by market forces which were already having devastating effects.

In spite of media manipulation, there is plenty of evidence that capitalism is not what Soviet-bloc people want. The *Boston Globe* of October 24, 1989 printed a picture of a mass demonstration in East Germany, with the caption, "Protestors in the East German city of Schwerin calling for democracy yesterday." In the picture one could just read the huge banner held by the demonstrators. It read, "Social-ismus Ja—Kapitalismus Nein": Socialism Yes, Capitalism No. This does not seem to be the demand of people calling for a society run by Bush and Exxon.

Once the Berlin Wall was opened, over two million East Germans visited the West in the first few days. According to reports, while they were excited by the chance to visit and shop, many were "appal-led" at what they saw. A West Berlin official, Hans Müller, said, "The East Germans, they just don't like capitalism. They don't like pornography, they don't like beggars, they don't like dirt on the street, they don't like expensive apartments." Müller continued, "The main difference is that on the other side of the wall the people have a strong sense of equality at every level....Being exposed to the ex-tremes of wealth and poverty is a shock to them."[286]

In October and November, 1989 East Germans had a powerful sense of possibility; they really thought that they could create a new alternative society. But while there was a huge mass movement ex-pressing very radical ideas about the future it wanted, there was no revolutionary leadership and no non-Marxist, non-capitalist model for establishing a new society. The leaders of New Forum, the broad-based movement which led the early demonstrations against the Com-munist government, seemed mainly interested in preventing the move-ment from taking radical action. The United Left, a coalition of anti-capitalist organizations, remained trapped within a discredited Marx-ism. In addition to these, East Germans had only the bourgeois par-ties—the Social Democrats and the Christian Democrats—and the Communists to choose from.

The government of West Germany, and indeed the entire world elite, was deathly afraid that East Germans would create a revolution-ary democratic society, which might quickly be imitated elsewhere. To get control of the situation, West German leaders took steps to bring about the reunification of Germany at an astonishing pace.

With West Germany's forceful moves toward reunification, the possibility of independent alternative development seemed suddenly to slip from the grasp of East Germans. Their hopes for the future rap-idly diminished—from creating a new society to merely making a suc-cess of reunification. In the April, 1990 elections, the conservative Christian Democrats, allied with the ruling party of West Germany, won an overwhelming victory—bringing another torrent of media claims that East Germans just want capitalism.

There had been a time, people in various East-bloc countries told me, when they thought they could create something new. In Poland, for example, back in 1980-81, when Solidarity was led by shipyard workers and miners and other ordinary people and had ten million members, Poles thought they could create what they called a "Solidarity Society"—a society not Communist and not capitalist, based upon the values and relationships of a democratic movement. Martial law put an end to the open mass movement in 1981; by 1990 millions had left Solidarity in disgust with its direction. The mass movement had been replaced by Solidarity politicians in a parliament, making laws designed to privatize public assets and to enforce labor discipline and to encourage Western corporations to establish factories in Poland. The Poles no longer felt that they were on a path to a bright and shining future, but to the only future which seemed possible—capitalism as the alternative to Communism.

In Romania the story was similar. The hopefulness of the days immediately following the December revolution was being replaced by a fearful realization that Romanians could either submit to continued domination by ex-Communist National Salvation Front politicians, or surrender to the same market forces which were beginning to ravage the rest of Eastern Europe.

If capitalism does not seem to be the real goal of Eastern Europeans, it also seems unlikely that more capitalism is what Chinese workers and peasants and students wanted in the spring of 1989, as they marched under red flags and sang the "Internationale." The "Internationale," written in 1872 in the wake of the Paris Commune, has been ever since then the international anthem of revolutionary workers' struggles. It is a call for revolution and democracy:

Arise, you prisoners of starvation; arise, you wretched of the
  earth.
For justice thunders condemnation. There's a better world in
  birth.
No more tradition's chains shall bind us, to the past no more in
  thrall.
The earth shall rise on new foundations. We have been
  nought, we shall be all.
'Tis the final conflict. Let each stand in his place.
The international working class shall be the human race.

"There is a legend spreading in China," reported Harrison Salisbury from Beijing, "of the hundred students who, when the tanks entered Tienanmen Square, locked arms and stood together singing the 'Internationale' while the bullets sprayed into their bodies. And then another 100 took their place and met the same fate. It makes no difference, really, whether this happened or not," said Salisbury. "Beijing simply believes that it occurred and the legend is spreading all over the country."[287]

We know enough about people to realize that the capitalist media are lying about the goals of the uprising in the Communist world. People everywhere want the same things, and neither capitalism nor Communism can provide them.

Revolution and the Twentieth Century

On the surface, the collapse of Communism and the adoption by Communist parties of capitalist economic and political forms do seem to represent victories for capitalism. But this would only be true in reality *if capitalism and Communism had truly been in a contest over conflicting social goals.* As we know, however, they were not; in spite of certain differences, they shared the same goal—control of the populace on behalf of the elite.

Communism was a means of creating economic development and enforcing elite control in places where private capitalism could not. The chief difference between the two systems lay in their strategies for control. Capitalism relies ideologically on the individual striving to enrich himself, backed up by the consequences of failure; Communism relies on an ideology of cooperation to produce for the common good, backed up by direct state repression.

Communism has long operated as a system of elite control in cooperation with world capital. While Communist domination of the "socialist bloc" restricted capital penetration of these countries and the growth of the world market, it represented the best *possible* alternative for capitalism. Communism was able to win people's allegiance only because it seemed revolutionary; the alternative to Communism in the areas of the world under Communist domination was not market capitalism but working class revolution.

Revolution is the driving force of the twentieth century. The rhythm of the century is revolution and counterrevolution; its defining events—World War I and World War II, the Bolshevik Revolution and the Chinese Revolution—were driven by the same force. World War I developed largely out of the world elite's fear of working class revolution. Desperate to maintain control, the ruling classes maneuvered their respective peoples into mutual national hatreds, and finally sent them to slaughter each other at Verdun and Ypres and the Somme. World War II also originated from world capitalism's struggle against revolution. The wealthy of England and France and America, as well as of Germany and Italy, admired and financed Hitler and Mussolini precisely because the Fascists were the only people capable of smashing the forces of workers' revolution in Italy and Germany. Capitalist politicians "appeased" Hitler because they wanted a strong Germany to rearm and attack the Soviet Union. It was only when Hitler double-crossed them and began to challenge their own power that British and American capitalists decided to fight him.

Capitalist strategies of counterrevolution succeeded only because of the assisting role played by Marxism. The Marxist parties of Europe, loyal to the elites of their own countries, led their working class members into battle against workers of other countries in World War I. In World War II, Marxist-Leninist parties cooperated with the ruling elites in the fight against Fascism, and then, when that fight was over, continued their alliance with capital to suppress working class revolutionary forces. Since the war, the Soviet Union has comanaged the world with its supposed bitter adversary, the U.S., behind the cover of the Cold War.

During the Stalin era, Communism destroyed many of the forces of working class revolution in Russia, and succeeded in trapping the conscious revolutionary movement of the world in a Marxist mythology which has until now proved an impenetrable barrier to the development of a new revolutionary movement. The last great wave of world revolution was defeated in 1968-69 by Communism. It had that power in part because it still had some revolutionary credibility, in part because there was no apparent alternative.

The revolutionary forces of the twentieth century have been thwarted and distorted because they have been trapped within an historical vision which does not see the source of the power to build a new world in the lives of ordinary people. Communism today seems utterly without revolutionary credibility. This lack of credibility does not in itself assure that the movement for change will adopt a new paradigm which can be the vehicle of its self-consciousness, but it creates that possibility as never before.

Capitalism has survived the twentieth century only because Communism has been there at every step along the way to prop it up. The collapse of Communism is a defeat for world capitalism of historic dimensions. The world elite may succeed in the short run in managing change from the top down in China and in the Soviet bloc. In the long run, however, they face the revolutionary aspirations of a world working class without the benefit of the organizational and ideological tools which Communism has provided to manage workers and suppress their struggles. The revolt against Communism shifts the forces of history immeasurably toward world revolution.

There are already models that authentic democratic revolution could take in the Communist world: the Kronstadt soviet of sailors, soldiers, and workers of 1921; the Hungarian workers' councils of 1956; the People's Commune of China of 1966-69—without Mao and without the Communist Party. All these represent forms of mass democracy, forged by working people in revolutionary struggle and expressing their will.

But models of democratic revolution are not enough. The crucial factor in the success of a revolutionary movement is the view of people upon which it is *consciously* founded. These previous efforts to overthrow the Communists failed because they did not understand why Communism had turned counterrevolutionary. Without a revolutionary critique of Marxism, the road to revolution is always blocked.

Revolution in the Communist world will only come when people consciously set out to make it, and only when they consciously reject Marxism and organize people on the basis of a new paradigm and a new vision. The way has been prepared for revolutionary democracy as never before. It is now up to revolutionaries to develop in these vast popular movements a consciousness of their tasks.

Those who believe that the collapse of Communism will usher in a period of world peace will find themselves sadly mistaken.[288] In fact the world is entering a period far more dangerous than the Cold War. Except for the chance that world leaders would misjudge each others' actions, there was never real danger of widespread war breaking out during the Cold War, for the simple reason that beneath the saber rattling and speechifying done for public consumption, the real relationship between the Soviet Union and the United States was cooperation to suppress popular struggle. The fake war against each other provided Communist and capitalist elites the perfect cover for their real war against democratic revolution.

No ruling class can long survive if there is no external enemy against which it can mobilize people; in the absence of an outside threat, people begin to look at the structure of society as the real source of their problems. A Soviet official said in 1988, "We are going to do something very terrible to you. We are going to deprive you of an enemy." Capitalist and Communist elites for years used the Cold War to control their own peoples. Communism having collapsed as a credible external enemy, the ruling classes will have to find new enemies for people to fight.

These new enemies have already been identified for Americans—Japan, a re-unified Germany, and perhaps others. The outbreak of near civil war conditions in some parts of the Soviet Union, as the government there maneuvers different populations against each other, foretokens the future gambit of the world elite. They will return with a vengeance to national rivalries as the basis of internal control. We can expect a great intensification of attempts to promote competition with Japan, and great fears raised about Germany. Don't expect the rulers to abandon their armaments, at least not for long. More likely, expect Japan and Germany to rearm, and for U.S. politicans to wring their hands about it and call for more weapons.

We are returning to the conditions which preceded two world wars. The choice again becomes, build a world revolutionary movement to overthrow the rulers and create society on a new basis, or be led to the slaughter, which is the only way the elite can continue their rule.

PART FOUR

Part Four describes an alternative view of history as the basis of a new kind of revolutionary movement. It discusses the meaning of political activity, the nature of the revolutionary movement, and the role of the revolutionary party which follow from a new model of social change and a new view of people.

12

HISTORY AND REVOLUTION

In 1851 a peasant revolt of exceptional size swept southwest China. The revolt had begun a few years earlier with the preaching of one Hung Hsiu-ch'uan, the educated son of a poor peasant family, in the mountains of Kwangsi province. Hung preached traditional peasant egalitarianism, mixed with Christian and ancient Chinese religious ideas, and leavened with modernizing concepts borrowed from the West. He recruited landless peasants, coolies, miners, charcoal burners, and disbanded soldiers to the movement, which then rose in open revolt against the traditional enemies of the peasants: landlords, gentry, and officials of the Manchu dynasty.

The peasant army left its home province in 1853 and marched through central China to the northeast. As they advanced, the troops were supported by spontaneous peasant uprisings; the peasants put officials and wealthy and unpopular landlords to death, burned tax registers and land registers, and sacked government offices. A contemporary chronicler described the progress of the peasant army:

> Each time they entered into a rich house, or into that of a great family, they would dig three feet into the ground [to find buried treasure]. But not only did they not plunder the peasants, on the contrary, wherever they passed they distributed clothes and other things they had taken to the poor, and announced a remission of taxes for three years, thus winning the gratitude of the villagers.[289]

The peasant army captured the ancient capital of Nanking, where it established a dynasty known as the "Tai-ping Heavenly Kingdom," or "The Celestial Kingdom of Great Peace."

In that same year, the Taipings promulgated their "Land System of the Celestial Dynasty." The dictates of the law clearly displayed the aspirations which lay behind the revolution:

All lands under Heaven shall be farmed jointly by the people
under Heaven....Land shall be farmed by all; rice, eaten by all;
clothes, worn by all; money, spent by all. There shall be no inequality, and no person shall be without food or fuel. No matter
whether man or woman, everyone over sixteen years shall receive land.[290]

The same collectivist ideas were to govern industrial production,
which was to be organized by means of "artisans' battalions," the
products of which were to go into "state treasuries," to be shared by
all.

The Taiping Heavenly Kingdom survived for eleven years. Nanking fell in the summer of 1864 to imperial armies aided by France
and England.

History is full of such uprisings of peasants and the urban
poor—the "toiling classes." The Chinese historian Wang T'ien-chiang
lists 58 revolts of various sizes in Hunan province alone from
1860-1895.[291]

Like many other movements of peasants and workers before the
twentieth century, the Taiping Heavenly Kingdom was characterized
by what Marxists call "primitive collectivism." It stood for equality,
collective working of the land, and communal sharing of all that is
produced. Like many other movements, it was savagely suppressed,
and is largely unknown to modern history.

Although history—as the real story of humanity's time on earth—is
full of such rebellions, recorded history is not. The history set down
by most bourgeois historians is filled with the strutting of kings and
the speeches of presidents; the struggles of the masses of people are
either entirely absent, or are accorded mere footnotes to texts which
describe the exploits of elites.

Marx rejected the bourgeois idea of history, which suggests that
the world is at the beck and call of ruling classes, to be shaped at
their will. His theory of historical materialism attempted to show that
larger forces of economic and technological development underlie the
actions and even the thoughts of men. According to Marx, the rulers'
apparent control of their destiny is illusory, because the actions of
ruling classes lead over time to results contrary to their intentions—in
particular, the actions of capitalists inevitably lead to capitalism's
destruction: "What the capitalists produce above all are their own
gravediggers." History is moving inexorably toward the triumph of
the working class.

The power of Marxism as an idea derived largely from the revolutionary significance it gave to history. But, as we have seen, the idea of history that was so powerful in Marx was also problematic. While it showed a different outcome to history from the capitalist view, it was based upon the same paradigm, which sees economic development as the driving force of history, and elites as the chief actors.

A new theory of revolution demands a new theory of history—a new explanation of how change develops in human society. The paradigm of society which I am proposing does in fact imply both a theory of history and a new way of understanding the historical record; it allows us to see conscious human agency in the activity of ordinary people in history, and to see the role this agency has played as an historical force.

"The World Turned Upside Down"

Thomas Kuhn explains that one aspect of the crisis in an existing paradigm is that scientists using it in their investigations turn up what Kuhn calls "counter-instances," phenomena which do not fit the existing model. In the past several decades—during the continuing crisis of the Marxist paradigm of history—two Marxist historians, E.P. Thompson and Christopher Hill, have written histories of England which show that the English working classes in two crucial periods, during the bourgeois revolution of the mid-seventeenth century and the industrial revolution of the nineteenth century, played dramatically different roles from what the Marxist paradigm would lead one to expect.

In *The Making Of The English Working Class*, Thompson challenges the Marxist idea that the working class can be properly understood as the creation of industrial capitalism. "The making of the working class," says Thompson,

> is a fact of political and cultural, as much as of economic, history. It was not the spontaneous generation of the factory sytem. Nor should we think of an external force—the 'industrial revolution'—working upon some nondescript undifferentiated raw material of humanity, and turning it out at the other end as a 'fresh race of beings'....The working class made itself as much as it was made.[292]

Thompson points out that the industrialists of the nineteenth century were forced to organize and become conscious of their class interests by the strikes and revolutionary activities of the working class—the reverse of the order which Marx described.[293]

Capitalist rule had been established in England in the Revolution of 1642-1660, long before the industrial revolution of which Thompson writes. In his book, *The World Turned Upside Down*, Christopher Hill explains that:

> There were, we may oversimplify, two revolutions in mid-seventeenth-century England. The one which succeeded established the sacred rights of property (abolition of feudal tenures, no arbitrary taxation), gave political power to the propertied (sovereignty of Parliament and common law, abolition of prerogative courts), and removed all impediments to the triumph of the ideology of the men of property—the protestant ethic. There was, however, another revolution which never happened, though from time to time it threatened. This might have established communal property, a far wider democracy in political and legal institutions, might have disestablished the church and rejected the protestant ethic.[294]

Hill argues that, "From, say, 1645 to 1653, there was a great overturning, questioning, revaluing, of everything in England....[T]here was a period of glorious flux and intellectual excitement, when, as Gerrard Winstanley put it, 'the old world...is running up like parchment in the fire.' Literally anything seemed possible; not only were the values of the old hierarchical society called in question but also the new values, the protestant ethic itself."[295]

The ferment ran through all parts of the society. Thousands of "poor mechanicks" took to the road as itinerant preachers, preaching a subversive mixture of religious and political ideas. Assisted by the spread of printing and literacy, radicals and preachers dressed the new ideas in religious garb with allegorical interpretations of the Bible. Private property was the Fall of Man. "The casting out of covetousness and the establishment of a classless society will be a 'new heaven and a new earth.'"[296]

In 1647, in the New Model Army, the troops elected Agitators, two for each regiment, to demand redress of their grievances.[297] Rank-and-file troops drafted petitions dealing with political as well as military matters. Army radicals established relations with their civilian counterparts. Hill cites another historian to the effect that "there had been nothing like this spontaneous outbreak of democracy in any English or continental army before this year of 1647, nor was there anything like it thereafter till the Workers' and Soldiers' Councils met in 1917 in Russia."[298]

The most radical and forward-looking movement of the time was that of the Diggers, led by a servant named Gerrard Winstanley. The Diggers were part of a wider movement known as the Levellers. Huge portions of England were uncultivated wastes and commons which had been enclosed or claimed by gentry or large landowners. Diggers proposed to "dig up, manure, and sow corn upon the common waste ground." They established colonies at St. George's Hill and in many other places: at Wellingborough in Northamptonshire, Cox Hall in Kent, Iver in Buckinghamshire, Barnet in Hertsfordshire, Enfield in Middlesex, Dunstable in Bedfordshire, Bosworth in Leicestershire, and at unknown places in Gloucestershire and Nottinghamshire.[299]

The Diggers sent pamphlets and emissaries all over England to organize support, and "called upon the poor to organize themselves for political action."[300] They were not a mere fluke; as another historian writes, "The whole Digger movement can be plausibly regarded as the culmination of a century of unauthorized encroachment upon the forests and wastes by squatters and local commoners."[301]

Gerrard Winstanley estimated that from one-half to two-thirds of England was not properly cultivated. He developed a program for communal cultivation, which would allow for "capital investment in improvements without sacrificing the interests of the commoners." Hill writes that:

> Winstanley's conclusion, that communal cultivation of the commons was the crucial question, the starting point from which common people all over England could build up an equal community, was absolutely right. Winstanley had arrived at the one possible democratic solution which was not merely backward-looking....Collective cultivation of the waste by the poor could have had the advantages of large-scale cultivation, planned development, use of fertilizers, etc....The Diggers sowed their land with carrots, parsnips, and beans—crops of the sort which were to transform English agriculture in the seventeenth century by making it possible to keep cattle alive throughout the winter in order to fertilize the land.[302]

The Digger colony at Burford was dispersed by troops in May, 1649 and other colonies were suppressed at later dates.[303] After the collapse of the Digger colony at Cobham in 1652, Winstanley prepared a draft constitution for a "communist commonwealth," entitled *The Law of Freedom in a Platform*. True human dignity, he wrote, would be possible only when communal ownership was established and buying and selling of land and labor ceased. Hill describes it as a "possibilist"—as opposed to utopian—document. Winstanley dedicated the work to Cromwell, in the hopes that he would implement it.

The constitution provides for economic development, for a popular militia, for universal education for both sexes while doing away with specialized scholars "'living merely on the labors of other men.'" It extends the death penalty to murder, buying and selling, rape, or following the trade of lawyer or parson.[304] Two Postmasters were to be elected by each parish, who would, among other things, publish and reward any new inventions. Other measures would be taken, not merely to increase production, but to add "'to the beauty of our commonwealth.'"[305]

While Winstanley saw himself speaking for 'the poor despised ones of the earth,' he also saw his proposals benefitting humanity as a whole. Private property is the basis of conflict among men; "once the earth becomes a common treasure house again, as it must...then this enmity of all lands will cease, and none shall dare to seek dominion over others, neither shall any dare to kill another, nor desire more of the earth than another."[306]

Speaking of Winstanley's plans for a democratization and dissemination of all knowledge, Hill comments: "We can hardly say that Winstanley's vision was impossible; we can only say that it was never tried."[307]

Marx Turned Upside Down

Marx and Engels had been aware, of course, if not of the extent and depth, at least of the existence of the Leveller movement which Hill describes.[308] They referred to such movements as "utopian," because, at the time of these early movements, the economic conditions which in their view would have made possible the realization of the social vision of such movements had not yet developed. Marx and Engels believed that inequality was the basis of economic development; any demands for equality before the full development of a capitalist economy were utopian.

But the second revolution in seventeenth century England which Hill describes was not a mere utopian dream. The proposals of the Diggers for communal cultivation of the soil, for the extension of education to all, and for the rapid development and dissemination of scientific knowledge were not only quite within the realm of possibility; they were exactly what was needed to develop the economy.

The revolutionaries pointed the way forward on a road that was not taken. The ideas and policies of the forces which opposed the common people—the propertied classes—were not more realistic. They were simply backward-looking; they resulted in the Restoration of the monarchy in 1660, and in vigorous suppression not only of the egalitarian and communistic ideas of the lower classes, but also of the modernizing ideas which working class revolutionaries were espousing. The bourgeoisie suppressed the new scientific ideas and anything else which smacked of revolution in favor of the restoration of Latin and Greek as the centerpiece of learning in the universities. The result was that "Not only did England enter the epoch of the Industrial Revolution with a ruling elite ignorant of science; the scientists of the Royal Society themselves abandoned the radicals' 'enthusiastic' schemes for equal educational opportunity."[309]

The crucial point here is not only whether the revolution of the working classes could have succeeded, but how it could have existed at all in Marx and Engels' scheme of things.

According to the Marxist view of history, mass rejection of capitalist values and relations could not have developed until a full-blown industrial economy had produced a proletariat which had experienced capitalist exploitation and been driven, on the basis of opposing interests, to oppose it. But the Diggers understood the nature of capitalist relations *before* these relations had produced any substantial economic effects. The vision and the consciousness of the Diggers do not seem to have been the less real for not yet having experienced the still-developing forms of capitalist exploitation; they had already perceived much of its content—enough, that is, to reject it as a form of social organization or a set of values fit for human beings.

Hill's description of the "second revolution" suggests that the old feudal order was not burst apart in seventeenth-century England as the fetters on burgeoning economic forces, as Marx believed; it was swept away on waves of popular struggle which was both anti-feudal and anti-capitalist—against hierarchy, individualism, and private property. The nascent bourgeoisie—the men of property—represented a particularly well-situated fraction in that struggle. Having the advantages of wealth, social position, organization, and the command of considerable social resources, and having made alliance with the defeated aristocracy to preserve not the particular form of hierarchical power but its essence, the bourgeoisie succeeded finally in crushing popular revolutionary struggle and in consolidating its own position.

Capitalism thus does not represent a progressive stage in history, as Marx thought, but the defeat of the popular revolution. With its victory, the new governing elite consciously created the conditions for capitalist development—that is, for economic and human development which reflected and reinforced the ideological, political, and economic conditions of their rule as a class. This development was by no measure—economic or human—superior to the development that a triumphant communal revolution could have created. Instead, it represented the suppression and distortion of the vital popular forces which had created the revolution.

The superiority of the young capitalist class to the feudal landowning class did not lay in its economic powers. The bourgeoisie in midseventeenth century England included more landowners than merchants and manufacturers; its economic base was very much like that of the elite group it was supplanting. The economic forces which it would unleash would not be developed to a significant extent for over a hundred years after its victory.

The superiority of the bourgeoisie to the old aristocrats was political and ideological rather than economic. These were men who were prepared to rule society on a new basis. The bourgeoisie represented ideas which could sustain social hierarchy clothed in different garb.

Capitalism won out over feudalism because it possessed means of asserting its dominance over the popular masses which feudalism did not. The capitalist concepts of society—of free men who rise by their own worth, of market relations based on competition, of wage labor and private property—and capitalist ideology, which justified the social order by an idea of human nature rather than the will of God, were far superior to feudal ideas and social relations for the purpose of preserving the social order. The masses of people had already rejected the ideas which sustained the rule of Church and king and aristocracy. The "Great Chain of Being" on which feudalism depended had been broken. Capitalism picked up the pieces and forged new chains to bind humanity.

The advantage of the incipient capitalist class over the laboring classes was not that the bourgeoisie represented Progress—for there were demonstrably different directions that progress could take—or that economic forces had not yet created a revolutionary class. The advantage was that by training and position the bourgeoisie were more used to seeing themselves as the leaders of society, had a more thoroughly developed and widely disseminated ideology justifying their leadership, and had more forces at their disposal to win.

The common people, through their relationships and organizing and agitation and writings, through their collective seizure of commons and wastes, had been preparing the conditions for their own rule—for a triumphant popular revolution. The ingredient which was missing from the history of the time which would have allowed them to succeed—and to create a successful communal society 350 years ago—was not greater capitalist economic development, but greater consciousness of themselves as the source of a new order, and sufficient organization to win. (The record suggests that the religious ideas which largely provided the vehicles for the working classes' revolutionary views also stood in the way of clearly seeing themselves as the source of a new moral and political order. During the period of upheaval, revolutionaries had attacked private property, exploitation, and waged labor as the Fall of Man. After the Restoration, "sin" became the explanation of continuing inequality and exploitation.[310] The propertied classes used religion to great advantage in suppressing the revolutionary movement. To prevail against the men of property, the commoners would have had to see themselves, not God, as the source of a new moral order.)

All this is not to reject economic development as a factor in history. But the Marxist paradigm and the relation it posits between human consciousness and material development is backwards. Capitalist ideology preceded capitalist economic development, and was a necessary condition of it; communalist and egalitarian ideas and relationships among people—in Marx's terminology, "socialist" ideas and relations—preceded the existence of the economic developments which Marx believed would spawn them.

The Marxist view of history proposes that economic forces drive history, shape human consciousness, and determine the possibilities of social transformation. The historical evidence suggests a very different relation, in which class consciousness drives political and economic development and creates possibilities for social transformation which are limited not by material conditions but by the people's collective understanding of themselves as actors in history.

Because of the power of the economic paradigm, espoused both by capitalist and Marxist historians, the role of human consciousness on "the wheel of history" has remained largely invisible and unexplored, so that our understanding of what drives history and how to affect its direction has remained profoundly distorted. Marx said that he had to stand Hegel on his head to set him right. Revolutionaries must turn Marx on his head if they wish to understand the role of human consciousness and aspirations in shaping the world, and if they want to learn how to change it.

Revolution and Human Nature

Marx called revolution "the locomotive of history"; but since his science of revolution was erected upon a view of human motivation in which individuals seek only their own self-interest, Marx had to find the source of revolution in economic forces beyond human control. Consciousness of the need for revolution would be impressed on men's minds by material forces, as economic contradictions developed to a crisis in need of revolutionary resolution.

A view of history which is truly alternative to the economic model must find the motive force of history and revolution in forces which are antecedant to economic development and which are within the realm of human control. I propose that revolution drives history, but in a way in which conscious human agency rather than economic forces is the determining factor.

What is the source of revolution? What other forces could give rise to revolutionary struggle, if not economic contradictions?

The source of revolution against class exploitation is to be found in human nature. Human beings are by nature social beings. Their collective nature leads people to value above others relationships which most fully reflect their social nature and which most completely support their development as human beings. Equal and collective relationships most support full human development; people have fought to establish these relationships throughout history, regardless of the state of economic development. What Marx referred to as "primitive collectivism" was really the irrepressible struggle of the human spirit for community and equality.

However much capitalist society may try to conceal the fact, human life is a collective product, from the beginnings of each individual to the development of human culture and society. The human child, conceived in a mutual act, is nurtured from his infancy with the love and warmth of other human beings. The child's full development as a person depends on his relations with his parents, brothers and sisters, relatives and friends, and how fully he is brought into the community of their affection. His dependence on them extends to the age when others can depend on him.

The language a child learns is itself a living, collective product of generations of human labor to shape the world to human ends. Learning to speak—to communicate as part of the human collective—marks an important stage in his development as a person. The environment which he experiences and which gives shape to his character and thoughts is a human environment. It consists primarily of the web of family and other relations which prepare him for the larger environment of society. The texture of life and culture which touch his life are all the products of collective labor, from the great cities to the works of the artist who builds on generations of human experience to create his apparently individual product.

Even the individual's experience of nature is shaped by collective human effort. The clothes he wears, the food he eats, the city or village he lives in, and all the human experience of the physical world that has gone before him mean that he sees nature not through his eyes alone but through the thoughts and feelings of generations.

The human individual cannot understand himself or be understood except as part of something larger. His ideas about himself and other people are rooted in society. They come from his interaction with other human beings and his understanding of his own relationship with them. He has no standard for judging the value or content of his own thoughts or feelings except in terms of their source—his independent experience of his interdependency with other human beings.

The human individual, in other words, is a collective being. Each person is a living and developing product of people working together. What distinguishes a human being from other animals is that he is capable of understanding the human and collective source of his development as a person, and by understanding it, to shape its direction.

But if it is true that human nature is social, what of the capitalists' claim that "capitalism is human nature"? By this they mean not only that people are naturally selfish, but that selfishness is the basis of human development. The individual develops through competition and the struggle to succeed, and society develops by giving free rein to competition and selfishness.

To weigh the merits of this claim, we must consider two things that we have observed about capitalism and people. One is that most people are engaged in their everyday lives in a struggle against capitalist relations. The other is that this everyday struggle requires the capitalist class, if it would maintain control over society, to attack relentlessly those things which are most fundamental to our humanity: our consciousness and our connectedness with other human beings.

We have here at least two bases for doubting capital's ultimate claim to legitimacy. If capitalism can only survive by attempting to destroy the fundamental human attributes of consciousness and connection with each other, and if people are daily engaged in efforts which contradict capitalist relations, it seems reasonable to suggest that capitalism is not human nature.

In fact we can go further, and say that this analysis suggests that capitalism is anti-human, and that the struggle *against* capitalism is rooted in human nature. When people rebel against capitalism—as they do everywhere, all the time—they are asserting their humanity against a system which would destroy it.

But how can capitalism be anti-human, since it obviously is one possible path of human development, however destructive it may be? And if the source of revolution is human nature, how could capitalism or any form of class society even exist?

To answer these questions, let us return to the discussion of the social nature of human beings. The social nature of human development leads us naturally to value relationships of solidarity and equality which fully express our social nature.

Human beings, however, do not exist as "communities" or "collectives" or "classes" or "nations," but as individuals. These collective terms merely define relationships among aggregations of individuals. While people's social nature has profound effects on their thoughts and actions, it does not determine their activities or efface their being as individuals.

There is always a contradiction between the individual and the aggregate of others; that is, the group and the individual are not the same thing. This contradiction is the basis of development. The group can grow and develop only through the actions of individuals, as the individual contributes his own perspective, experience, work, ideas. At the same time, the group unites the contributions of many individuals in a formulation of knowledge or wealth that is always greater than the product of any individual; each individual is developed by this greater collective knowledge or wealth. Thus the group is the basis of the development of the individual; the individual is the basis of the development of the group.

The contradiction between the individual and other individuals can be complementary or antagonistic. One can contribute to others or exploit them. Human beings shape their relationships to other people through choices made more or less consciously and more or less freely; though the choices of the individual are always conditioned by circumstances, the individual is always capable of choosing different paths. There is nothing to insure that the individual will understand the "source of his development as a person" to be collective, or that, having so understood it, he will choose to contribute to the human collective—rather than stealing from it—as the basis of his own further development.

"Human beings," in the words of the philosopher Charles Taylor, are "self-interpreting animals." Moral choices are the bases of human existence as human; they are the way in which human beings create their own self-definition.[311] Since in human activity people are always in some respects defining their relationships with other human beings, they are always engaged in creating themselves. In addition, through their relationships and the character they choose to give them, people are always engaged in defining what they believe it means to be human.

As ways of relating to other human beings are repeated and patterned over time, they constitute cultures. Cultures encode values and ideas concerning what is appropriate and possible in human relationships. To the extent that cultures reflect the practices and values of people in terms of their relationship to the creation or destruction of the means of human existence—that is, in relation to work—they are class cultures. As they erect standards of morality and self-definition, class cultures are themselves important, sometimes decisive factors conditioning the choices individuals make in their lives.

The culture of capitalism—the ideas and relationships which it sanctions—are a function of the relationship of capitalists to productive activity. Capitalists as capitalists do not labor; instead, they profit from the labor of others. In capitalist culture, the sanctioned relationship of the individual with other individuals is competition; with the group, it is exploitation. The sanctioned ideas of capitalist culture are egotism and inequality.

The values and ideas about human life encoded in working class culture and in work itself reflect the relationship of working people to production, which is also necessarily a relationship to each other. These values and ideas—cooperation, solidarity, equality—have their roots in human nature, and are continually recreated by people as they engage in productive activity.

The struggle to transform the inhuman into the human includes both the struggle with nature, to shape it to human ends, and the struggle with other human beings, to shape relationships to the ends of human development. Class struggle and the struggle with nature are two activities of the same force.

In class struggle as in the struggle with nature, working people act on values and ideas which are properly their own to achieve goals which reflect their idea of human life; that is, they act as self-determining subjects, striving to achieve goals which oppose those of the master class. The fundamental resource people have in this struggle is their shared and irreducible humanity.

The goal of class struggle is the transformation of class society with values and relationships which express human nature and support the full development of human beings. Revolution is the fulfillment of people's struggle as human beings to assert their role as conscious creators of the world and of their collective self, and as interpreters of their own acts and history. Revolution comes from the struggle to create human life and to fill it with meaning.

This struggle, as we know, does not go on in a vacuum. Capitalists, like Communists now and other ruling elites in the past, have powerful means at their disposal to enforce their culture: to break relationships among people and to distort their consciousness of themselves and other people.

Capitalism is anti-human because it can only survive as a system by attacking the collectivity and consciousness which are the historic bases of human life and culture. While capitalism represents a possible form of human development, it is one which requires the destruction of human development as the basis of its continued existence. The working class creates the bases of human existence; the capitalist class destroys them.

Since Marx believed that economic development was the motive force of history, he thought that each new ruling elite in turn had its role to play in developing the economic resources at its disposal. History, Marx thought, develops in stages, each of which is a necessary economic foundation of the next; feudalism was a necessary stage before capitalism, and capitalism before socialism. Class society prepares the way for classless society. The basis of classless society, in Marx's view, is a fully-developed capitalist economy.

By continuing to place the source of history and human development outside humanity (in the economy), the Marxist theory of history has played a counterrevolutionary role in the last century. The religious and aristocratic view of the world under which man labored for centuries was replaced by the "scientific" view of Marx and Lenin, in which political and economic experts are the new mediators between ordinary people and their consciousness of their role in history.

In the view which I have proposed, the motive force of history is working people's struggle to humanize the world. Inequality serves only to distort and retard human development in all its aspects, including economic development. Progress in history does not result from and is not marked by any necessary stages of technological development. Progress comes rather from the increasing consciousness of the people who create the moral and material wealth of society of themselves—not gods or priests or politicians or capitalists or experts or the party—as creators.

The revolutionary movements of ordinary people, except for brief moments, have always been under the cloud of some form of the idea that positive values proceed from the top of society. It is because the revolutionary struggles of ordinary people have always been trapped within ideas which negate their meaning that they have never triumphed.

The condition for world revolution is greater consciousness among working people of themselves as the collective creators of human society. The condition of this greater self-consciousness is a new paradigm of history and society which shows the role of ordinary people in creating them.

Values and Conciousness

Since human nature is by definition a constant, and in this sense a-historical, how can it give rise to revolutionary consciousness, which develops with historical experience and is therefore an historical artifact? What is the link between human nature and revolutionary consciousness?

Marx thought that material conditions shaped men's consciousness. He believed that capitalism, as it organized workers into factories and taught them discipline and cooperation, showed workers the social nature of human labor and made them aware of the contradiction between social labor and private appropriation. Marx thought that in this way capitalism was responsible for creating modern revolutionary consciousness.

Marx's view was mistaken, however. Human labor was no less collective before the advent of capitalism. The ancient pyramids, the cathedrals and great cities of the Middle Ages, the development of agriculture: all these depended upon conscious cooperation. Laboring people possessed revolutionary ideas long before the factory system was in existence; other classes, such as peasants, whom Marx believed incapable of revolutionary consciousness, have at many times in history possessed it.

Capitalism has not itself had the effect which Marx described. While the tendency of capitalism has been to centralize production, capitalism is the first social system in human history which has strived to *conceal* the social nature of production by all the means at its disposal: by organizing work, technology, and ideology in such a way as to fragment people's lives and work relationships. The fragmentation and concealment of the collective wellsprings of human life are the essence of capitalism as a system of class domination. The product of the factory system was not class consciousness but Taylorism, management's science of controlling workers by attacking the bonds between them and wresting knowledge and control of the production process out of their hands. The collective consciousness which workers have developed under capitalism is not a product of the system but of workers' struggle *against* it.

The link between human nature and consciousness is formed by people's values. Values have their source in human nature, and take shape in the context of people's role in society. Working class values lead people to struggle with the conditions of their existence to shape these conditions to accord with their vision of human life. This struggle to shape reality leads to consciousness. In struggle people become more aware of the goals and possibilities of revolutionary change, and more cognizant of the obstacles in their path.

The distinction between values and consciousness is crucial to realize how working class consciousness can develop in history and yet not be determined by it. We have already seen, in the strikes of the British miners and Hormel meatpackers, that workers in class struggle act on the basis of goals rather than interests; the strikers' goals in those struggles led them to sacrifice their self-interest to their values. Working people are conscious human subjects, because they pursue *goals* which are internal to them as a class, rather than merely pursuing *interests* forced upon them by historical circumstances. Their goals precede their historical experience, because they are a function of human nature. Consciousness develops through people's struggle against the conditions of their existence to fulfill their vision of human life.

There are both enduring and historical elements in class struggle. While the consciousness of the masses of people has developed through historical experience, the values which are the driving force of struggle are rooted in human nature and have been shared by working people throughout history. It is no accident that demands for equality and solidarity arise again and again in the history of popular revolts. The struggles of toiling humanity are linked across time and space. The slave uprisings and peasant revolts in Roman times, the peasant uprisings that shook medieval Europe and 19th century China, the revolt of urban workers in the French Revolution and the Russian Revolution, are part of the same struggle and have been driven by the same force. The contemporary struggles of workers in El Salvador and the U.S. and South Africa and Poland and China and the Soviet Union are linked not only by the threads of an international economy, but by the common longings of the human spirit.

Revolutionary values are internal to working people rather than contingent on any historical conditions. Revolutionary movements are more than anything movements in which people stand above society, to fashion it according to their vision of what it should be like. Human nature is the solid basis outside any set of historical conditions on which they place their lever, and, as Archimedes wished, move the whole world.

This explains how the values and consciousness which allowed the working people of seventeenth century England to struggle against capitalism could have preceded capitalist development. Their values—their view of what was important in life, encoded in centuries-old customs and ways of relating to each other—were rooted in their nature as human beings, mediated by their role as the creators of the wealth of society. Their consciousness was not created or determined by a set of material circumstances; rather, it was a function of the relation between their values and the struggle with the conditions of their existence to which their values led them. Their consciousness had developed through centuries of experience and struggle—with the material conditions of their lives and the human relations and ideas of which the material conditions were but a part. Their consciousness was not primarily of conditions but of themselves and of their relationships to each other. From this consciousness, rooted in their values, they erected standards by which to judge the newly-developing capitalist relations and devised the means to struggle against them.

As they work together to create human society, people always to a greater or lesser extent share an understanding of the collective nature of human beings. When people fight on the job to reassert the human dimensions of their work; when they strive in the face of media disinformation to understand the world; when mothers and fathers work in the face of the hardness and pressures of life to maintain a family or guide their children's education: when people do any of these things, they do so on the implicit understanding of the relationships central to human development. The best aspects of the life in every workplace and family and neighborhood—especially where life is hardest and people humanize it against the greatest odds—are the products of the ongoing struggles, rooted in this understanding, which people wage to transform the inhuman into the human.

It is true that people's struggles vary widely in the clarity and explicitness with which their underlying motivation is developed. The extent of this development—that is, the extent of the conscious articulation of revolutionary goals and recognition of the obstacles to their fulfillment—grows out of the historical circumstances of the struggles, the ideological and organizational structures within which they develop, and the presence or absence of explicitly revolutionary ideas. And yet all working class struggles tap the same essential strength and share the same essential goals.

People's consciousness tends to lag behind their values, in the same way that people's belief in what human society *can* be lags behind their view of what it *should* be. While people's values and ways of relating to each other are under constant attack and influence by ruling class culture, consciousness is more susceptible than values to these attacks because of the dominance of the ruling class in the field of culture and people's vulnerability to misinformation in those areas in which they cannot have direct knowledge.

The only exception to the dissonance between values and consciousness is in revolutionary movements, when people's belief in what life should be and what it can be coincide. Revolution is the explosion created by the fusion of people's belief in what is necessary and what is possible.

An Alternative Model of History and Society

I can now summarize the key elements of the model of history and revolution which I am proposing:

—The fundamental contradiction in society is between the values and vision of human life of the people who create human society and the values and vision of the people who exploit it—between slaves and masters, peasants and lords, workers and capitalists.

—Class struggle is a war over what it means to be human; this struggle goes on in every aspect of human existence: personal and social, political and ideological, cultural and economic.

—History is driven not by economic or technological development but by class struggle.

—The working class—whether slave, peasant, or proletarian, blue collar or white—creates all values necessary to the creation and development of human life; that is, it creates both the material wealth of society and the values and relationships conducive to human development.

—Human nature is social; the social nature of human beings leads them to value relationships most conducive to collective human development: relations based on solidarity and equality.

—Human beings are both products of society and products of their own creation; human beings create themselves in all their acts as they develop relationships in ways which reflect their vision—their values interacting with their consciousness—of what it means to be human.

—While all values are rooted finally in human nature, all values are mediated by class roles, class cultures, and individual choices bearing on one's relation to other people.

—Capitalism is not primarily an economic system but a system of human relations and class control; the force that drives it is not its own, but the power of the working class which it strives to contain.

—Capitalism contradicts human nature as it disguises, undermines, and attacks the social nature of people and turns all their works into weapons to assault the roots of their humanity: their consciousness and relationships with other people.

—The drive to revolution is rooted in human nature.

—Consciousness develops in history as the toiling classes encounter new problems to solve; these problems—such as capitalism—do not constitute necessary "stages of history," however, but obstacles to human development which could have proceeded more swiftly by different paths. Capitalism represents the defeat of the popular revolution against feudalism. One can only guess at the progress that would have been achieved if the popular revolution had crushed incipient capitalism as well.

—There is nothing internal to capitalism as an economic system which makes its destruction inevitable; it will be destroyed because it contradicts human nature.

—The revolutionary transformation of class society—the destruction of capitalism and Communism and the creation of a new society—is the only possible fulfillment of the goals and values of the vast majority of the people of this society and of the world.

—Most people are already engaged in important parts of their lives in a struggle to transform capitalist relations into their opposite; most people are already in a struggle to create a new world.

13

REVOLUTION
AND DEMOCRACY

On Christmas Day, 1914, in the first year of World War I, German, British, and French soldiers disobeyed their superiors and fraternized with "the enemy" along two-thirds of the Western Front. German troops held Christmas trees up out of the trenches with signs, "Merry Christmas." "You no shoot, we no shoot." Thousands of troops streamed across a no-man's land strewn with rotting corpses. They sang Christmas carols, exchanged photographs of loved ones back home, shared rations, played football, even roasted some pigs. Soldiers embraced men they had been trying to kill a few short hours before. They agreed to warn each other if the top brass forced them to fire their weapons, and to aim high.

A shudder ran through the high command on either side. Here was disaster in the making: soldiers declaring their brotherhood with each other and refusing to fight. Generals on both sides declared this spontaneous peacemaking to be treasonous and subject to court martial. By March, 1915 the fraternization movement had been eradicated and the killing machine put back in full operation. By the time of the armistice in 1918, fifteen million would be slaughtered.

Not many people have heard the story of the Christmas Truce. Military leaders have not gone out of their way to publicize it. On Christmas Day, 1988, a story in the *Boston Globe* mentioned that a local FM radio host played "Christmas in the Trenches," a ballad about the Christmas Truce, several times and was startled by the effect. The song became the most requested recording during the holidays in Boston on several FM stations. "Even more startling than the number of requests I get is the reaction to the ballad afterward by callers who hadn't heard it before," said the radio host. "They telephone me deeply moved, sometimes in tears, asking, 'What the hell did I just hear?'"

I think I know why the callers were in tears. The Christmas Truce story goes against most of what we have been taught about people. It gives us a glimpse of the world as we wish it could be and says, "This really happened once." It reminds us of those thoughts we keep hidden away, out of range of the TV and newspaper stories that tell us how trivial and mean human life is. It is like hearing that our deepest wishes really are true: the world really could be different.

My purpose so far in this book has been to show that the possibility of revolutionary change lies in seeing the world, and in particular seeing people, in a new way. In this chapter, I deal with some practical questions about the society toward which a new view of people seems to lead, and describe some elements of the revolutionary movement I believe it will take us to get there. I also deal with one of the most vexing problems of revolutionary movements: the question of organization, and specifically, the need for a revolutionary party.

Is Democracy Possible?

Bertolt Brecht once wrote:

The leaders who have brought the country into the abyss
Call ruling too difficult
For ordinary men.[312]

Is ruling too difficult for ordinary people? Do we live in a "meritocracy," in which the most fit to rule have risen to the top? Aside from individual personalities—to call Ronald Reagan or George Bush or Dan Quayle "the best and the brightest" seems preposterous—would the social problems which seem so daunting now seem even more insoluble if the important decisions of the society were being made of, by, and for the people rather than the elite?

There are some very important questions here. But before we can answer whether ordinary people are capable of tackling difficult issues, we must ask, "Where do the most serious problems facing us come from?"

What are some of those problems? Inequality of every sort—of wealth and poverty, of gender and race. Ethnic and national conflict.

Unemployment, homelessness, costly and uneven medical care. Boring and stupid jobs. A mis-education system. Consumerism. Alienation, isolation, and loneliness. Crime and drug addiction. The degradation of the environment. Weapons build-ups. Wars and threats of war. Malnutrition and starvation in some countries. Torture and repression of working people in Third World countries.

These are certainly daunting problems. It is important to see, however, that these and other problems facing us have something in common. That is, while these are serious problems for ordinary people, *for the ruling elite, they are not problems but solutions*—solutions to the problem of how to stay in power.

Each of the terrible problems we face is a source of profit or control for the ruling class. Each is an instrument of class rule: inequality to encourage people to fight each other; unemployment and other terrors to make them frightened and controllable; isolation to weaken them; crime to justify more police power; drugs to keep people passive; a natural environment raped for the sake of profit; torture to keep people subdued.

Look again at the story of the Christmas Truce. The men in the trenches in World War I knew how to end that war, but the power of the generals and political elites they represented depended on the war continuing. For the ruling elites, the war was not a problem but a solution. In the same way, most Americans and most Russians did not want to kill each other during the Cold War; the arms race, and the fear and hatred that went with it, were generated by the U.S. and Soviet elites to strengthen their own grip on power.

The fact is that the rulers have no intention of solving the key problems, because their continued existence as rulers depends on the problems continuing in some form. Sure, they will focus on one problem or another, and make a big deal about solving it—but they can never point to the real solution. Instead they will use the problems to create further division among people, by offering misleading explanations and destructive solutions. Gender inequality? Men are no good. Unemployment? The Japs are taking your jobs. Crime and drugs? Blacks are criminals. Boring job? If you weren't a loser, you would'nt be stuck in it.

These problems are not technical problems, which depend on greater know-how to solve. They are political problems, which stem from the system of class rule. They can *only* be solved by democracy—by placing the direction of the society in the hands of the vast majority of people for whom these really are problems and not solutions.

Democracy, then, is necessary. Still, is it possible? Would ordinary working people be capable of creating solutions to major problems? I think we have seen enough in this book and in our own lives to know that they could. How often have people proposed better ways of doing things in this society, only to have their ideas struck down—not because they would not work, but because they conflicted with powerful interests?

Could parents and teachers and students working together design a better education system? Of course they could. Not only do they have more intimate knowledge of schools and kids than the people now in charge; they have a completely different set of goals from the goals of the present system. As we have seen, the present system, based on the needs of capitalism, is designed for failure. Working together in a real democracy, people could fashion schools for the real success of students, in new and exciting ways that we can hardly imagine.

Could doctors and nurses and other hospital staff and other working people design a better health care system? Obviously they could, if they were freed from the constraints of the profit system. The root of the crisis in health care is not lack of resources or an aging population or an unfeeling staff or any of the other false explanations which are offered to us by the apologists of the existing system; the root of the crisis is a health care system driven by the needs of profit and social control.

Could people working together figure out solutions to the environmental crisis? Of course they could. Much of the technology already exists. The problem is that it contradicts the needs of the capitalists. There was a saying during the "energy crisis" of the '70s that, "If Exxon owned the sun, we'd have solar power." The capitalists can only tolerate solutions to the energy crisis which enhance their profits and control—which is why they would rather sink billions into nuclear power than a fraction of that amount into solar power. With revolutionary democracy, people would have a new relationship to the earth as well as to each other. All kinds of ideas for living with and preserving the earth would spring forth from that new relationship.

These few examples reveal an important aspect of a revolutionary democratic society: that the intelligence and creativity of people would be unleashed in new and unexpected ways. We live now in a society controlled by an elite which depends for its continued existence on suppressing people's intelligence and ideas; this is, in fact, one of the most unfulfilling things about life in this society—people's talents are never really used to the fullest. The ruling class needs to prevent people from collectively discussing and solving their problems for the simple reason that, at bottom, elite control *is* the problem. In a revolutionary democratic society, all the talent and intelligence that people could bring to bear on the world's problems would be used to solve them. People would find undreamed-of levels of personal and collective fulfillment in contributing all that they can really do to the common cause of humanity.

What Would Revolutionary Democracy Mean?

We have seen that revolutions are shaped by the ideas about people on which they are based. If we believe that the people who do the work of the society share goals which constitute a vision of human life fundamentally opposed to that of the ruling class, then revolution for us means the transformation by working people of every sphere of society to fulfill their vision of human life.

No area of society in which human life is invested can remain untouched by this revolution. Political and economic, personal and social life: all should be transformed by popular initiative to reflect truly human goals and values. Such a revolution must be democratic to the core, expressing the goals and vision of the great majority of people, and resulting from their conscious action on society.

This description of revolution may sound like common sense. It is important to see, however, that it is quite different from the economic model of change, in which revolution essentially consists of the imposition on society of new economic structures—either market relations or a centrally-planned economy—governed by a new elite. Capitalist and Communist revolutions amount essentially to a change of management.

The new paradigm of which I have been speaking does not consist primarily of a new structure, but of a new understanding of human motivation which makes new structures possible. People will learn how to create new, democratic structures for society in the struggle to overturn existing structures of exploitation and inequality.

The essence of revolutionary democracy will be a revolution in human relationships, to reflect the values of democracy, equality, and solidarity which are its driving force. The revolution in human relations is both the goal and the method, the test and the fulfillment, of the revolution.

Transforming human relations will include destroying the capitalist and Communist states and all their apparatus—the military, the police, the courts, the legislative and executive bodies. It will include the active suppression of counterrevolution by armed working people. It will mean the mobilization and participation of people, under conditions of equality, in the investigation and debate of all questions of importance to the life of the people. It will mean the creation by ordinary people of appropriate bodies for democratic planning and coordination, consistent with their values and goals.

Transforming human relations will also include destroying capitalist and Communist economic relations and creating new economic relations in their place. All the means of production will be appropriated and managed by the workers themselves. It will mean, on the initiative of working people, the creation of workers' councils at every level to oversee the democratic transformation of the relations, goals, and structure of work and production. It will mean producing for use, not for profit, those products identified as needed.

Changing other spheres of life—education, health care, communications and transportation, and all the rest—and creating racial and gender equality cannot be assumed to follow automatically from changes in economic and political areas. Ordinary people will have to deal consciously with these areas so that they too reflect the values and goals which shape discussion on all other matters.

It is not possible or desirable to impose a blueprint for a new society on the revolutionary process. There is only a need for clear revolutionary principles to guide the way. These principles are the same values which are the best part of people's lives now. The new world will be built on a foundation of equality and solidarity, as people discover how to extend these values to all of life.

The new society will consist of the flowering into social reality of people's deepest shared aspirations, made collective, conscious, and free. It will be created by people whose full creative power, so long suppressed, will at last be able to find its expression.

Building a Revolutionary Movement

The two different paradigms which I have explored in this book—the economic model common to capitalism and Communism, and the new model which I am proposing—lead to very different ideas of political practice.

The model which sees economic forces driving society also sees ordinary people as quite limited in their willingness to entertain ideas which challenge capitalism. If people are motivated chiefly by self-interest, then the way for a movement to reach them lies in explaining where their immediate interests lie and offering them tactical leadership. For these reasons, and also because the possibilities for change seem so limited in the economic model, it is important to limit the movement's agenda to very modest, defensive goals ("No Concessions," "No Intervention," "Stop The Cuts"), and to avoid discussion of the capitalist system. Modest and defensive though these demands may be, few people really expect to achieve them—precisely because they do not deal with the system which is producing concessions and military intervention and funding cutbacks.

The political practice which follows from the new paradigm I am proposing is quite different from this. If people are already motivated by values and engaged in struggles which are implicitly revolutionary, then political practice consists essentially of making the implicit meaning of people's goals and struggles explicit. The movement should reveal the hidden meaning of everyday life: the daily struggle waged by millions of people in the midst of capitalist society to create a new world. It should lay bare capital's attack on people's lives in all its ferocity and illuminate people's struggles in all their humanity. The movement should clarify the connections between the specific problems confronting people—say, education or wage cuts—and the broader issues and texture of capitalist rule. It should encourage people to extend and strengthen the relationships in which their struggles are embodied. It should encourage them to examine the significance of their struggles for all of society.

If the view of people which I have proposed is accurate, then it is possible to build a broad-based revolutionary movement which reaches deeply into widely-shared values and expresses these as a social vision.

The paramount political task in this new paradigm is to present and fight for a revolutionary democratic vision of society. Precisely because it is based on ordinary people as the makers of history, a revolutionary democratic movement must openly challenge capitalist goals, values, plans, policies, and power with its own revolutionary vision.

The primary condition for the advance of working class struggle is that people become more conscious of themselves as the collective source of human values—not only of material wealth, but of all the other values that provide the bases for human life. The fundamental condition for transforming society is for working people to realize that they are the source of it.

The Question of Revolutionary Organization

The question of organization has played a central role in the history of revolutionary movements. Some of the most important battles in the working class movement have been fought over it. With the occasional exception of anarchists, revolutionaries have always sought to create appropriate organizational forms for waging their battles. Yet these organizations have always ended up betraying the movements from which they emerged in one way or another.

In the 1960s, particularly within the New Left, there was widespread rejection of established organizational forms, and even rejection of the very notion of organizational structure, in the hope of creating more democratic movements.

But the experimentation of the 'sixties did not yield a satisfactory solution to the problem. People found that, in every movement or organization, some people always exercised formal or informal leadership, and that informal leadership was simply unaccountable leadership. Informal leadership took different forms. Sometimes the more active or organized or articulate minority would act the part of leaders, without election or discussion. At other times, the media would designate someone the "leader," who would then express his or her own opinions as the opinion of a whole group or movement. In any case, what developed were not leaderless movements, but movements with no democratic control over the leaders who had emerged.

But formalized rules and procedures do not insure democracy either. Democratic centralist parties, trade unions with membership voting rights, the Democratic Party, large formal organizations: all of these are more or less controlled by small elites not truly answerable to the members. In each of them, a small leadership group dominates a membership which is largely excluded from determining the direction of the organization.

In short, no particular organizational forms guarantee democratic control and effective organizational action: the organization question cannot be answered on the basis of organizational structure alone. The view of people on which an organization is based and the goals it is designed to achieve together play a profound role in shaping the relationships within it.

The Meaning of Leadership

The dominant concept of leadership in capitalist society is based on the dominant view of people. In this view, the majority of people are passive; their "leaders" act on their behalf. If they are good leaders, the passive mass will benefit from their actions; if they are not, the mass will suffer.

This is the notion of leadership which is fundamental to representative democracy, and to most institutions within this society. It characterizes the present trade union organizations, for example, which follow the model of "service" or "business" unionism. Union officials "service" the members; they speak, negotiate, make deals, direct the union on their behalf. The more competent the leader, the more he will be able to "take care of business" by himself. This idea of leadership is based on the idea of a passive membership, and it may actively enforce passivity—by intimidation, withholding information, isolating members from each other, dealing behind the members' backs, and other well-known techniques.

If leaders are sincere and well-intentioned, the top-down leadership model defeats their efforts. The more a leader acts on the members' behalf, the more they are encouraged to say "Let Joe do it." It's not that they are lazy or unwilling; it's just that Joe seems to know the ropes better than they do and to be more self-confident. In many union locals, energetic and competent leaders unwittingly discourage the participation of the members, all the while providing them many "services." The result is that the leaders grow cynical and burned-out, because they feel like they are carrying the whole load, while members feel excluded from decisionmaking and grow resentful.

Clearly a different concept of leadership is called for. The new paradigm suggests one. Most people, far from being passive, are already engaged in a struggle to create a new world, but they are held back by lack of clarity or self-confidence or support for their efforts. Leadership in the new paradigm means enabling other people to act. Leadership means producing more leadership in an expanding circle of people. It means helping to clarify thinking, to create self-confidence, to create supportive relationships. It means helping a movement that already exists to become more clear, more self-confident, more aware of its collective power.

Who exercises leadership? The collective nature of human development means that leadership comes from many different sources in any group of people. Think of being in a conversation, trying to figure

out how to change a bad policy in your school. At different points in
the discussion, one person explains how the policy came about, while
someone else corrects that version a bit and adds something new;
another person gives an example of how some students have been
affected by the policy, while still another relates a story from the
teachers' lounge about it. Another helps sort things out to get a clear,
total picture. Each of the people contributing to the discussion, though
they might not think of themselves as "leaders," is exercising leadership to one extent or another.

Where does leadership come from? The paradigm which sees most
people as passive sees leadership coming from a few individuals who
are sufficiently skilled, educated, or talented to lead—or who are
"born leaders"—and who rise above the mass. "Leaders" in the dominant paradigm are those who participate in the superior culture of the
dominant class.

But if human development and consciousness are really produced
by people working together, then real leadership is an organic expression of the mass. People engaged in collective struggle produce their
own leaders, whose job is to push on the development of the collective.

The real situation in life is not a vast mass of people who know
nothing and a few militants or activists who know a great deal. The
masses of people are already engaged in a struggle with reality; what
the leaders know is only a fraction of the ideas and relationships of
the mass.

Revolutionary understanding is a product of the collective. Democratic leaders themselves are produced by the collective. They are
trained and developed by a multitude of interactions, and are thrust
forward by the people themselves when people think they are worthy
of trust.

These leaders are legitimate as long as they continue to articulate
the goals of the collective and to enhance its development. It is when
the knowledge and ablity of leaders is seen as separate and coming
from themselves as individuals, or when their ideas in fact come from
the opposing class, that they begin to play a counterrevolutionary
role. They become illegitimate when they begin, intentionally or not,
to express the goals and relations of the opposing class, and begin
thereby to discourage the development of the collective.

The working class is always engaged in the work of creating leaders. The only guarantees on the direction of leadership are the
strength of the collective relations which create the leaders and bind

them to the mass, and the consciousness of the collective that it is the source of leadership. The solution of the problem of leadership is that workers understand that they have created their leaders.

The Need for a Revolutionary Party

Lenin based his arguments for a disciplined party with revolutionary goals on the need for conscious human subjects to create revolutionary change. His concept of the party depended on his belief in the primacy of consciousness in shaping society. His Economist opponents, who believed in raising only economic, not political, issues, thought that economic forces would create revolutionary change spontaneously. They were economic determinists who believed that capitalism would collapse of its internal contradictions.

As we have seen, while Lenin was correct about the importance of consciousness, he was wrong about where revolutionary consciousness comes from and of what it consists. Lenin believed that political consciousness consists of knowledge of capitalism and the laws determining its operation in society, and that the working class of itself is capable only of consciousness of its interests within the capitalist system. He thought that bourgeois intellectuals are the source of revolutionary consciousness, and that it is the role of the party to supply political consciousness to the working class.

The premises of revolutionary democracy are very different, both from Lenin's and from his opponents. Capitalist society is not driven by forces or laws which develop independently of human will or consciousness, but by the ideas, hopes, goals, values, struggles of contending classes. Workers participate in class struggle as human subjects. So Lenin was correct in his argument against the Economists, that consciousness *is* primary in class struggle. But if the driving force of history is not the economic system but working class struggle, then Lenin was wrong about political consciousness. Political consciousness does not consist of knowledge of the system but knowledge of people. Revolutionary consciousness consists of workers' consciousness of themselves as the collective source of value in society and the source of revolution.

In revolutionary democracy, political consciousness is not technical knowledge of the system, but a way of thinking about and relating to other people. Political consciousness is value-laden and value-based: it expresses and reflects human relationships based on solidarity and equality. The fundamental ideas of revolutionary democracy and the relationships in which these ideas are embedded and expressed are deeply intertwined in the life of the working class. They consist of an understanding of people and society inseparable from certain shared goals for human society, certain shared beliefs in what society should be like. They cannot be the products of economic "experts" or the property of a political party separate from the working class. Political consciousness is the organic product of people working together to create the bases of human life, who then reflect upon the meaning of their actions.

To Lenin's point, that the working class left to itself is not capable of developing revolutionary consciousness, we reply: Yes, it is capable. But the working class is not left to itself; it is under constant attack by capitalist and Communist culture. The revolutionary consciousness which workers develop spontaneously from the interaction of their values with their experience is constantly quashed before it can be further developed, consolidated, expanded, and spread; it is smothered before people can become conscious of its significance.

The problem of the working class is not that it does not know enough to make a revolution, or that it has insufficient or false consciousness. People collectively know enough now to crush capitalism and to create a new world. The problem is that the working class does not know what it knows. The knowledge, insights, and consciousness among people is broken into many pieces; everyone has at least a bit of the whole truth, but the bits and pieces of collective knowledge have not been brought together into a critical mass, a whole vision to transform the world. People remain unsure of what they know, because what they know contradicts everything that they have been taught. Because they are not together to confirm the validity of what they each know and to assemble it into a whole, the earth-shaking, world-creating significance of their knowledge is hidden from view.

Being fragmentary, this consciousness can also be an inadequate instrument for practical use: for seeing the connections among issues, or for sorting out the misinformation and misleading ideas from the useful and accurate, or for developing strategies for building a movement. Without a developed movement, conscious of its goals and tasks, the normal state of people's consciousness is a mixture of ideas, some of them true and revolutionary, some of them quite contradictory.

Why is this consciousness fragmentary? There are three important factors. One is capitalist control. Capital dominates all the public organs of consciousness—the media, the schools, the churches, the politicians. Revolutionary views are seldom voiced, and are given no legitimacy by the organs of capital. At the same time, the ruling class works constantly to break the collective relationships among people which would allow them to pool and develop what they know into a more comprehensive understanding.

Secondly, there has been no revolutionary paradigm which articulates the significance of working class struggle and consciousness. The Marxist model is as blind to the significance of people's struggles as the capitalist model. As long as a way of understanding the world which displays the meaning of working class consciousness has not been set forth, workers' consciousness cannot become conscious of its own significance, and thus able to proceed in its work of transformation. As long as it is unaware of its own significance, working class consciousness cannot defeat the other models for understanding and organizing human reality.

A third factor concerns the nature of knowledge and human consciousness. Knowledge comes from the struggle with reality to change it. Knowledge is always based on experience—either our own or someone else's—and it always has a collective aspect to it; our knowledge is always built on a base of what others have known before us. Knowledge and experience are always fragmentary: there is always more to be learned, and what is already known is always known to some extent in discrete pieces by numbers of people. Learning thus is always in some respects a collective process; learning the truth about a many-sided reality requires drawing together the experiences and perceptions of many people. The organization of people and the development of consciousness are in some respects the same process, whether we are discussing how to build a car or raise children or how to make a revolution.

The need for revolutionary organization arises from the nature of the contradictions in class society, from the nature of political knowledge, and from the nature of human intelligence and development. A revolutionary organization is needed to draw together the best of what people know into a whole vision of society; to further develop an understanding of society which reveals the revolutionary meaning of working class values and struggles; and to wage war with capitalist culture for "the hearts and minds" of the people.

The role of a revolutionary party is not to bring to the working class a consciousness from outside, but to uncover and bring together the fragments of consciousness that are already there, rooted in workers' experience and their values and social relations. Its role is to make more clear the significance of these values and relations, to develop them as a vision of a new world, and to use them as a revolutionary standard with which to judge every aspect of the world as it now exists.

A party integrates the experiences of many people, and perceives the whole of society; it places developments in a historical framework; it develops the ideas which people bring to it. It is precisely because people have a great many ideas that a party is able to play a positive role in developing them. The essential activities in which a revolutionary party would engage, people already do informally and in piecemeal fashion: people already subject society and their own experience to analysis, and spread the results of their thinking, if just on their coffee break or at the local tavern. A party would also do this work, self-consciously, systematically, and in a sustained manner, and by doing it encourage wider and wider circles of people to do it themselves, but with more awareness of the significance of their efforts.

Every idea people have which challenges the dominant ideology is developed in the face of tremendous pressure from a powerful culture and in the absence of any fully articulated alternative basis for conceptual development. It is not that people do not have alternative conceptions, but that the pressure of the hegemonic culture keeps their ideas from being articulated and developed in all their implications, much as the lack of an alternative paradigm kept the meaning of the miners' and meatpackers' strikes from being fully articulated.

The revolutionary party crystallizes a revolutionary point of view and legitimizes revolutionary ideas and values generated by workers against the hegemonic culture. As it makes people more aware of the significance of their ideas and actions, it becomes the instrument of the revolutionary self-knowledge of the working class. It is this self-knowledge which enables working class culture to become hegemonic; that is, that allows it to see itself and be seen as the salvation of the human race.

In this way the revolutionary party is an essential element of a revolutionary movement. The revolutionary party is not the repository of working class self-consciousness; this can only reside in the class. But the party plays an essential role in the development of this self-consciousness, by articulating and applying to every aspect of class struggle the paradigm which shows its significance.

The relationship between the working class and the revolutionary party is a function of the collective nature of human consciousness and development. The people taken together always know more than the party, because in their numbers and variety they comprehend greater class experience. But they do not always know what they know. The conscious organization and articulation by the party of its ideas is fundamental to the further development of mass consciousness. The party leads the working class to the extent that it articulates and spreads ideas embedded in the class; the party's effort leads to the greater self-consciousness of workers individually and generally, who in turn lead the party as they drive it forward to new comprehension of their experience and new levels of articulation.

CONCLUSION

As the twentieth century draws to a close, there is one thing missing from the upheavals shaking the East and the less obvious struggles pervading the West: an alternative to the existing systems.

In these pages I have tried to show that an alternative to capitalism and Communism has been there before us all along, in the pervasive struggles of toiling humanity to create a world in their vision of it as it should be. We do not have to create a new alternative out of thin air. We have merely to see it already being created before our eyes—see it, develop it, and bring it to fruition.

Revolutions are built on hope. There can be only one solid basis of hope now, at the end of the twentieth century: a view of people that allows us to see the values and aspirations and struggles which most people share, and from which a new world can be created.

Marx once said that "the revolution will draw its poetry from the future." He was wrong about this. The revolution will draw its poetry from the past and the present: from the meaning of people's lives finally revealed.

What does joining in the struggle to create a new world mean for us personally? It means making more conscious and explicit and collective the best of what we do now, and bringing into conscious harmony the deepest goals of our lives with the day-to-day activities of living.

Being a revolutionary means freedom in the fullest sense, because it means fulfilling our freedom through all those commitments to other people that give our individual lives dignity and significance. It means being more fully in control of where we are going in our lives, and having the joy and strength of sharing these goals and struggles with other people.

Working for world revolution means taking a full and conscious role in the most important struggle of all, one which constructs a new world from the dreams and hopes which have always shined beneath the surface of the old.

NOTES TO CHAPTER ONE:

1.Thomas S. Kuhn, *The Structure of Scientific Revolutions* (2nd ed., enlarged; Chicago: University of Chicago Press, 1970), p. 77.
2.*Ibid.*, pp. 121-122.
3.*Ibid.*, p. 113.

NOTES TO CHAPTER TWO:

4.Quoted in Huw Beynon, ed., *Digging Deeper: Issues in the Miners' Strike* (London: Verso, 1985), p. 99.
5.Quoted in Beynon, p. 32.
6.Quoted in Geoffrey Goodman, *The Miners' Strike* (London: Pluto Press, 1985), p. 200.

NOTES TO CHAPTER THREE:

7.Cited in Harry Braverman, *Labor and Monopoly Capital: The Degradation of Work in the Twentieth Century* (New York: Monthly Review Press, 1974), p. 102.
8.*Ibid.*, p. 86.
9.David F. Noble, *Forces of Production: A Social History of Industrial Automation* (New York: Alfred A. Knopf, 1984), p. 383.
10.I am indebted for some of the arguments in this paragraph to Stuart Ewen, *Captains of Consciousness: Advertising and the Social Roots of the Consumer Culture* (New York; 1976).
11.*Ibid.*, pp. 17-18.
12.Barbara Garson, *All The Livelong Day: The Meaning and Demeaning of Routine Work* (New York: Penguin Books, 1975), xii-xiii.
13.Rick Fantasia, *Cultures of Solidarity: Consciousness, Action, and Contemporary American Workers* (Berkeley: University of California Press, 1988), p. 72.
14.*Ibid.*, p. 64.
15.*Ibid.*, p. 80.

NOTES TO CHAPTER FOUR:

16.Quoted in *Teacher Education Reports*, Vol. 7, No. 8 (April 25, 1985).
17.*Boston Globe Magazine*, Oct. 6, 1985.
18.Samuel Bowles and Herbert Gintis, *Schooling in Capitalist America: Education Reform and the Contradictions of Economic Life* (New York: Basic Books, 1976), p. 44.
19.Paolo Freire, *Pedagogy of the Oppressed* (New York: Herder and Herder, 1971), pp. 58-59; cited in Bowles and Gintis, p. 40.
20.Freire, pp. 58, 60.

280 NOTES

21. Michelle Fine, "Examining Inequity: View From Urban Schools,"
Univ. of Pennsylvania, Unpublished Manuscript; cited in Stanley
Aronowitz and Henry Giroux, *Education Under Siege: The Conservative, Liberal, and Radical Debate Over Schooling* (South Hadley,
Massachusetts: Bergin and Garvey, 1985), p. 98.
22. Barry Bluestone and Bennett Harrison, *The Deindustrialization of
America: Plant Closings, Community Abandonment, and the Dismantling of Basic Industry* (New York: Basic Books, 1982), p. 32.
23. Bob Kuttner, "The Declining Middle," *The Atlantic Monthly* (July,
1983), pp. 60-72.
24. Paul Berman et al., *The Minnesota Plan: The Design of a New
Education System* (Berkeley: BW Associates, 1984), 2 Vols.
25. *New York Times*, June 4, 1989.

NOTES TO CHAPTER FIVE:

26. Marc S. Miller, ed., *Working Lives: The Southern Exposure History of Labor in the South* (New York: Pantheon Books, 1974), p.
121.
27. *Ibid.*, p. 184ff.
28. Cited in Ronald Fraser et al., edd., *1968: A Student Generation in
Revolt* (New York: Pantheon Books, 1988), p. 54.
29. Otto Kerner et al., *Report of the National Advisory Commission on
Civil Disorders* (New York: Bantam Books, 1968), p. 114.
30. *Ibid.*, pp. 128-129.
31. *Ibid.*, p. 146.
32. Miller, p. 365.
33. *Boston Globe*, October 18, 1988.
34. *Boston Globe*, November 4, 1988.
35. Printed in Judith Clavir Albert and Stewart Edward Albert, *The
Sixties Papers: Documents of a Rebellious Decade* (New York: Prae-
ger, 1984), pp. 82ff.
36. *Ibid.*, p. 216.
37. Herbert Marcuse, *An Essay on Liberation* (Boston: Beacon Press,
1969), p. 11.
38. *Ibid.*, p. 17.
39. *Ibid.*, p. 16.
40. *Ibid.*, p. 58.
41. *Ibid.*, p. 16.
42. *Ibid.*, p. 56.
43. Albert and Albert, p. 216.
44. Marcuse, p. 65.
45. George Katsiaficas, *The Imagination of the New Left: A Global
Analysis of 1968* (Boston: South End Press, 1988), p. 120.
46. Samuel Bowles, David M. Gordon, and Thomas E. Weisskopf,
Beyond the Wasteland: A Democratic Alternative to Economic Decline
(Garden City: Anchor Press, 1983), p. 74.
47. Katsiaficas, p. 135.

48.*Ibid.*, p. 137.
49.*Monthly Review*, vol. 40, no. 5 (October, 1988), 51-52.
50.Katsiaficas, p. 141.
51.*Monthly Review, loc. cit.*
52.Cited in Jeremy Brecher and Tim Costello, *Common Sense For Hard Times* (New York: Institute for Policy Studies, 1976), p. 124.
53.Cited in Bowles et al., p. 107.
54.Ken Knabb, ed. and trans., *Situationist International Anthology* (Berkeley: Bureau of Public Secrets, 1981), p. 225.
55.Knabb, p. 141.
56.*Ibid.*, p. 63.
57.*Ibid.*, p. 69.
58.*Ibid.*, p. 122.
59.Guy Debord, *Society of the Spectacle* (Detroit: Black and Red, 1983), paragraph 1; first published as *La société du spectacle*, 1967.
60.Raoul Vaneigem, *The Revolution of Everyday Life* (London, 1983), p. 12; first published as *Traité de savoir-vivre a l'usage des jeunes générations*, 1967.
61.Knabb, p. 126.
62.*Ibid.*, p. 72.
63.*Ibid.*, p. 285.
64.*Ibid.*, p. 75.
65.For the French Communist Party's role in the strike, see Daniel Singer, *Prelude To Revolution: France in May 1968* (New York: Hill and Wang, 1970), pp. 162, 171, *et passim*; and Fraser, pp. 218-219.
66.Knabb, p. 235.
67.*Ibid.*, p. 234.
68.*Ibid.*, p. 351.
69.Yu Shuet, "The Dusk of Rationality," in The 70's, ed., *China: The Revolution Is Dead; Long Live The Revolution* (Montreal: Black Rose Books, 1977), pp. 182, 187.
70.Mao Tse-tung, *Selected Works* (Peking: Foreign Languages Press, 1965), Vol. I, pp. 23-24.
71.Jean Daubier, *A History of the Cultural Revolution* (New York: Vintage Books, 1974), pp. 67-70.
72.*Ibid.*, p. 14.
73.*China*, p. 147.
74.Hong Yung Lee, *The Politics of the Chinese Cultural Revolution* (Berkeley: University of California Press, 1978), pp. 87 ff.
75.Li I-che, *Concerning Socialist Democracy and Legal System—Dedicated to Chairman Mao*, printed in *China*, pp. 213-241.
76.*China*, p. 186.
77.*Ibid.*, p. 187.
78.Lee, p. 301.
79.*China*, p. 147.
80.*Ibid.*, p. 167.
81.*Ibid.*, p. 171.
82.*Ibid.*, 172.

83.*Ibid.*, pp. 179-180.

NOTES TO CHAPTER SIX:

84.Bluestone and Harrison, p. 147.
85.David Brody, *Workers in Industrial America*, p. 209; cited in Kim Moody, *An Injury To All: The Decline of American Unionism* (London: Verso, 1988), p. 86.
86.Cited in Samuel Bowles, David M. Gordon, and Thomas E. Weisskopf, *Beyond the Wasteland: A Democratic Alternative To Economic Decline* (Garden City: Anchor Press, 1983), p. 103.
87.*Ibid.*, p. 104.
88.Bureau of Labor Statistics Handbook, 1980, p. 415; cited in Moody, p. 86.
89.Bowles, Gordon, and Weisskopf, pp. 98 ff.
90.Thomas Ferguson and Joel Rogers, "The Knights of The Roundtable," in *The Nation*, December 15, 1979, pp. 620-625.
91.Holly Sklar, "The Commission's Purpose, Structure, and Programs: In Its Own Words," in Holly Sklar, ed., *Trilateralism: The Trilateral Commission and Elite Planning for World Management* (Boston: South End Press, 1980), pp. 83-89; and Jeremiah Novak, "Trilateralism and the Summits," in Sklar, pp. 190-196.
92.*Business Week*, October 12, 1974.
93.Bowles, Gordon, and Weisskopf, p. 111.
94.*Ibid.*, pp. 109-110.
95.*Ibid.*, p. 111; Frances Fox Piven and Richard Cloward, *The New Class War: Reagan's Attack on the Welfare State and Its Consequences* (New York: Pantheon Books, 1982), p. 25.
96.Bowles, Gordon, and Weisskopf, p. 111.
97.Sklar, p. 2.
98.Cited in Piven and Cloward, p. 27.
99.As he left office, Reagan Administration Budget Director David Stockman admitted that the Administration had purposely created a "strategic deficit" to be used as a weapon against programs it did not like. Reported by Senator Daniel P. Moynihan in a press conference; *Boston Globe*, July 11, 1989.
100.*TIME*, January 13, 1983.
101.*TIME*, January 13, 1983.
102.*Boston Globe*, February 1, 1983.
103.John Lacombe and Joan Borum, "Major Labor Contracts in 1986 Provide Record Low Wage Adjustments," *Monthly Labor Review*, May 1987, p. 11; cited in Moody, p. 2. US Bureau of Labor Statistics, *Handbook of Labor Statistics*, Washington 1985, pp. 332-33; cited in Moody, p. 2.
104.AFL-CIO, *The Polarization of America: The Loss of Good Jobs, Falling Incomes and Rising Inequality*, Washington 1986, p. 15; cited in Moody, p. 6.

105.According to Lester Thurow, writing in the *Boston Globe*, November 11, 1989.
106.*Boston Sunday Globe*, December 24, 1989.
107.*Boston Globe*, August 8, 1989.
108.AFL-CIO, *Polarization*, cited in Moody, pp. 9-10.
109.*Boston Globe*, March 19, 1987.
110.Moody, p. 100.
111.Bluestone and Harrison, p. 42.
112.*Ibid.*, pp. 6-7.
113.*Ibid.*, 113-114.
114.Labor Institute, "Shifting Balance of Power: An Education Program for UAW-Region 9A," mimeo, 1986, p. 5, cited in Moody, p. 112. Bureau of the Census, *Statistical Abstract, 1986*, p. 833; cited in Moody, p. 112.
115.Bluestone and Harrison, p. 42.
116.*Boston Globe*, July 17, 1990.
117.Bluestone and Harrison, pp. 175-76.
118.*Ibid.*, p. 176.
119.*Capital* I, ch. 15, sec. 5.
120.Barbara Garson, *The Electronic Sweatshop: How Computers Are Transforming The Office of the Future Into The Factory of The Past* (New York: Penguin Books, 1989), pp. 74-75.
121.Steve Early, in *Boston Globe*, November 21, 1989.
122.Reported in *Bureau of National Affairs Employee Relations Weekly*, Vol. 3, No. 7 (February 18, 1986)
123.Moody, p. 172.
124.Noam Chomsky and Edward S. Herman, *The Washington Connection and Third World Fascism; The Political Economy of Human Rights*, Vol. I (Boston: South End Press, 1979), p. 9.
125.Daniel B. Schirmer, "Whatever Happened To Cory Aquino," in *Monthly Review*, Vol. 40, No. 1 (May, 1988), 9-20.
126.Chomsky and Herman, p. 16.
127.Norman Girvan, "Economic Nationalists vs. Multinational Corporations: Revolutionary or Evolutionary Change?" in Sklar, p. 441.
128.Quoted in Bluestone and Harrison, p. 114.
129.*Ibid.*, p. 145.
130.*Boston Globe*, December 1, 1987.
131.Gerald Epstein, "Domestic Stagflation and Monetary Policy: The Federal Reserve and The Hidden Election," in Thomas Ferguson and Joel Rogers, edd., *The Hidden Election: Politics and Economics in the 1980 Presidential Campaign* (New York: Pantheon Books, 1981), p. 144.
132.See, for example, Harry Magdoff and Paul M. Sweezy, "The Stock Market Crash and Its Aftermath," in *Monthly Review*, Vol. 39, No. 10 (March 1988), 1-13.
133.*Boston Globe Magazine*, December 6, 1987.
134.*Boston Globe*, November 24, 1987.
135.*Boston Globe*, January 31, 1991.

136.William Tabb, "The Trilateral Imprint on Domestic Economies," in Sklar, pp. 212-237.
137.Bowles, Gordon, and Weisskopf, p. 7.
138.Cited in Bowles, Gordon, and Weisskopf, p. 112.
139.Tabb, *loc. cit.*

NOTES TO CHAPTER SEVEN:

140.Voline, *The Unknown Revolution* (New York: Free Life Editions, 1975), pp. 212-213; emphasis in original.
141.Maurice Brinton, *The Bolsheviks and Workers' Control: 1917 to 1921* (Montreal: Black Rose Books, 1975), p. 84.
142.Brinton, viii.
143.R.V. Daniels, *The Conscience of the Revolution* (Harvard University Press, 1960), p. 81; cited in Brinton, iii.
144.*Ibid., loc cit..*
145.Frederick Kaplan, *Bolshevik Ideology* (P. Owen, London, 1969), p. 128; cited in *ibid.*, p. 33.
146.*Ibid.*, p. 37.
147.Before the revolution, Lenin had attacked Taylorism as "the enslavement of man by the machine." In April, 1918 Lenin published an article in *Isvestiya* proposing to restore piece-work, to establish a card system to check the productivity of each worker, and other measures. The article called for adopting "all that is valuable in the achievements of science and technology" in the Taylor system. The Soviets soon became some of the world's most enthusiastic practitioners of Taylor's methods for labor control. *Sochinenya*, XVII, 247-8; cited in Daniels, p. 40.
148."Large-scale machine industry—which is the material and productive source and foundation of socialism—calls for absolute and strict unity of will...How can strict unity of will be ensured? By thousands subordinating their will to the will of one." *"Unquestioning submission* [emphasis in original] to a single will is absolutely necessary for the success of labor processes that are based on large-scale machine industry...today the Revolution demands, in the interests of socialism, that the masses *unquestioningly obey the single will* [emphasis in original] of the leaders of the labour process." V.I. Lenin, *Selected Works*, Vol. VII, pp. 332-33, 340-42; cited in Brinton, p. 40-41.
149."In late 1920, of 2051 important enterprises for which data were available, 1783 were already under 'one-man management.'" L. Kritzman, *Geroicheski period russkoi revolutsii* (The Heroic Period of the Russian Revolution), Moscow and Leningrad, 1926, p. 83; cited in Brinton, p. 64.
150.Trotsky, pp. 162-63; cited in Brinton, p. 67.
151.Paul Avrich, *Kronstadt 1921* (New York: W. W. Norton and Company, 1974), p. 14.
152.*Ibid.*, pp. 166-167.
153.*Ibid.*, p. 215.

154.*Ibid.*, p. 231.
155.Voline, pp. 194-95.
156.Fernando Claudin, *The Communist Movement: From Comintern to Cominform*, Trans. by Brian Pearce (New York: Monthly Review Press, 1975), 2 Vols., p. 619.
157.*Ibid.*, p. 618.
158.Felix Morrow, *Revolution and Counterrevolution in Spain* (London: New Park Publications, 1976; first published, 1938), p. 94.
159.Claudin, p. 388-89.
160.*Ibid.*, p. 317.
161.*Ibid.*, p. 325-26.
162.*Ibid.*, p. 329.
163.*Ibid.*, p. 331.
164.*Ibid.*, pp. 346-347.
165.*Ibid.*, p. 358.
166.*Ibid.*, p. 360.
167.*Ibid.*, p. 361.
168.*Ibid.*, p. 361.
169.*Ibid.*, p. 18 notes.
170.*Ibid.*, pp. 372-373.
171.*Ibid.*, p. 376.
172.*Ibid.*, pp. 480 ff.
173.*Ibid.*, p. 452.
174.Noam Chomsky, *Towards A New Cold War: Essays on the Current Crisis and How We Got There* (New York: Pantheon, 1982), p. 218.
175.Gabriel Kolko, *Anatomy of a War: Vietnam, The United States, and the Modern Historical Experience* (New York: Pantheon Books, 1985), pp. 49-57.

NOTES TO CHAPTER EIGHT:

176.Luxemburg declared, "...we can conceive of no greater danger to the Russian party than Lenin's plan of organization. *Nothing will more surely enslave a young labor movement to an intellectual elite hungry for power than this bureaucratic strait jacket, which will immobilize the movement and turn it into an automaton manipulated by a Central Committee.*" Rosa Luxemburg, *The Russian Revolution* and *Leninism or Marxism?* (Ann Arbor: University of Michigan Press, 1961), p. 102; emphasis in original.
177.Maurice Brinton and Fernando Claudin, for example.
178.David W. Lovell, in a full length study written to show that Lenin's authoritarianism is foreign to Marx's intentions, remarks that, "Leninism is generally accepted as the authentic Marxism...because there has been no serious and lasting non-Leninist Marxist challenge to Leninism." David W. Lovell, *From Marx to Lenin: An Evaluation of Marx's Responsibility for Soviet Authoritarianism* (Cambridge:

1984), p. 195. The interesting question, of course, is why this should be so.

179.Marx to Joseph Wedemeyer, in *Marx and Engels: Basic Writings on Politics and Philosophy*, Lewis S. Feuer, ed.(Garden City: Anchor Books, 1959), p. 457.

180.Frederick Engels, "Speech at the Graveside of Karl Marx,"(1883), *Selected Works*, vol. I, p. 16; cited in Howard Selsam and Harry Martel, *Reader in Marxist Philosophy: From the Writings of Marx, Engels, and Lenin* (New York: International Publishers, 1963), p. 189.

181.Cited in Robert C. Tucker, *The Marxian Revolutionary Idea*, p. 3.

182.Marx, *Theories of Surplus Value*, ch. 19, sect. 14; cited in Tom Bottomore et al., *A Dictionary of Marxist Thought* (Cambridge: Harvard University Press, 1983), p. 75.

183.Bottomore, p. 178.

184.*Capital*, Vol. I, p. 763. Marx sums up his approach in this way: "In the social production which men carry on they enter into definite relations that are indispensable and independent of their will; these relations of production correspond to a definite stage of the development of their material powers of production. The sum total of these relations of production constitutes the economic structure of society—- the real foundation, on which rise legal and political superstructures and to which correspond definite forms of social consciousness. The mode of production in material life determines the general character of the social, political, and spiritual processes of life. It is not the consciousness of men that determines their existence, but, on the contrary, their social existence determines their consciousness.

"At a certain stage of their development, the material forces of production come into conflict with the existing relations of production, or—what is but a legal expression for the same thing—with the property relations within which they had been at work before. From forms of development of the forces of production these relations turn into their fetters. Then comes the period of social revolution. With the change of the foundation the entire immense superstructure is more or less rapidly transformed.

"In considering such transformations, the distinction should always be drawn between the material transformation of the economic conditions of production, which can be determined with the precision of natural science, and the legal, political, religious, aesthetic, or philosophic—in short, ideological—forms in which men become conscious of this conflict and fight it out. Just as our opinion of an individual is not based on what he thinks of himself, so we can not judge such a period of transformation by its own consciousness; on the contrary, this consciousness must rather be explained from the contradictions of material life, from the existing conflict between the social forces of production and the relations of production. *Basic Writings*, pp. 43-44.

185.Cited in Bottomore, p. 206.

186.Marx, *Economic and Philosophic Manuscripts of 1844*, Dirk Struik, ed. (New York: International Publishers, 1964), pp. 125ff; emphasis in original.
187.*Capital* I, p. 362.
188."*Communism as the positive* transcendence of *private property*...[is] the real *appropriation of the human* essence by and for man...the complete return of man to himself as a *social* (i.e., human) being....Communism is the riddle of history solved, and it knows itself to be this solution." *Economic and Philosophic Manuscripts*, p. 102; emphasis in original.
189."Since the abstraction of all humanity, even of the *semblance* of humanity, is practically complete in the full-grown proletariat;... since man has lost himself in the proletariat, yet at the same time has not only gained theoretical consciousness of that loss, but through urgent, no longer disguisable, absolutely imperative *need*—that practical expression of *necessity*—is driven directly to revolt against that inhumanity....The question is not what this or that proletarian, or even the whole of the proletariat at the moment *considers* as its aim. The question is *what the proletariat is*, and what, consequent on that being, it will be compelled to do." Marx and Engels, *The Holy Family*, p. 53; in Selsam and Martel, p. 310. Emphasis in original.
190.Marx and Engels, *The German Ideology*, in *Basic Writings*, p. 255.
191.Cited in Tucker, p. 19.
192.In Marx's view, only the economic forces which exist independent of and often contrary to men's thoughts and intentions are the proper study of revolutionary science. It is only because there are ascertainable and objective laws of economic development that a science of history or revolution is possible. It is the task of the scientist of revolution to discover these laws, to observe their operation on society, and to use them in making revolution. It is these forces which finally, in socialist revolution, destroy the contradiction between the interests of the individual and the community, to create a society in which "the free development of each is the condition for the free development of all."
193."The proletariat," Marx and Engels wrote, "can and must free itself. But it cannot free itself without abolishing the conditions of its own life. It cannot abolish the conditions of its own life without abolishing *all* the inhuman conditions of life of society today which are summed up in its own situation." Marx and Engels, *The Holy Family*, p. 53; in Selsam and Martel, p. 310. Emphasis in original.
194.Marx and Engels, *The Holy Family*, p. 52; in Selsam and Martel, p. 310.
195.The sharpest critic of Lenin's idea of a party, Rosa Luxemburg, herself subscribed to a thoroughly economistic idea of political development. She believed—in 1904—that working class revolution was fast approaching because capitalism had nearly exhausted its economic possibilities. Once it had reached them, she thought, capitalism's

disintegration would bring forth a revolutionary workers' movement spontaneously. Thus there was no need for a party of the Leninist type, and such a party would only retard the historic process.

NOTES TO CHAPTER NINE:

196.For example, Jackson defended the interests of US imperialism. In a nationally televised debate, asked whether the presence of "a Soviet satellite [Nicaragua] in Central America" would bother him, Jackson responded: "If we support self-determination and aid economic development...we can win Nicaragua." Leftist journalist Alexander Cockburn, formerly a Jackson supporter, quoted Jackson's further comments:

> Yes, we should negotiate bilaterally with Ortega. No Soviet base. No foreign military advisors. And if they, in their self-determination, choose to relate to the Soviets in that way, they must know the alternative. If they are with us, there are tremendous benefits. If they are not with us, there are tremendous consequences. If we are clear...the response will be clear."

Cockburn commented: "In other words, if you are not with us, you are against us—and in case you are wondering what this means, read up on the history of Guatemala." *In These Times*, Dec. 23, 1987.
197.*Business Week*, June 1, 1988.
198.*New York Times*, Nov. 1, 1987.
199.Rosa Luxemburg, from her draft of "The Russian Revolution," reprinted in *Rosa Luxemburg Speaks* (New York: Pathfinder Press, 1970) p. 382.
200.Lenni Brenner, *Zionism in the Age of the Dictators: A Reappraisal* (Westport, Connecticut: Lawrence Hill, 1983), p. 1.
201.Patai, *Complete Diaries of Theodore Herzl*, vol. III, p. 729; cited in Brenner, p. 5.
202.*Ibid.*, p. 13.
203.*Ibid.*, p. 13.
204.*Ibid.*, pp. 38-43.
205.*Ibid.*, p. 45.
206.*Ibid.*, p. 55.
207.*Ibid.*, p. 65.
208.*Ibid.*, pp. 267-68.
209.*Ibid.*, p. 265. Was Rabbi Shamir aware of the proposed alliance with Hitler? Brenner cites an interview with Baruch Nadel, who joined the Stern Gang in its post-Nazi period and who had thoroughly researched Shamir's role. "Baruch Nadel is absolutely certain that ...Shamir was fully aware of Stern's plan: 'They knew all about it.'" *Ibid.*, p. 269.

NOTES TO CHAPTER TEN:

210.Kim Moody, *An Injury To All: The Decline of American Unionism* (London: Verso, 1988), pp. 1-4.
211.Richard O. Boyer and Herbert M. Morais, *Labor's Untold Story* (New York: United Electrical, Radio, and Machine Workers of America, 1970), p. 311.
212.*Ibid.*, p. 310.
213.See, for example, Nelson Lichtenstein's description of this process in Big Steel in *Labor's War At Home: The CIO In World War II* (Cambridge: Cambridge University Press, 1982), pp. 22-23.
214.Interview with John Sargent, in *Rank and File: Personal Histories of Union Organizers*, Alice and Staughton Lynd, edd. (New York: Monthly Review Press, 1988), p. 101.
215.Lichtenstein, p. 141.
216.*Ibid.*, p. 145.
217.Claudin, vol. 2, p. 395.
218.Lichtenstein, p. 214.
219.*Ibid.*, p. 213.
220.*Ibid.*, 121.
221.Moody, p. 18.
222.Lichtenstein, pp. 217, 219.
223.*Ibid.*, 237.
224.Quoted in William Bollinger, *The AFL-CIO in Latin America*, Interamerican Research Center, np.
225.Barbara Garson, *All the Livelong Day*, p. 97.
226.Lichtenstein, p. 1.
227.Bollinger, np.
228.Moody, pp. 165 ff. Note that my analysis differs from Moody's, who believes that AFL-CIO leaders suffer from "a disabling myopia" which has led them to "forget how to organize" workers. Labor leaders may have forgotten how to organize, but they know very well how to *dis*-organize. The union leaders are clear-sighted and skilled at what they do; they just happen to be on the other side.

NOTES TO CHAPTER ELEVEN:

229.Robert Heilbroner, *The New Yorker*, January 23, 1989.
230.*Boston Globe*, June 3, 1989.
231.*Boston Globe*, July 15, 1989.
232.*U.S. News and World Report*, November 20, 1989.
233.*New York Times*, July 26, 1989.
234.*New York Times*, July 26, 1989.
235.*Boston Globe*, September 12, 1989.
236.*Boston Globe*, November 3, 1989.
237.*Boston Globe*, May 23, 1990.
238.*Boston Globe*, July 12, 1990.
239.*Boston Globe*, July 19, 1989.
240.*International Herald Tribune*, February 20, 1990.

241.Abel G. Aganbegyan, "Introduction: The Language of Perestroi-ka," in Aganbegyan, ed., *Perestroika: 1989* (New York: Charles Scribner's Sons, 1988), p. 3.

242.Nieves Bregante, "Nationalist Unrest in the USSR and the Challenge to the Gorbachev Leadership," in Susan L. Clark, ed., *Gorbachev's Agenda: Changes in Soviet Domestic and Foreign Policy*, Westview Special Studies in the Soviet Union and Eastern Europe (Boulder, Colorado: Westview Press, 1989), p. 103.

243.*International Herald Tribune*, February 20, 1990.

244.The Soviet government is hardly alone in understanding how to manipulate ethnic groups against each other, of course. On March 21, in the Transylvanian city of Tirgu Mures, Romanian mobs attacked ethnic Hungarians, until tanks and troops sent in by the National Sal-vation Front government intervened. This incident represented the first time the beleaguered government had been able to use armed force since the December revolution. A British newspaper, *The Guar-dian*, reported that the Romanian mob consisted largely of members of the Securitate, the secret police force under Ceausescu which had supposedly been disbanded by the National Salvation Front. *The Guardian*, March 22, 1990.

245.*Boston Globe*, December 14, 1989.

246.The details of Walesa's actions were explained to me by Solidar-ity officials who still supported Walesa but were critical of his un-democratic approach.

247.*Boston Globe*, May 28, 1990.

248.*Boston Globe*, November 19, 1989.

249.*Boston Globe*, July 14, 1990.

250.*Boston Globe*, May 6, 1990.

251.*Boston Globe*, July 14, 1990.

252.*Boston Globe*, November 19, 1989.

253.Jan von Yoost, Director of PLANECON, interviewed on Nation-al Public Radio, November 28, 1989.

254.These details were given to me by two Solidarity officials, who found them "troubling."

255.*Boston Globe*, May 28, 1990.

256.*Boston Globe*, June 30, 1990.

257.*Boston Globe*, September 12, 1989.

258.*TIME*, September 25, 1989.

259.*Boston Globe*, December 14, 1989.

260.An important exception to this pattern is in East Germany, where intellectuals of the United Left have made scathing attacks on capital-ism and warned East Germans of the disastrous economic effects to be expected from reunification. Their critique of capitalism, however, is made wholly within a discredited Marxist framework, and they have little apparent following among workers.

261.For discussion of the economics of the Cultural Revolution, see E. L. Wheelwright and Bruce McFarlane, *The Chinese Road to Socialism: Economics of the Cultural Revolution* (New York: Monthly Review Press, 1970) and Jan Myrdal and Gun Kessle, *China: The Revolution Continued* (New York: Vintage Books, 1970).

262.*Boston Globe*, April 29, 1989.

263.*Business Week*, October 31, 1988.

264.Porus Olpadwala, "Problems With China's Agricultural Modernization," *Monthly Review*, Vol. 41, No. 7 (December, 1989), 9-12.

265.William Hinton, "Dazhai Revisited," in *Monthly Review*, Vol. 39, No. 10 (March 1988), 34-50.

266.Nicholas D. Kristof, *New York Times Magazine*, June 4, 1989.

267.Liu Guogang, "Socialism Is Not Egalitarianism," *Beijing Review*, No. 39 (September, 1987), 16-18.

268.*Boston Globe*, May 7, 1989.

269.*New York Times*, May 24, 1989.

270.*New York Times Magazine*, June 4, 1989.

271.*Boston Globe*, April 24, 1989.

272.Report of New China News Agency, quoted in *Boston Globe*, April 25, 1989.

273.*Boston Globe*, December 11, 1989.

274.*New York Times*, May 21, 1989.

275.*Boston Globe*, June 18, 1989.

276.*New York Times*, May 5, 1989.

277.Western news coverage must also have affected the understanding of Chinese about events unfolding in their own country, as Voice of America broadcasts and countless "fax" reports became their chief sources of information.

278.Trini Leung, "Workers, Students, and Intellectuals in the Chinese Democracy Movement," *New Politics*, Vol. IV, No. 1, 41-49.

279.*Boston Globe*, May 7, 1989.

280.The press's way of dealing with the slaughter has been curious to watch. At the time of the massacre, the *Boston Globe* referred to "thousands killed." A few months later, it began to refer to the "hundreds, even thousands killed." By July, 1990, the *Globe* referred only to the "hundreds killed." Thus thousands of corpses disappear, and history is rewritten before our eyes.

281.*Boston Globe*, November 9, 1989.

282.*Boston Globe*, November 15, 1989.

283.*Boston Globe*, December 7, 1989.

284.*Boston Globe*, July 24, 1989.

285.True to their word, thousands of East German workers went out on strike in the first few days after reunifaction, to warn against lay-offs. Three hundred and fifty thousand metallurgical workers in the East Berlin area struck for five days against threatened cuts.

286.*Boston Globe*, November 15, 1989.

287.*New York Times*, June 6, 1989.

288.Five short months after these lines were written, the U.S. launched a war against Iraq. Shortly before Saddam Hussein's invasion of Kuwait, the U.S. had assured him that it would not interfere, saying, "We have no opinion on the Arab-Arab conflicts, like your disagreement with Kuwait."(*NYT*, September 23, 1990) After the invasion, the U.S. rejected meaningful negotiations. The U.S. leadership wanted this war for many reasons. The war showed the American people that we still live in a dangerous world, and still need the elite and their weapons; it drew attention away from ever more devastating domestic problems; it seemed to justify the enormous arms expenditures of the Reagan years, and created a need to replace all the expended bombs and missiles; it recast Israel as victim rather than as merciless oppressor of the Palestinians; it sharply exacerbated all the nationalist hatreds in the region on which elite rule depends.

One of the more important reasons may have been finally to cast off the "Vietnam syndrome" and create in Americans who had grown skittish about war a new sense of national purpose. Conservative columnist Charles Krauthammer exhulted that "[this war] may turn out to have been a war about America," rather than about gulf oil or Kuwait. From it, "A new, post-gulf America will emerge, its self-image, sense of history, even its political discourse transformed....A post-gulf America might see its economic problems in perspective." Eventually the euphoria will fade, says Krauthammer; "But it will leave something behind: a renewed America, self-confident and assured." (*TIME*, January 28, 1991) With no "Evil Empire" to threaten people, the U.S. had to create an enemy "worse than Hitler," and then make war on it—to restore a sense of common purpose to a nation grown weary of the greed and individualism of the last two decades of American life.

NOTES TO CHAPTER TWELVE:

289.Quoted in Jean Chesnaux, *Peasant Revolts in China, 1840-1949*; trans. C.A.Curwen, (London: W.W. Norton & Co., 1973), pp. 25-26.
290.Chesnaux, p. 28.
291.*Ibid.*, p.44.
292.E. P. Thompson, *The Making of the English Working Class* (London: Penguin Books, 1970), p. 213.
293.*Ibid.*, p. 12.
294.Christopher Hill, *The World Turned Upside Down: Radical Ideas During the English Revolution* (London: Penguin Books, 1975), p. 15.
295.Hill, pp. 14-15.
296.*Ibid.*, p. 144.
297.*Ibid.*, p. 62.
298.*Ibid.*, p. 63.
299.*Ibid.*, p. 124.

300.*Ibid.*, p. 131.
301.E. Kerridge, *The Agricultural Revolution* (1967), ch. VII and VIII; cited in Hill, p. 130.
302.*Ibid.*, p. 130.
303.*Ibid.*, p. 345.
304.*Ibid.*, p. 136.
305.*Ibid.*, p. 138.
306.Cited in *Ibid.*, p. 139.
307.*Ibid.*, p. 304.
308.Engels described the phenomenon in *Socialism: Utopian and Scientific*:
But, side by side with the antagonism of the feudal nobility and the burghers, who claimed to represent all the rest of society, was the general antagonism of exploiters and exploited, of rich idlers and poor workers....[I]n every great bourgeois movement there were independent outbursts of that class which was the forerunner, more or less developed, of the modern proletariat. For example, at the time of the German Reformation and the Peasants' War, the Anabaptists and Thomas Munzer; in the great English Revolution, the Levelers; in the great French Revolution, Babeuf." *Basic Writings*, p. 70.
309.Hill, p. 305.
310.Hill, pp. 351-352.
311.Charles Taylor, *Human Agency and Language*(Cambridge: Cambridge University Press, 1985), p. 45 and ff.

NOTES TO CHAPTER THIRTEEN:

312.Bertolt Brecht, "Those Who Take The Meat From The Table," trans. by H. R. Hays; from "A German War Primer"; in John Willett and Ralph Manheim, edd., *Poems 1913-1956* (London: Methuen London Ltd., 1987), p. 287.

INDEX

ORDER FORM

NEW DEMOCRACY BOOKS
P. O. BOX 427
BOSTON, MA 02130

Number of copies of *We CAN Change The World*:

_____ Paperback copies @ $9.95 $_____

_____ Hardback copies @ $19.95 $_____

Add 5% Mass. Sales & Use Tax: $_____
(including out-of-state orders)

Add Book Rate Shipping:

$1.75 for first book $_____

$ .75 for each additional book $_____

TOTAL COST: $_____

(Enclose check payable to "New Democracy Books")

Send to: Name _____

           Address _____

                      _____

       State _____ Zip _____

Please send me _____ brochures to give to friends and colleagues on *We CAN Change The World: The Real Meaning of Everyday Life.*

If you would like to see this book in your local bookstore, please give this form to its proprietor. Inquiries on bulk sales welcome.

ORDER FORM

NEW DEMOCRACY BOOKS
P. O. BOX 427
BOSTON, MA 02130

Number of copies of *We CAN Change The World*:

_____ Paperback copies @ $9.95 $_____

_____ Hardback copies @ $19.95 $_____

Add 5% Mass. Sales & Use Tax: $_____
(including out-of-state orders)

Add Book Rate Shipping:

$1.75 for first book $_____

$ .75 for each additional book $_____

                    TOTAL COST: $_____

(Enclose check payable to "New Democracy Books")

Send to: Name_____

             Address_____

             _____

             State _____Zip_____

Please send me _____ brochures to give to friends and colleagues on *We CAN Change The World: The Real Meaning of Everyday Life*.

If you would like to see this book in your local bookstore, please give this form to its proprietor. Inquiries on bulk sales welcome.